From Generation to Generation

A Centennial History of Congregation Ahavath Achim
1887-1987

Dedicated to the generations of men and women of Ahavath Achim
whose vision and devotion have nurtured
and sustained this institution.

May each succeeding generation do likewise.

By Doris H. Goldstein

Norman Shavin, Editor

Ahavath Achim Synagogue   600 Peachtree Battle Avenue, NW   Atlanta, Georgia 30327

ISBN 0-910719-22-5.

Design by Kathleen Oldenburg King

Mechanicals by Olio-2 Advertising

Printing by Phoenix Communications, Inc., Atlanta, Ga.

Typography by Clopton Typography and Graphics, Inc., Atlanta, Ga.

Binding by National Library Bindery, Atlanta, Ga.

Additional copies of "From Generation to Generation" are available from the Synagogue Gift Shop.

Doris H. Goldstein
Author

Norman Shavin
Editor

The Centennial

The planning for the commemoration of an event as momentous as the 100th anniversary of Ahavath Achim Synagogue was of major proportions. A successful and meaningful celebration could not have been achieved without the cooperation and dedication of Congregants and Staff. Their contributions are noted with great appreciation.

A diverse schedule of events took place throughout the Centennial Year (1986-87) providing an opportunity for the entire membership to participate. The enthusiastic response by our members and the community

at large was gratifying.

The story of the past century recorded in this book is presented with affection. Innumerable hours have been spent tracing the evolution of this institution from 18 struggling immigrants who met in each others homes to the over 2000 families who are today's members.

It is our sincere wish that those future generations who will be responsible for the next 100 years will have the same dedication to the perpetuation of our precious heritage as have those of the past century. Hazak, Hazak, V'Nithazek.

David S. Alterman & Norman H. Diamond
Co-Chairmen, Centennial Committee

David S. Alterman
Centennial Co-Chairman

Norman H. Diamond
Centennial Co-Chairman

Rabbi Emeritus
Harry Epstein and Reva

The Congregation pays tribute to the 54 years of devoted leadership of Rabbi
and Mrs. Epstein. Their presence in the community has truly been
"Livraha. . .for a blessing."

TABLE OF CONTENTS

Janet & Phillip Sunshine

Amy & Louis Taratoot

Sponsors of the Centennial History

"We Jews are a community based on memory."
Martin Buber

Annette Srochi

Mynette & Mendel Segal

Susan & Raymond Schoenbaum

Hank & Buster Oxman

Elizabeth & Abe Alterman

Helen & Sidney Cavalier

Bunny & Dave Center

The men and women whose generosity has made possible the publication of this book have created a repository of memory for present and future generations. The recording of the events and personalities important to the development of Ahavath Achim gives each member instant access to a rich past and makes possible the bonds which hold us together.

The Congregation is deeply indebted to these sponsors and all who participated in the creation of this volume.

Shirley & Irwin Greenbaum

Barbara & Sanford Orkin

Sherry & Harry Maziar

My first congregation, located in Chicago's South Side, had a meteoric existence. It was founded in 1953, but was disbanded in 1971, a victim of neighborhood changes. During the century of Ahavath Achim's existence, many congregations came into being only to disappear within a brief period of time. Ahavath Achim, however, met the powerful challenge of changing neighborhoods and the march to suburbia; far too many synagogues did not.

We are fortunate to be part of a Synagogue that has reached its centenary and now looks forward to its second century. Thus, this year, we celebrate the hearty pioneers who founded this Congregation; the second generation of leadership that gave Ahavath Achim a firm base; and the subsequent generations that built upon the infra-structure they inherited having vision to relocate the Synagogue not once, but twice. We rejoice because of the many in our midst who continue to give of their time, effort, energy and resources to assure Ahavath Achim's status as a jewel in the crown of American Jewry.

This volume is a celebration of the many successes achieved and enjoyed by our Congregation. It is a proud record of the dedication of thousands of Jews to interface Jewish teachings with American values. It is a written testimony to the effort of Jews in our community to balance loyalty to our Tradition with a commitment to modernity.

This centennial volume, crafted so beautifully, is a tribute to all our leaders past and present, but especially to Rabbi Harry and Reva Epstein whose vision, courage, and steadfastness during more than five decades of service to Ahavath Achim helped make our Congregation what it is today.

The past, of course, must be a prologue to the future. May our Centennial celebration inspire us to greater devotion to G-d, to increased loyalty to our People, and to deeper commitment to help our society reflect those moral and ethical teachings that flow from Judaism at its best.

Rabbi Arnold M. Goodman
Congregation Ahavath Achim

" . . . A Brave and Beautiful City"

" . . . we have raised a brave and beautiful city; that somehow or other we have caught the sunshine in the bricks and mortar of our homes, and have builded therein not one ignoble prejudice or memory."

Henry W. Grady, 1886

Members of the staid New England Society of New York listened spellbound to the first Southern speaker in their 81-year history paint a glowing vision of Atlanta and the New South. In the two decades since Gen. R.E. Lee's surrender at Appomattox Court House, Grady proclaimed, Atlanta and the South had risen from the ashes and were on their way to solving their economic and social problems.

Grady, the young managing editor of the *Atlanta Constitution* since 1880, had acquired national recognition as a journalist and, after his speech in New York, was the acknowledged, preeminent representative of the South in America. He was a man of boundless faith in the region of his birth, and the prophet of hope and optimism for a white population whose entire way of life was dramatically altered.

The reality of the New South was not yet as glorious as Grady desired. Per capita wealth and income were at least 50% below the national average while racial tensions intensified rather than modified.

Atlanta, in contrast to the rest of Georgia, was a thriving center of commerce with a population of about 40,000. The city's manufacturing capacity, destroyed during the Civil War, was being rebuilt and by 1886 Atlanta boasted 303 different businesses which employed 6,674 people. Initially responsible for Atlanta's birth, the railroads continued to find the city a natural hub. Each new line connected Atlanta to a wider area and increased its status as a transportation center.

Peachtree St., 1872, looking north. Horsedrawn trolley heading south on Whitehall St. which Peachtree was called on the south side of the railroad crossing.

To attract Northern investment, Grady published a series of articles in the *New York Ledger* preaching the gospel of faith and confidence. He referred to Atlanta in *The Constitution* as the "Chicago of the South...a giant young metropolis." A reporter for the *London Daily Telegraph* called the city "swaggering."

For all its swagger, Atlanta in 1886 was a small town trying to convince the world it wasn't. Although there were 140 miles of streets, only 16 of them were paved; rainstorms created havoc for horse and man. For the pedestrian, there were more than 200 miles of sidewalks but most were rough planks. Buildings in the center

THE ATLANTA CONSTITUTION.

VOL. XIX.   ATLANTA, GEORGIA, SATURDAY MORNING, SEPTEMBER 17, 1887.   PRICE FIVE CENTS

PASSING IN REVIEW.

Grand Army Men Cheer the President.

AND IN TURN HE LIFTS HIS HAT.

Great Day in Philadelphia—Thirty Thousand Soldiers in the Parade—The Receptions at Night.

ALL ESCAPE CUT OFF.

A Whole Family Burned to Death.

THEIR FRANTIC CRIES FOR HELP.

A Horrible Catastrophe in New Orleans—A Candy Factory Burned—Other Destructive Blazes.

Large Fire in Shreveport.

An Ice Factory Destroyed.

TRYING TO SAVE THEIR NECKS.

The Anarchists Hold a Consultation About Their Condition.

THE CASE IN COURT.

The Nashville Americans Under the Eye of the Law.

THE ALABAMA SOCIALISTS

Meet in State Convention to Air Their Grievances.

THE PRESIDENCY AT THE CLOVER CLUB.

THE AMERICAN PARTY.

Proceedings of the First Convention at Philadelphia.

Playing With a Gun.

A CHILD THE PAWN.

Cross Purposes Between an Alabama Husband and Wife.

A STATE FUNERAL.

Burial of the Remains of Governor Bartlett, of California.

A Lady Crosses the Bridge.

DRESBACH'S LIABILITIES.

The Most Remarkable Collapse in the History of the Country.

REVIEW OF BUSINESS.

A Severe Pressure in Money—Effects of Recent Failures.

A National Bank Closes.

New Cotton Rules.

Type Founders Fail.

THE WRECKED BAROUCHE.

Five Ladies Have a Narrow Escape from Death.

TWENTY-FOUR KILLED.

A Collision on an English Railway the Signaling the Cause.

WE'LL GET A REST

Parliament Prorogued Until November Next.

READING OF THE QUEEN'S SPEECH

Last Day in the Commons—Large Funeral—The Victims of the Mitchellstown Fight—Other Foreign News.

THE MITCHELLSTOWN AFFAIR

Burial of Another Victim—The Coroner's Inquest.

League Meetings Next Sunday

Russian Nihilists Organize.

The Scots Desire Home Rule.

Front page of Atlanta Constitution, Sept. 17, 1887.

10

of town were only two or three stories, and a maze of railroad tracks ran helter-skelter over the streets. Woodrow Wilson, after closing his unsuccessful short-lived law practice in Atlanta, complained about the "humdrum life down here in slow, ignorant, uninteresting Georgia...where the chief aim of men is certainly to make money."

There were, however, glimmers of the future in 1886.

A pharmacist named John Pemberton invented the formula for a new elixir (Coca-Cola), which would, in years to come, make Atlanta the world headquarters for a corporate giant. A new Capitol was nearing completion on the corner of Mitchell St. and Capitol Ave. for which the General Assembly had allocated $1,000,000. Twenty two miles of street rail lines connected downtown to West End via horse-drawn streetcars.

The only telephone exchange had been located in the opera house, Atlanta's tallest and grandest building, on the corner of Forsyth and Marietta. There was a paid fire department and police services, and the Georgia Institute of Technology had been launched.

Despite Wilson's assessment of the city as crass and uninteresting, there was an opera house, newspapers, and an incumbent president, Rutherford

John Pemberton, inventor of the patent medicine which would become Coca-Cola.

B. Hayes, came on a good will visit in 1887 to help cement warmer feeling between North and South.

A nascent group of benevolent institutions had been organized and would evolve into a network of groups whose purpose was to be of assistance to their fellow men. Among these were The Hibernian Association, St. Joseph's Infirmary, B'nai

Henry Woodfin Grady, 1850-1889, part owner and managing editor of the Atlanta Constitution *and prominent publicist for Atlanta and the "New South."*

St. Joseph's Infirmary, founded 1880, is Atlanta's oldest hospital. This original building was located on present-day Courtland St.

Unpaved Hunter St. (now Martin Luther King Jr. Dr.) looking east. Spires of the Church of the Immaculate Conception tower above the trees. 1875

B'rith Orphan Asylum, and the home of the Women's Christian Association.

The religious community had developed a large number of churches ...black and white.

All major Christian denominations were represented, including one Lutheran and two Roman Catholic churches. A number had imposing structures; one, the Church of the Immaculate Conception (completed in 1873), is still in its same location and restored building. The religious minorities with established congregations were the Unitarians and the Jews.

The Hebrew Benevolent Congregation

When Rabbi Isaac Leeser, a prominent leader of 19th Century American Judaism, visited Atlanta in 1852, he noted that although a few ladies and gentlemen assembled for prayers, there was no "congregational union in this place."

Although Jacob Haas and his family had come to the village known as Marthasville in 1844, very few co-religionists had followed. Two years after his initial visit, Leeser wrote that the High Holidays had been observed in Atlanta by many Israelites because of the prevalence of yellow fever in Savannah, Charleston, and Augusta. The mere handful of Jews who were permanent Atlanta residents did, however, establish regular instruction for their children very soon after their arrival.

Rabbi Leeser returned in 1867 to perform a wedding and urged the residents to form a congregation. Upon hearing they had rented a hall, purchased a Torah and planned to hold regular Sabbath services, Lesser commented, "We expect much from Atlanta...The city has been fearfully devastated during the late war...Still, it is a center of commerce, and the reasons which caused it to be built are yet active enough to be the means of its restoration. Israelites will, to a certainty, take their share in the regeneration of Georgia..."

The Hebrew Benevolent Congregation was chartered in April,

Isaac Leeser one of the foremost leaders of American Jewry in the 19th Century. Founder of The Occident and American Jewish Advocate *and Maimonides College in Philadelphia. Also translated the Bible into English.*

Second Kimball House, built in 1885, was a familiar landmark near Five Points until it was demolished in 1959.

The advent of electric powered trolleys enabled the northern suburb of Inman Park to flourish.

1867. It is estimated there were approximately 300 Jews then living in Atlanta, consisting mainly of Central European immigrants and their native born children. Since the city was not a point of entry, most Jewish adults began their Americanization in other cities and came to Atlanta with a basic knowledge of English and some capital. They were predominately retail merchants, young, and ready to participate in Grady's dream of the New South.

The new congregation's mode of worship was Orthodox. Men and women sat separately, *tallit* and *kipah* were worn by male worshipers, two days of Rosh Hashanah and the Festivals were observed, and the service was led in Hebrew by lay leaders until a rabbi was hired. The religious ideology vacillated for many years between the tradition which most members had learned in childhood and Reform, an American version of what had begun in Germany earlier in the century.

After a series of rented facilities, the congregation moved into its first building, at the corner of Garnett and Forsyth on Aug. 31, 1877. It was an impressive edifice inside and out, its Moorish design and onion-domed spires adding an exotic flavor to a skyline which was hardly notable.

Only adult males were counted as members, of which there were 60. Including women and children, the total membership was approximately 300, half the total Jewish population of Atlanta in 1877.

Annual dues were $30 per year and the fee for a designated seat was $50, payable with interest over two years. Those unable to pay were admitted free of charge.

A Jewish presence had been firmly established to begin fulfilling Rabbi Lesser's prophecy of the "Israelites ...share in the regeneration of Georgia."

First building of the Hebrew Benevolent Congregation, corner of Garnett and Forsyth, 1877.

The "Russian" Congregation

"There are in Atlanta a community of Israelites, principally from Poland and Russia, who do not subscribe to the reformed or American ritual . . . and who have services of their own."

Atlanta Constitution, Oct. 8, 1886

The arrival of Eastern European Jews in Atlanta was precipitated by events far from the unpaved streets and railroad yards of a town struggling to become a city.

A succession of Russian czars, princes and religious leaders had led a series of *pogroms* and expulsions of Jews for over a century. A new wave of terror, engineered by the state and the church, began in Odessa in 1871 and spread in all directions.

A decade later, in May, 1882, the government promulgated the so-called May Laws which in effect constituted *"pogrom by law"* on a national scale. The trickle of immigrants from Russia became a torrent as Jews fled the murder and rape of their families and pillage of their homes. A small number of them came to Atlanta.

Rosters of members of the Hebrew Benevolent Congregation in 1877 list Morris Wiseberg from Russia and Max Marcus from Poland. Others probably came and went but they were not numerous enough to be noticed.

Upon arrival, East European immigrants tried to feel at home in the imposing brick building on For-

Peachtree St., from R. R., Atlanta, Ga.

syth and Garnett but the solemnity and unorthodox mode of the service combined with the condescending attitude of their German cousins were too distant from the noisy prayer halls and easy fellowship of their *shtetl* homes.

By Rosh Hashanah, 1886, their numbers had grown and they rented Concordia Hall at the corner of Marietta and Forsyth for High Holiday services, and were duly recognized as a separate religious entity.

Peachtree St. at the railroad tracks. Note the tower of the artesian well located at Five Points. 1887

Atlanta Historical Society

I. Balagur
1887-1888

N.A. Kaplan
1892-1893

Philip Elson
1893-1894

D. Zaban
Date Uncertain

Morris Lichtenstein
Date Uncertain

Leon Eplan
Date Uncertain

Steerage Deck aboard the S.S. Pennland. 1893

Eye examination of arriving immigrants, Ellis Island.

Russian Jew in New York carrying all his earthly possessions.

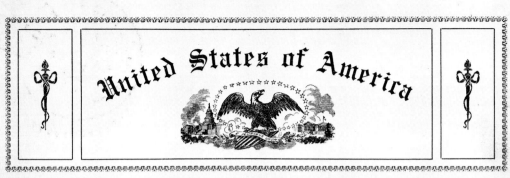

United States of America

The President of the United States of America

To all who shall see these presents, Greeting:

Know Ye, that on the **2** day of, **May** Anno Domini, 19**05**, at a term of the Circuit Court of the Sixth Judicial Circuit of Tennessee, in and for the County of Hamilton, personally

came **ISRAEL ABELSON**

a native of **RUSSIA**

who produced a Certificate of his intention to be **Naturalized,** and become

A CITIZEN OF THE UNITED STATES

and also proved to the satisfaction of the Court that he has behaved as a man of good moral character, attached to the principles of the Constitution of the United States, and well disposed to the good order and happiness of the same. That he is a person who does not disbelieve in and is not opposed to all organized government, and is not a member of or affiliated with any organization entertaining and teaching such belief in or opposition to all organized government and does not advocate or teach the duty, necessity or propriety of the unlawful assaulting or killing of any officer or officers either of specific individuals or officers generally of the government of the United States or of any other organized government because of his or their official character, and has not violated any of the provisions of the Acts of the Fifty-Seventh Congress entitled "an Act to regulate the immigration of aliens into the United States."

The Court having made careful inquiry into all the matters herein recited touching the granting and issuing of this the final order or certificate of Naturalization caused to be entered of record the affidavit of the applicant, to-wit:

the said **ISRAEL ABELSON** and of his witnesses to-wit:

A. Block, Mike Silverman, A. Abelson, G. Edelstein

which were duly made and recorded, and which recite and affirm the truth of every material fact requisite for naturalization. And he the said **Israel Abelson**

having fully complied with the laws of the United States in relation to the Naturalization of Aliens, the said

Israel Abelson being admitted by the Court, took the oath to support the Constitution of the United States of America, and to **absolutely and entirely renounce and abjure** all allegiance and fidelity to every **Foreign Prince, Potentate, State or**

Sovereignty, whatsoever, and particularly to **Nicholas II The Czar** whose subject he was.

This is, Therefore, to Certify, that the said **Israel Abelstein** is **a Citizen of the United States.**

In Testimony Whereof, I have hereunto subscribed my name officially, and affixed the Seal of said Court, at the City of Chattanooga, this **Second** day of **May** A. D., 19**05**

R B Howard
Clerk of the Circuit Court of Hamilton County, Tennessee

Per **J P Pemberton**
Deputy Clerk of the Circuit Court of Hamilton County, Tennessee

Final Citizenship certificate of Israel Abelson.
1905

State of Georgia } To the Superior Court of said County
Fulton County } Petition for Charter for Religious & Charitable institution

The petition of Barnet Wolbin Julius Jaffa Harry Rudich Jacob Schultman & Thomas Eplan Respectfully show that they & their associates & successors desire to be incorporated as a religious & charitable institution to be known as the Congregation Ahawas Achim (Congregation of Brotherly Love) The object of said institution is the Establishing of a Church of the Jewish faith for promoting the Cause of the Jewish Religion Education & Charity

The particular business will be the Conducting of religious Services Collecting of dues from the Members of the Congregation in Manner & form according to the Constitution and by Laws of said Congregation, the reception of such donation as May be Made by others interested which shall be expended according to the Constitution and by Laws of said institution among such of its Members as May be in Need by reason of sickness or abject poverty or in other declines that May under them objects of Charity. They desire to be incorporated in accordance with Section 1676 Code of State of Georgia for the Space of Twenty Years With the privilege of renewal at the Expiration of said Time. The Capital shall consist of the Monthly dues from the Members & such donations Made as above stated. The business of said Corporation shall begin upon the granting of its Charter and the payment of the dues Which shall be fixed by the Constitution & by Laws To the above end they desire the power to receive in its distinct and proper Name by its officers & trustees donations both of real & personal property And to hold title to property both real and personal & to convey the Same if necessary, to make a constitution & by Laws, to elect such Officers or trustees as May be necessary to be capable in Law of suing or being sued Pleading & being pleaded defending & being defended Contracting and being Contracted With and to have all powers and rights to do all things as are Common to Corporations of like Character and necessary to the objects of said institution. The Location of said Church to be in the City of Atlanta County & State aforesaid The Petitioners pray the passing of an order granting them order Petition & incorporating them their associates & successors as above set forth and in duty bound & petitioner will Ever pray &c

Morris Mack
Atty for Petitioners
E. H. Strong Cxc
A. H. Strong

Filed in Office Septr 17th 1887
Recorded Sept 17/87

Original, hand written petition for incorporation of Congregation
AHAWAS ACHIM, filed Sept. 17, 1887, Superior Court of
Fulton County.

Their numbers had increased dramatically, from a handful to more than 100, and growing almost daily.

It is little wonder that the original petition filed for a charter on Sept. 17, 1887, listed the name as Congregation Ahawas Achim — Congregation of Brotherly Love. Named in the petition were Barnet Walberg, Julius Jaffa, Harry Rudick, Jacob Schniltman and Louis (i.e. Leon) Eplan.

In addition to those named in the charter petition the original members were I. Balaguer, Isaac Caplan, Leon Fresh, J. Gross, L. Grudkovsky, N.A. Kaplan, A. Posner, F. Rabinovitz, F. Rogovin, L. Sax, I. Sinkovitz, Charles Taylor and J. Teplitzky.

The Atlanta City Directory of 1888 lists only six of these names and gives the following information as to their occupations and business address.

I. Balaguer, tailor, 38 Ivy St.; Leon Eplan, clothing, 94 Decatur St.; L. Grudkovsky, tailor, Hirsch Bros.; Nathan Kaplan, notion stand, Peachtree St.; F. Rabinowitz, grocer, 290 Marietta; and I. Sinkovitz, clothing, 62½ Decatur St.

The fact that these men were even

listed is a sign that they had attained a certain degree of financial success. It can be reasonably assumed that most of the others lived with family or friends and were not listed independently.

They were predominantly young men who ventured South, leaving wives and children behind until there was enough accumulated capital for their passage. Clustering in rented lodgings in the vicinity of Decatur St., the Russian Jews began their trek toward acculturation together, comforted by their shared backgrounds. The Eastern European community was overwhelmingly poor, most earning their meager living via the peddler's pack.

In spite of their circumstances, the need to establish a cosmic center for their lives was paramount. The cycle of the Jewish calendar and Jewish observance had sustained their ancestors under horrendous circumstances, and it was this familiar tradition they sought for themselves. Religious life was not a mere trapping; it was the core of their existence.

A rented room at 106 Gilmer St. was the congregation's first known official address although in the forma-

Left: Decatur St. between Central and Pryor, looking toward Five Points. Circa 1890.

Above: Female street merchant selling her wares from a wooden crate, Decatur St.

Minutes N° 1.

Meeting held at meeting room of Congreg. Ahavath Achim on the 27th of July 1890, opened by pres¹ D. Rabinnovis in presence of a quorum.

V. Prest. B. Wolberg was absent. Secy Chas. Taylor read the minutes of previous meeting. Moved and seconded to declare the minutes adopted. Motion carried. Minutes adopted.

Br. Eplan brought in an application from Mr. Jacob Gross with $5⁰⁰ of membership fee. Mr. Gross was balloted for and the ballot proving favorable he was accepted and initiated.

Report of committee on ark. Committeemen D. Rabinnovis and A. Posner reported that the cost will be between 40 and 50 dollars and that $10⁰⁰ has been paid as a deposit to secure the construction of the ark by the School of Technology. Nominated for trustee: Ch. Taylor. The nomination of two more was postp. for next regular meeting.

The elected officers were duly installed

First page of earliest known records of the Congregation, July 27, 1890. Previous minutes, 1887-1890, if they were kept have not survived. Note spelling of "Ahavath" (Hebrew) in second line compared to "Ahawas" (Yiddish) used in petition for Charter on Page 18.

20

tive period members met in each others' homes for services. A short time later they moved a few doors away to 120 Gilmer St. where a larger space was rented for $6.25 per month. Congregational meetings and regular services were held there with additional space leased for Rosh Hashanah and Yom Kippur.

The earliest congregational minutes known begin on July 27, 1890. F. Rabinovitz, the grocer who lived behind his store on Marietta St., was conducting his last meeting as president.

An interesting item discussed was the allocation of between $40 and $50 for the construction of an Ark (spelled Arc) by the "School of Technology" (Georgia Tech). A $10 deposit was paid.

Other business conducted was the installation of new officers (A. Posner became president), the renting of adjacent rooms, the appointment of a committee to investigate the renting of an electric fan, the acceptance of Jacob Gross to membership, the reading of a proposed version of a constitution and, finally, an appeal for a loan of $50 to cover current expenses, to be repaid after

the Feast of Tabernacles.

"The following brothers promptly responded to the appeal: L. Eplan, $10; J. Jaffa, $10; J. Gross (the new member), $10; L. Grudkovsky, $10, and I. Caplan, $10. This makes a total of $50 to which the above named have subscribed with the understanding to deliver the money to the Congregation as soon as called for by the proper authorities."

The following items culled from early minutes give a flavor of the times:

Dues were collected at each meeting, usually in increments of 50¢. Yearly membership fee was $3, which was often reduced or waived completely.

Committees were fined between 25¢ and 50¢ for failure to make their report without a "legal excuse."

Officers were fined 50¢ for failure to attend special meetings.

Applicants for membership were investigated and voted upon with the possibility of being rejected by one negative vote.

An initiation fee of $1 was charged to each new member.

Congregation allocated money for burial expenses for all members. This was often raised by donations of those

Faculty and students of Georgia Tech posed on what is now North Ave., formerly a dirt road called Cherry St. Original 1888 Academic Building (on right) is still a campus landmark.

Pioneer Families

Those who migrated before the turn of the century from the port cities of New York, Philadelphia, and Baltimore to the Jewish outpost of Atlanta were a hardy lot. Drawn by family ties, prior friendships, or mere happenstance, they were bonded to each other by a common language (Yiddish), religious observances, and shared circumstances. Ahavath Achim was where these individual families became a community.

Hannah and Morris Gavronski, young Russian immigrants married in Atlanta in 1899.

The parents of Meyer Rich (a future Synagogue president), Freda and Velvel Rich joined their son in Atlanta in 1915.

Esther and Hyman Mendel pose with their first child, Sarah, shortly after arriving in America. 1894

Early members, Nechama and Kohlman Koplin, with the first of their eight children born in Atlanta. Pincus, second from left, was Synagogue treasurer for many years.

Riga natives, Rachel and Zelig Goldberg with their daughters. Nessie, standing behind her father, was an early president of the Sisterhood. Circa 1900

Rosa and Abraham Jacobs and family. Children are (left to right) seated: Minnie and Joseph and standing: Annie, Rebeeca, Hyman, and Edward. 1895

Rev. Abraham Jaffe, Ahavath Achim's
first cantor was also a mohel and
officiated at weddings.

Above: Jewish section of Oakland
Cemetery containing children's graves.
Below: Ahavath Achim section

present at the meeting.

President was reimbursed for his streetcar fare when he traveled on congregational business (30¢).

$2 donated to the Hebron Hospital, Palestine.

Member assigned to collect fees owed was given a commission on total.

Secretary paid $25 per year.

Loans made to needy members on an ad hoc basis.

One of the most pressing needs of the Orthodox Jews was a reliable source of kosher meat that necessi-

tated a *shochet*, a ritual slaughterer, and Abraham Jaffe was employed. (It is not known if he was the brother or relative of Julius Jaffa who is mentioned in the earliest minutes. Abraham Jaffe's granddaughter, a current member of Ahavath Achim, notes that the correct spelling of his name is Jaffe but she knows little of his early history.)

He was employed as *shochet* in January, 1892, at a salary of 15¢ per member per month. In May that year another problem arose: It appears the congregation had arranged with the butcher, W. Cohen, to pay Jaffe and another *shochet*, J. Schein, for their services. Cohen refused to pay Jaffe unless he agreed to slaughter animals for him exclusively.

After lengthy debate it was decided that "an appropriation of fifty (50) dollars be made for the purpose of opening a butcher shop controlled by the congregation in opposition to Cohen until the latter is brought to terms."

At a meeting in August it was reported that the shop had an operating deficit of $22 in outstanding accounts, and a claim of $10 to Jaffe for "cattle killing." How long it remained in operation is not known.

Another immediate concern of the congregation was securing burial plots, one of the benefits of member-

ship. Since the overwhelming majority of the members were young, the issue did not arise until 1891 when an infant died.

Arrangements were made with the Hebrew Benevolent Congregation for the purchase of a grave for $5, plus $10 for a site for an adult. The oldest cemetery in the city was Oakland, which had opened in 1850 and in which The Temple, the name by which the Hebrew Benevolent Congregation was known in later years, had secured a portion for its own use.

A year later Ahawas Achim purchased from them for the sum of $500 one quarter of the new section it had recently acquired. Thus Oakland Cemetery became the final resting place of Eastern European Jews who slept beside Confederate generals, wealthy land developers, hardworking railroad men, slaves and other men and women who pioneered Atlanta.

First male members of the *Hevra Kadishah* were Bros. Wilensky, Schein, Slutzky and Kramer. The first female members of the *Hevra Kadishah* were Mrs. Lichtenstein, Mrs. L. Sax and Mrs. Jacob Gross.

The new congregation functioned for a number of years without a rabbi. The members were sufficiently literate to lead the daily and Shabbat services, and Jaffe was engaged as *chazan* for Rosh Hashanah and Yom Kippur. It appears he performed weddings also and was for years the community's *mohel*. A sexton was employed and required to be in attendance every day. His salary was $2 per month plus a percentage of donations collected.

The internal organization seemingly was based on the Masonic order, the one group which crossed religious and economic lines and admitted Jews. The members were called "brother"; there was a formal application procedure which included an "investigating committee" and an "initiation fee"; and a vote was taken on each member who could be rejected on the basis of a "clouded" vote, i.e., black-balled.

Most meetings were concerned with the matters of finance — collecting dues and donations, voting for the payment of bills, determining the price of tickets, and the distribution of seats for the High Holidays. Next in importance were matters concerning the cemetery and the care of deceased members. Infant mortality was high and is reflected in frequent mention

"Mounted" division of Atlanta Police Dept. in front of the recently completed station on Decatur St. between Butler and Piedmont Ave. 1899

Wedding portrait of Fannie and Morris Lichtenstein, outstanding leaders of the Eastern European community. 1893.

Piedmont Park as it looked during the highly successful Cotton States Exposition of 1895. This event attracted wide media attention and brought many visitors, some of whom became permanent residents.

The original structure of Grady Hospital. It opened in 1892 with 100 beds for the indigent and 10 private rooms for paying patients.

of the deaths of babies and young children.

On occasion individuals were censured for inappropriate behavior, such as speaking maliciously about the congregation or a "brother." At one meeting events aroused such passions that a committee was appointed to consult an attorney as to a parliamentary rule.

Presidents resigned and were reinstated during the same meeting, and there was a committee appointed for every minute detail. A limited number of members did the work of the evolving congregation while working long hours to support their families.

Ahawas Achim was not, however, the only Orthodox choice in town. Congregation B'nai Abraham was chartered in September, 1890, and Congregation Chevra Kaddisha in 1896. Both were short-lived groups who obviously had not found "brotherly love" in some of the raucous meetings of Ahawas Achim.

In January, 1893, a delegation from B'nai Abraham attended the regular meeting of the Congregation "for the purpose of negotiations in view." By August a merger had been effected. Both presidents and secretaries presided at their initial combined meeting on Sunday, Aug. 20, 1893.

The influx of Jews continued. By 1895 the rooms on Gilmer St. were inadequate and a hall was leased on Decatur St. across from the police station. The total Jewish population of the city was close to 1,500, a majority being Eastern Europeans and their children.

Nor had Atlanta stood still. The highly successful Cotton States & International Exposition of 1895 had attracted national attention and created a new wave of commercial expansion. Grady Hospital had been built and the Cyclorama painting of the Battle of Atlanta installed in Grant Park. New buildings of major proportions were planned and completed in the Five Points area while the city's residential areas were expanding northward. New residents continued arriving, looking for jobs and opportunity.

According to some sources, the Congregation's first rabbi was Jacob Simonoff. The 1893 minutes mention, at the time of the merger with B'nai Abraham, that "Mr. Simonoff should remain with this congregation on conditions as before." Exactly what those conditions were is not stated in previous or later entries.

Simonoff was a learned man but was never ordained. Perhaps when the membership grew and the move was made to the new hall, he was officially called "rabbi." His name also appears in the handwritten list of members deposited in the cornerstone of the Gilmer St. *shul* on Oct. 4, 1900.

The small group of unskilled, poor immigrants had held their fledgling enterprise together by providing for the most basic needs of their members. They recognized opportunities for growth and made the most of them. They established organizational structures which tapped the energies and talents of the men who would continue what they had started.

Coming of Age

"Dirt was broken yesterday morning for the building of the church of the Ahavath Achim or Congregation of Brotherly Love at the corner of Piedmont Avenue and Gilmer Street."

Atlanta Constitution, August 9, 1900

No one minded the summer heat when they gathered for the ground-breaking of their first synagogue building, at 37 Piedmont Avenue. Just 13 years after the issuing of the original charter to four men and their 14 fellow members, a congregation of 125 "prominent Hebrews" had contracted for a building which was to cost between $8,000 and $10,000. It was an appropriate way to mark the Bar Mitzvah year of the growing institution.

The lot had been purchased in June, 1898. According to a short history written in 1911, the building fund had requested and received a donation of about $500 from Baroness de Hirsch, who administered her husband's enormous philanthropic activities after his death. The Baron had established a special fund in 1891 for assisting and settling immigrants in the U.S.; it is possibly this source to which an enterprising Ahavath Achim member addressed an appeal.

A ceremony to lay the new building's cornerstone was presided over by Rabbi David Marx of The Temple in October, 1900, and the building was completed and dedicated on Mar. 31, 1901. The Young Ladies Auxiliary Benevolent Society, assisted by the Hebrew Ladies Society, furnished the interior and established the precedent of service the women of the congregation have maintained ever since.

The building was two-stories high which allowed room for a small balcony for the ladies. It was 90′ long and

Marietta Street, circa 1900.

Atlanta Historical Society

40′ wide and built of plentiful red brick. Its main architectural features were two square spires on each side of the entrance, each one capped by a squat, onion dome. Whether this feature was a conscious attempt to imitate The Temple's architecture or a coincidence is not known.

A round stained glass window was in the center above the main entrance on Piedmont Ave., and other stained glass windows were used throughout the building. The main entrance led to the sanctuary; an entrance on Gilmer led to a daylight basement housing a chapel and a few classrooms.

The sanctuary was dominated by a carved wood *bimah* in the center of the room from which the Torah was read. The Ark which housed the Torah scrolls was set into a large

27

Above: First permanent home of Ahavath Achim, corner of Gilmer St. and Piedmont Ave. Now a parking lot for Georgia State University. Right: Minnie Solomon Kolodkin with nephews Bernard and Zack Lifchez in front of the wrought iron gate at the entrance of the building.

ORTHODOX JEWS BUILDING

Dirt Broken Yesterday Morning for a New Church.

BUILDING TO COST $10,000

Located at Corner Piedmont Avenue and Gilmer Street—Congregation Has One Hundred Members.

Dirt was broken yesterday morning for the building of the church of the Ahavath Achim or Congregation of Brotherly Love at the corner of Piedmont avenue and Gilmer streets.

The edifice is to cost about $10,000 and is to be of elegant design and handsome finish.

The Ahavath Achim is the congregation of Orthodox Jews in Atlanta and there are about 125 of the most prominent Hebrews of that denomination interested in the building of the new church.

About a year ago a lot was purchased at the corner of Gilmer street and Piedmont avenue and since then the money for the church has been partially raised by subscription.

The orthodox Jews believe in the rituals and ceremonies of the ancient Jewish church and follow all the teachings of Moses and the prophets closely, their form of worship being as nearly as possible such as is laid down in their version of the Holy Writ.

The Ahavath Achim has been using any convenient building for a church, at one time utilizing the Lyceum theater. The congregation grew so that it was decided to erect a place of worship.

Joel Dorfan is president of the congregation and T. Wineberg, of No. 191 De-catur street, is chairman of the committee to receive donations for the new church.

Mr. Dorfan stated to a representative of The Constitution yesterday that the congregation had not quite raised all the money necessary for the erection of the new building.

"We have not more than eighty or ninety men in our congregation," said Mr. Dorfan, "who are able to aid in the building of our church. A number of public-spirited citizens have donated handsome contributions and we will be glad to receive any others which might be made. We desire to have a good and comfortable building and one that will cost between $8,000 and $10,000. We have a convenient site on Piedmont avenue and a lot large enough to give us a building which will meet our demands."

The new church is to be ninety feet long and forty feet wide.

Walter Smith is the architect who drew the plans and who will superintend the construction of the building.

Atlanta Constitution article announcing ground breaking for the building. Aug. 9, 1900.

Wedding ceremony, Mr. & Mrs. Joseph Freedman, Nov., 1913. Only known photograph of the interior of the Gilmer St. Shul.

Cantor I.M. Lubel

Translation of article in Yiddish press, March, 1908: "Cantor Lubel is beloved and well known in Atlanta. Besides the fact that he is one of the best musical cantors in the South, he is also a very good and capable mohel. Rev. Lubel is a disciple of Nisam Beker (famous cantor of Russia) and a past cantor of Yagistov shule in New York City. He was also cantor and mohel for two years in Los Angeles.

arched recess and was capped by a pair of lions on either side of the Tablets of the Law. A center aisle separated the long wooden pews in front of the *bimah*. Additional benches lined the walls facing the center.

Thomas Martin, writing a history called *Atlanta And Its Builders* in 1902, remarked, "The Atlanta synagogue is considered one of the largest and handsomest Orthodox houses of worship in the Southern states."

The Congregation had engaged its first bonafide rabbi, Berachya Mayerowitz. Rabbi Mayerowitz received his *smicha* from the Kovno Theological College (Lithuania) and also studied in Riga (Latvia). After serving congregations in Kansas City and Toledo, the 37-year-old Mayerowitz came to Ahavath Achim.

He had written a book on the ethics of the Talmud and, unlike so many European-trained rabbis, was fluent in English. The rabbi was also unusual in that he actively participated in community affairs to the extent that he was praised by the *Atlanta Constitution* as being "fully imbued with the spirit of American liberty."

At about the same time, a new *chazan* replaced Jaffe. Cantor I.M. Lubel, who reportedly served a large congregation in New York, came to Atlanta in the summer of 1901. He was

said to have had a fine musical voice and to be well liked by the members.

The hiring of these two religious functionaries and the construction of a building were major milestones accomplished in a relatively short time.

The Fulton County Tax Digest of 1896 reveals that only 37 of 142 Eastern Europeans had a net worth of over $50 and only one, Aaron Lansberger, had assets of more than $1,000.

Considering that the Russians had arrived in Atlanta with little more than a few personal possessions and had grown prosperous enough to support their own families in addition to organizing and building a synagogue, the opening of the Gilmer Street *shul* was quite remarkable.

While religious education for the young was vital, the Congregation did not organize a full school program for many years. Attempts had been made to bring an existing Talmud Torah under Ahavath Achim auspices in previous years but had failed as the members realized it would mean an increase in their dues.

Preparation for Bar Mitzvah was helter-skelter, usually involving a private *melamud* who tutored the boys after school. A weekly Sunday School had begun as had weekday classes but most education was done at home and only for boys. Yiddish

No. *335* Section *2* Pew No *17* Seat No .

Congregation Ahavath Achim.

SERVICES FOR

ROSH HASHONO AND YUM KIPUR,

—— 5664 ——

Sept. 22nd, 23rd and Oct. 1st, 1903.

SYNAGOGUE, 37 PIEDMONT AVE., COR. GILMER.

LEON EPLAN, Pres.   M. NEY, Sec.

High Holiday ticket, 1903. The practice of issuing admission tickets was established very early and has continued throughout the years.

was learned because everyone spoke it, and customs absorbed because they were part of everyday living.

Services at Ahavath Achim could be as raucous as membership meetings. A pot-belly stove and cuspidors were basic furnishings, and boxes of snuff dotted the *bimah*. The elders of the congregation sat along the eastern wall swaying in prayer or heated discussion behind individual lecterns in which they stored *siddur* and *tallit*.

Yiddish was the *lingua franca* for everything except the prayers in spite of the fact that Rabbi Mayerowitz had excellent command of English. Women, of course, sat in the balcony where they clustered around the few female members who could read either Hebrew or Yiddish, both of which were in the prayer books brought from Europe.

For the children, principally boys, the major holidays were a social event. Their time was spent in front of the three archway entrances on Piedmont Ave. or amusing themselves in the small classrooms downstairs.

Life in America demanded compromises. Those peddlers who had "graduated" to small proprietor soon found that Saturday was the most profitable business day of the week and most opted to remain open. A motion had been passed that those who were not *Shomer Shabbat* be denied certain honors but it was generally ignored.

The less affluent and newer arrivals were still scrupulous in their observance and resented the slippage of their brethren. The cleavage became an open break shortly after the new building opened.

Struggling with a greatly increased financial burden, the congregation decided to deny free admission to High Holiday services for non-members and those who could not afford the price of a ticket. Enraged, a small group left and became the founders of Shearith Israel Congregation.

Tensions continued between the German Jews and the Russians as the former found themselves part of an ever-shrinking minority.

One confrontation erupted when The Temple decided to open a cheap bath house on Decatur St., with the obvious implication that their co-

Page of prayer book brought from Europe printed in Hebrew and Yiddish. While most men could follow the service in either language, women were not given the opportunity to learn to read. Those who could, like Elka Raizel Goldstein, were exceptional. Her daughter, Ida Levitas, has vivid memories of her mother reciting the prayers aloud so that those around her could participate in the service.

The first successful joint venture of the German and Russian communities completed in 1911. This building was the meeting ground of Atlanta Jewry for 40 years.

Joel Dorfan, an exceptional community leader, served as president of the congregation longer than any person before or since. Elected first in 1900, he held the office almost continually until 1928 and then served again from 1931-32.

religionists could benefit. Led by Leon Eplan, Ahavath Achim responded vehemently, and it soon closed.

In times of trial, however, the community did come together. Following the brutal Kishinev massacre in 1903, Rabbi Mayerowitz called for the creation of a fund to aid the survivors. Leaders of both communities worked together and in three weeks raised $900.

The most successful communal effort of the era was the founding in 1909 of the Jewish Educational Alliance. In reality it was a merger of the Young Men's Hebrew Association and the Kindergarten Association, both of which had been established to serve the educational needs of immigrants.

The YMHA had conducted a night school to teach English, while the Free Kindergarten and Social Settlement cared for children and taught women the rudiments of the domestic arts. Meeting in the vestry room of The Temple, representatives from these groups and other philanthropic organizations voted to combine to form the Alliance whose purpose was educational, social and religious.

Combining funds which had been collected for independent ventures, the Alliance purchased a lot on Capitol Ave. between Fair and Woodward, and its building was completed in the spring of 1911. Because the German community had raised most of the $35,000 required, its members were allotted two-thirds of the seats on the Board of Trustees.

The officers were V. H. Kriegshaber, president; Miss Melanie Friedman and Morris Lichtenstein, vice presidents; L. J. Trounstine, treasurer, and

J. HYMAN, President
S. BOORSTEIN, Vice-President

RABBI P. HIRMES, Principal

M. YUDELSON, Treasurer
M. SHEINBAUM, Rercording Secy.

United Hebrew School

„עץ חיים היא למחזיקים בה ותמכיה מאשר"

90 CAPITOL AVENUE

ATLANTA, GA.,

OSCAR GERSHON,
Finance Secretary

Honorary Directors

RABBI P. HIRMES
RABBI T. GEFFEN
RABBI BLOOM

Board of Directors

D. BERGER
I. BERMAN
B. CLEIN
JOEL DORFAN
M. GAVRONSKI
J. H. GOLDSTEIN
M. GERSHON
S. GOLDSTEIN
S. J. GOLD
JAKE JACOBS
K. KOPLIN
M. LICHTENSTEIN
I. MELNICK
H. MENDEL
I. J. PARADIES
L. PFEFFER
J. RAUZIN
ALBERT ROTH
H. SMITH
S. SOLOMON
S. SMULLIAN
A. TENENBAUM
N. WEITZMAN

№ 907

Benefit-Raffle
For Purchasing Truck
for the United Hebrew School

For the Purpose of securing a Truck for the Hebrew School a $20.00 Gold Piece will be given away to the
LUCKY NUMBER

TICKET 10c TRY YOUR LUCK
Raffle will take place at the Annual Purim Ball

3 Elegant Prizes will be awarded to those who will be successful in selling the most Tickets.

Letterhead naming the leadership of the United Hebrew School; almost exclusively Ahavath Achim members.
Inset: Raffle held to benefit the school.

Heyman Jacobs, secretary.

Litchtenstein and Jacobs were Ahavath Achim members as were board members J. J. Saul, Dr. B. Wildauer, H. Mendel and J. Dorfan. A full-time director, Joseph Heyman, came from Cincinnati to head the staff.

Its stated purpose was "to help in the education of those who have come to our city from across the ocean…to offer innocent pleasures and amusement under proper auspices, to dispense happiness…".

In addition to a large hall, classrooms, library and meeting rooms, a free clinic was housed in a separate structure immediately behind the building. Because the more Americanized and established German community did not need the Alliance services offered, it quickly became the focus for the communal activities of the continually growing immigrant group.

Built largely by German Jews, it became home to Russian Jews and the predecessor of the Jewish Community Center which decades later became the meeting place for all Jews.

Ahavath Achim members were instrumental in founding the United Hebrew School, which was chartered in 1913 and met in the Alliance. Representatives of all the congregations were invited to participate in order to provide a systematic Jewish education to all children whatever their affiliation.

From its inception, the Ahavath Achim Congregation considered it their obligation to provide financial

Hyman Mendel and his enlarged family. Besides developing a most successful wholesale dry goods business, Mendel was active in a variety of communal activities.

H. Mendel & Co. on Decatur St. from which he operated a private Free Loan Society.

RECEIVED at 790 Broad St., near Market St., Newark, N. J.
TELEPHONES: Nos. 207 AND 307.

95 RI RA   6 paid

NY Harbor NY July 31-1906

Jacob Andranowsky

21 twenty one Beacon St Newark NJ

Arrived steamer woordam meet me EllisIsland

Joseph Galupceck

10 32 AM

ALWAYS OPEN.   MONEY TRANSFERRED BY TELEGRAPH.   CABLE OFFICE.

Telegram sent from N.Y. harbor in 1906 announcing the arrival of Joseph Galupceck whose name was "americanized" to Goldberg. He settled in Atlanta soon after and married Sarah Annie Levitt.

Sarah and Jacob Heiman, active and devoted members. Parents of Mary Dwoskin and Fannye Galanty.

An early photograph of Betsy and Charles Goldstein whose many descendents are present-day members.

34

Above: Wedding photo of Minnie Jacobs who married Max Kessler, Thanksgiving Day, 1907.
Above right: Isadore Heiman, Bar Mitzvah, 1913.
Right: Hand painted pictures and wedding invitation of Mr. & Mrs. Morris Nissenbaum, 1905.

Mr. and Mrs. A. Berger
request the honor of your presence at the
marriage of their neice,
Rosa,
To
Mr. Morris Nissenbaum
Thursday Evening, April 6, 8 o'clock,
1905.
Ceremony and Reception at
Columbia Woodmen Hall,
122 1-2 Peachtree Street,
Atlanta, Ga.

Pioneer Families

The Orthodox community continued to grow as more new arrivals found the notion of leaving the over crowded tenements of northern cities attractive. Here they struggled to establish small businesses some of which eventually became highly successful corporations.

Brit Milah invitation, 1913.

Mr. and Mrs. S. Parks

request the honor of

your company

at the

ברית מילה

of their new born son

on Tuesday, Feb. 18, 1913

at 11 A. M.

...residence

...nau St.

Atlanta.

Rebecca and Israel Barnet arrived in Atlanta with their sons and daughter. Israel sold dry goods from a horse drawn wagon.

Dot's Grandfather
Samuel Harris
Mrs J's Father

*Sam Harris operated a grocery store on
Magnolia Street.*

*Faggie and Solomon Zion. Faggie was the sister of
Joel Dorfan, Rev. Zion was the shochet.*

*Bressler children, Ben, Hannah, Lizzie, and David with their
mother, Ida Jacobs Bressler, and grandmother, Freda Jacobs. 1901*

Willie Reisman's grocery store, circa 1915.

Society was the vehicle through which a family became self-sufficient.

An early member of the Congregation, Hyman Mendel, operated his private Free Loan Society. Coming to Atlanta in 1893 because a friend from his *shtetl*, Sam Harris, was already here, Mendel advanced rapidly from peddler to wholesaler. By 1900 he was established at 86 Decatur St. where he remained for 44 years.

Many newly-arrived immigrants made their way to that address where they received a parcel of merchandise, encouragement and advice — all interest free. In some cases the potential entrepreneur was established in a small community outside Atlanta with enough merchandise to open a store.

There are a number of present-day businessmen whose parents or grandparents were beneficiaries of Mendel's fulfillment of the highest form of Jewish concern for the dignity and welfare of his neighbor.

Early minutes make several references to the reading of sections of a proposed charter or constitution. The earliest one known is dated 1907. It lists 206 members (men only), three of whom lived out of town — S. Ginsburg in Washington, GA, J. A. Wolfson, Greensboro, GA, and A. Samuel in New York City.

Dues had risen to $6 per year for seat holders and $9 for non-seat holders, payable monthly. An initial "admission fee" of $5 was charged to new members.

The Investigation Committee was still functioning and three black balls were required to reject an applicant. English was designated the official language of all business of the Congregation, but "a brother has the right to address the chair in Jargon (Yiddish) if he so desires."

support and leadership. Ahavath Achim members who served as president in its early years were I. J. Paradies, H. Mendel, J. H. Rodbell, Oscar Gershon and S. Boorstein. Harris Bergman was treasurer for many years. Later, when the Washington St. *shul* was built, the United Hebrew School was housed there rent free, and two Ahavath Achim rabbis, Abraham Hirmes and Harry Epstein, served as superintendents of the school.

Other important communal institutions were the Montefiore Relief Association, organized by Ahavath Achim in 1896, and the Free Loan Association, one of whose leaders was Morris Lichtenstein. While the Montefiore organization dispensed *tzedekah* to the needy, the Free Loan

Jewish calendar advertising M. Lichtenstein's insurance agency. Message is in Yiddish.

Stationery: Joseph Saul's wholesale clothing business.

Fines were imposed for a variety of offenses: 25¢ for disregarding a call to order by the president, from 25¢ to $1 for black-balling a candidate "from private revenge," and from $10 to $25 for "organizing or aiding in the building or maintaining a synagogue or *minyon* within five blocks of this synagogue."

From other provisions the concerns of the times are evident.

No children under four years were admitted to services except during Simchat Torah and all members were responsible for their children's behavior. No one was allowed to stand in the aisles or speak during the services, "especially during the reading of the Torah." Any member who intermarried or converted to another faith was to be "expelled from the congregation without any notice."

If a member died without a male descendant to recite *Kaddish*, the Congregation was obligated to hire a man to recite the daily prayers for 11 months. Honors during all holidays were sold to the highest bidder but specified times are mentioned when a member is entitled to an *Aliyah* (spelled "Alije" in the document).

A most interesting sentence provides that "It shall be the duty...for the Cantor to recite memorial prayers for Baron and Baroness De Hirsh and Doctor Theodore Hertzel" *(sic)* at appropriate times during the year.

Coinciding with the publication of this constitution and by-laws was the election of Rabbi J. M. Levin, who came to Ahavath Achim in November, 1907.

Born in Colelishok, Russia, he had studied in the famous Talmudic academies of Meer, Eshishock and Valosin, and was ordained at 18. Before coming to Atlanta, Rabbi Levin held pulpits in Fall River, MA.; Bayonne and Jersey City, N. J.; and Wilkes-Barre, PA. An emotional orator, he was among the early leaders of the Zionist movement in Atlanta. Other cantors during the time were N. Abelson and M. Rabinovitz.

An important member of the synagogue was the *shammes*. This position, which dates from Talmudic times, combined the duties of dues collector, janitor, record keeper and partial religious functionary. Such a person was indispensable to even the smallest and poorest congregation.

S. Feen is first mentioned in this position, followed by Samuel Solomon. Solomon's real name was Solomon Kabatzky, a peddler who came to Augusta, GA., before the turn of the century to join relations already there. Perhaps thinking business would be better in Atlanta, he

Rabbi Joseph Levin and his family. His great niece, Judy Finkel, is a current member.

Aaron Salensky, an early member whose name appeared on a membership list prepared in 1900.

moved and "Americanized" his name to Samuel Solomon.

A pious and learned man, he found a life which revolved in the synagogue more to his liking than commerce and became *shammes* shortly after the Gilmer St. building was finished. He remained in that position until his death in 1925.

Many of his descendants remained in Atlanta and are still affiliated with Ahavath Achim (*e.g.*, the Kolodkin and Hillman families).

For unknown reasons Rabbi Levin left Atlanta and was followed in the pulpit by Rabbi Dr. Hyman Yood. Very little is known of his background except that he received part (or all) of his education in London and was a "medical qualified *mohel*" who advertised that his operations healed in 24 hours.

Along with Rabbi Yood, Rev. Solo H. Goldstone, also a *mohel*, served the Congregation as cantor. From an ad for his services, it is learned that Goldstone was from Vienna, and called himself the "Obercanter of the Ahavath Achim Congregation."

In the years preceding World War I, the pattern of Jewish immigration from abroad repeated itself and another strain of Judaism came to the community. Political and economic turmoil as well as a series of natural disasters caused severe upheaval in Turkey, Rhodes and surrounding territories. Sephardic Jews who had lived in that part of the world since the Spanish Inquisition began to flee, gravitating to a few cities in the U.S. — San Francisco, New York, Seattle and Atlanta.

The two Sephardic families who arrived here in 1906 were, within a decade, joined by many more. Now it was the turn of the Russian community to be condescending to their strange cousins from the East. Indeed, the breach between the basically European community and the Levantine community was wide.

Their cultural overtones were completely different, in food, dress,

Rabbi Yood and Cantor Goldstone advertise their services in The American Jewish Review, Jan., 1916. *Both men were employed by the Congregation for relatively short periods. Rabbi Yood, it is said, was dismissed for behavior unbecoming a man of his position.*

Above, top of page: A. Silver family celebrates Seder with soldiers stationed in the area. March 28, 1918
Above: Camp Gordon near Chamblee. 1918
Right: Jake Abelson

Kobryner Relief Society, spearheaded by Sam Gershon who actually travelled to Kobryner (Russia) his native city to help those impoverished by the war.

Letter of introduction (in Yiddish) for Sam Gershon to help in his fund raising activities. Signed by Rabbi Hirmes and officers of the Congregation.

Lynch mob poses readily for the photographer beside the body of Leo Frank. None of them were brought to justice. Aug. 17, 1915

Sketch of the house on Central Ave. purchased by Cong. Or Ve Shalom. 1920

liturgy, world view and even the pronunciation of Hebrew. Poor and uneducated like the Russians before them, the young men came first to establish a foothold and then sent for wives and families.

But again the centuries-old tradition of one Jew reaching out to another Jew was replayed in Atlanta as Ahavath Achim's Free Loan Society and other communal organizations did their part. Petty traders, artisans and laborers, the Sephardic Jews began on the bottom of the heap and worked hard to build a future for their children.

At first they worshipped at Ahavath Achim and Shearith Israel but their religious traditions were so different it was only a matter of time before they formed their own *shul*. By 1914 the Oriental Hebrew Association Or Ve Shalom was organized, and by 1920 its new synagogue structure stood on the corner of Central and Woodward Avenues.

The bleakest episode in Jewish life in Atlanta and the entire South concerned the arrest, trial and subsequent lynching of Leo Frank, the manager of a pencil factory. Arrested and convicted on the flimsiest circumstantial evidence of the 1913 murder of a 14-year-old female employee, Frank was the subject of intense public scrutiny. The entire Atlanta Jewish community felt the glare of ugly publicity and squirmed in its light. During the trial many men sent their wives and children out of town to relatives in other cities, and some Jewish families left permanently.

Throughout the next two years, Frank's lawyers appealed his case all the way to the Supreme Court, which refused to hear it. In June, 1915, Gov. John Slaton commuted his death sentence to life imprisonment, unleashing a new wave of mob violence. On Aug. 17, 1915, hooligans dragged Frank from his cell in Milledgeville, GA, took him to Marietta, and hanged him.

Frank was a member of The Temple, but the entire Jewish community lived with a gnawing insecurity for years.

The Corner of Washington and Woodward Avenue

"The lot on Cor Washington and Woodward Ave. was purchased from Wm. Tontak. Ex Treasurer on March 25, 1919."

Deposited in cornerstone, Nov. 28, 1920

By 1920 Atlanta had changed considerably since the first Eastern European Jews trickled onto Decatur St. in the 1880's. Electric lights long illumined major downtown streets, and the suburbs extended all the way to Morningside Heights. Street cars powered by overhead wires rode the shiny rails as far as Stone Mountain and Marietta, costing the passenger 6¢.

The first "Chicago School" skyscraper — the first Equitable Building on the corner of Pryor and Edgewood — had been joined by other impressive structures: the Candler Building, the Peachtree Arcade, the Flatiron Building, the Winecoff Hotel, the Carnegie Library and the Grant Building.

An exuberant Chamber of Commerce writer exclaimed that "the city looks like the lower part of Manhattan Island."

The population was well over 150,000, of whom it was estimated some 4,000 were Jewish. Decatur, Gilmer, Butler and Piedmont were still heavily Jewish streets — both business and residence — but the influx of rural blacks, adding to the black population which predated the Jews, caused the more affluent Jews to move further south just across the Georgia Railroad tracks. The Ger-

Junction of Peachtree and Forsyth, known as the Atlanta "theatre district." Howard Theatre, on right, became the Paramount. 1921

Joel Dorfan
1900-1928

Lizzie Jacobs
1920-1924

Lillie Faeman
1924-1927

Nessie Rich
1927-1930

The Equitable Building, Atlanta's first skyscraper, became The Trust Company of Georgia Bldg. in 1913.

The tri-level Peachtree Arcade, the city's first shopping mall, connected Broad and Whitehall (now Peachtree) Sts.

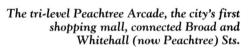

Rabbi Abraham P. Hirmes and his wife Freida.

In July, 1921, a petition was submitted to Fulton Superior Court for an official name change from "Ahawas Achim" to "Congregation Ahavath Achim." Petition stated that corporate business was conducted under the later name therefore that name should appear in official records.

man Jews had preceded them to the southside and would soon begin to migrate to the newer neighborhoods to the north.

Years of hard work and business acumen had brought the Ahavath Achim community gradual financial stability. Former peddlers were now proprietors of small businesses, wholesalers and semi-professionals. Many were property owners and had acquired savings. In the less than four decades since most arrived, they had become the newest embodiment of the American Dream.

The declaration of war in April, 1917, brought the establishment of Camp Gordon in DeKalb County and the expansion of Ft. McPherson. Before the war ended, more than 233,000 men passed thru these facilities, some of them Jews. The community opened its doors to them, especially during Pas-

sover and other holidays. Ahavath Achim members sent their sons to fight for their adopted country.

Rabbi Abraham P. Hirmes was elected rabbi in 1919. In the year preceding his appointment he had been in Atlanta at least twice as a guest speaker at Zionist-related events; once at the celebration of the first anniversary of the Balfour Declaration (Nov. 1, 1918) and again at a combined meeting of Young Judea and the Atlanta Zionist group (Dec. 8, 1918).

Born in Tren, Lithuania, in 1883, Rabbi Hirmes studied in the Slobadka Yeshiva before coming to America in the early 1900's. Records at Yeshiva University in New York indicate he was ordained at the Rabbi Isaac Elchanan Theological Seminary in 1919 before arriving in Atlanta at age 36.

Shortly after coming to Ahavath Achim, he was married and during the

Building Committee, Washington St. synagogue which included Joel Dorfan, 3rd from left, and Rabbi Hirmes, next to Dorfan.

Cornerstone for new building, set Nov. 28, 1920.

Washington St. building soon after completion. 1921

Atlanta Historical Society

course of his years in Atlanta, a son and two daughters were born. Rabbi Hirmes was a modest, soft-spoken man who moved with ease among his European-born, Yiddish-speaking congregants.

Kind and gentle, he emphasized the noble human traits and tried to overlook the darker side of individual behavior. One of his favorite comments on relationships was to "look for love and you will find little to hate." He had a custom of ending each marriage ceremony by wishing the couple "Peace and 'appiness." Hs is still remember by congregants with affection.

His sermons on the High Holidays were always in Yiddish and he was content to allow Joel Dorfan, Morris Lichtenstein, Hyman Mendel, Isidor Jacobs and other leaders to, in large measure, determine the direction of the Congregation.

Freida Hirmes, in contrast to her husband, had a commanding *persona* which was immediately apparent. More than 10 years younger than the

Rabbi, she was assertive, energetic and active in the affairs of the Congregation. Her name appears on certificates issued by the Sunday School as the "Superintendent." Wags of the day commented privately that she should have been the rabbi.

Despite his wife's reputation, Rabbi Hirmes is credited with originating the Sisterhood. A Ladies Auxiliary of some kind is mentioned during the building of the Gilmer St. *shul*, but either it had disintegrated or was not clearly defined.

In June, 1920, after the purchase of the lot for the new building, Rabbi Hirmes called 10 ladies together to reorganize a previous group or form a new one. After some discussion, Lizzie Jacobs (Mrs. Isidor) agreed to become the first president. Dues, $2, were to be paid semi-annually and the minutes were kept in a black spiral notebook in Yiddish.

The Sisterhood's first project was a four-day bazaar for which its 18

Photo by Doris Goldstein

First Church of Christ, Scientist, corner of Peachtree and 15th, erected in 1914.

Interior of Washington St. shul. Note extensive use of paint to create illusion of marble and other classic decoration.

Morris Dwoskin, a master of trompe l'oeil, was responsible for the decoration.

members baked cakes and collected merchandise from Jewish merchants on Decatur St. At the end of the last day, the total income was $1,858.12, all of which was donated to the building fund to furnish classrooms. It was quite an accomplishment!

Synagogue membership had soared from the 125 who had participated in the dedication of Gilmer St. in 1901 to the 395 families whose names were placed in the cornerstone of the new building on Nov. 28, 1920.

Construction lasted a year, and on Sept. 25, 1921, an official dedication ceremony was held. As the members ascended the steps and passed the massive Corinthian columns, their pride and joy in the completion of this impressive, neo-classical building knew no bounds.

Inside the sanctuary, which could accommodate between 1,500 and 1,800 people, sunlight poured in through a series of two-story, arched, stained-glass windows. The center *bimah* was 10 rows from the front, and a small reader's desk was immediately in front of the pulpit. A large domed ceiling extended over the major part of the central pews and artificial light was provided by over a dozen fixtures hanging from heavy brass link chains. The Holy Ark from the old building was painted and installed *in toto* complete with the pair of carved wooden lions which flanked the Ten Commandments. The only addition were 200-watt red electric lights in the lions' eyes.

Members of the newly-formed Sisterhood served refreshments and helped distribute the program books during the ceremony. An orchestra played, Cantor Abraham Selsky sang, Mayor James L. Key and Gov. Thomas W. Hardwick spoke, and Rabbis Tobias Geffen, David Marx and Hirmes participated.

It was said that the building was a scaled-down replica of the First Church of Christ, Scientist, which had been

Program

2 P. M.

Informal reception in the vestry of the Synagogue by the Sisterhood and the Reception Committee of the Congregation.

3 P. M.

Turning over the keys by the Chairman of the Building Committee, Mr. Morris Lichtenstein, to the President of the Congregation, Mr. Joel Dorfan.

OPENING THE MAIN AUDITORIUM FOR THE GENERAL PUBLIC

1—Overture .... Orchestra

2—Opening Prayer .... Rabbi Tobias Geffen

3—"Star Spangled Banner and Hatikvoh," lead by the children of the Hebrew and Sabbath School, accompanied by Orchestra and Cantor Abraham Selsky.

4—Address by the Rabbi of Congregation— Rabbi Abraham P. Hirmes

5—Placing of the Holy Scrolls and Prophets in the Ark—

"Vaehy Benshea Ho-oron and Vaenucha Yomar— By Cantor Abraham Selsky

6—Placing of the Porechoth in position on the Holy Ark.

7—Psalm 30 .... Cantor Abraham Selsky

LIGHTING "NEYR TOMED" (PERPETUAL LIGHT)

8—Address .... His Excellency, Thomas W. Hardwick, Governor of the State of Georgia

9—Music .... Orchestra

10—Address .... Honorable James L, Key, Mayor of the City of Atlanta

11—Music .... Orchestra

12—Address .... Rabbi David Marx

13—Music .... Orchestra

14—Address .... Mr. Joel Dorfan, President of the Congregation

15—Benediction .... Rabbi Abraham P. Hirmes

Mr. Joseph Goldberg, chairman of the Ways and Means Committee and Mr. Jake Jacobs, Treasurer of the Building Committee, will have charge of distributing the honors of unlocking the door, placing the Holy Scrolls and Prophets in the Ark, putting in position the Porechoth, and lighting the Neyr Tomed

Above: Dedication program, Sept. 25, 1921
Right: Cover of souvenir book printed for the dedication.

Souvenir Program

Dedication

—of—

Synagogue Erected 1920-21, 5681

—at the—

Corner of Washington Street and Woodward Avenue

September 25, 1921

Atlanta, Ga.

completed in 1914 at the corner of Peachtree and Fifteenth Streets. For many years it was believed that the Congregation could not afford the services of an architect so they bought the plans used for the Church. Records show, however, that the plans for the synogogue were prepared by Charles H. Hopson and Harry I. Hirsch, Associated Architects, while the Church had been designed by Arthur Neal Robinson.

Yet, there are striking similarities between the two buildings. A yellow brick facade, soaring columns, arched windows and a domed roof are featured in both structures. Inside the recessed alcove flanked by columns (which in the church houses a huge Moller organ) where the ark and pulpit were located and the dark wooden pews show the relation of the two buildings. Both structures were of the Classical Revival style, a mode of architecture popular in public buildings.

The interior decoration of the synagogue sanctuary was a marvel. Unable to afford the hand-cast plaster decorations associated with the Revival style, the building committee turned to

Notice of early event held in the new building; 2nd anniversary of the Sisterhood. 1921

Sisterhood Gives Synagogue Banquet

An afafir of Wednesday evening was the banquet given by the A. A. Sisterhood, at the Synagogue on Washington Street, to celebrate their second anniversary.

The hall was decorated with flowers and ferns, and silver vases with cut flowers adorned the tables from which refreshments were served.

The program consisted of the following numbers:

Addresses by Rabbi A. P. Hermes, J. Dorban, (president of synagogue), J. Jacobs, M. Lichtenstein.

Violin Solo—Messrs Prayer and Siegal.

Vocal Solo—Miss Bertie Eisenberg.

A Playlet—Sunday School Class.

Another important feature of this occasion was the sale of books for the A. A. Library. A large amount of money was raised.

Dinner in Honor

of

Morris Lichtenstein

Jewish Educational Alliance
Atlanta, Georgia

March 24, 1926

Tribute Dinner in honor of Morris Lichtenstein, widely respected community leader. 1926
Right: List of attendees which included both the German and Russian communities.

Morris Dwoskin who had a small interior decorating business and was a master at the art of *trompe l'oeil*...or "fooling the eye."

Over many weeks Dwoskin painstakingly painted all the "marble" columns as well as the moon and the stars in the dome. A Greek key design decorated the ceiling, and other classic borders were painted instead of using costly moldings. Dwoskin's 13-year-old son Harry helped his father paint the synagogue during vacations, and was paid 30¢ an hour.

Below the sanctuary were four large classrooms used by the United Hebrew School during the week, and the fledgling Sunday school on weekends.. A chapel for daily services was also on the lower level. *Shammes* Solomon agreed to continue his duties in the new building and everything was in place for the beginning of a new era.

Joel Dorfan, who had been president since 1900 and who remained in that office until 1928, received the keys from Morris Lichtenstein, chairman of the building committee. Both men had been important leaders of the Russian community for many years.

Dorfan, in addition to serving as president of the congregation, was instrumental in the early development of the synagogue's educational programs as well as the Chevra Tehilim and Free Loan Association. He was so well-known among the immigrant generation that it is said one congregant, when asked while applying for citizenship the name of the president of the United States, replied without hesitation, "Joel Dorfan."

Lichtenstein had the distinction of being respected by the German community as well as his natural constituents at Ahavath Achim. He became the second president of the Alliance and was a leader in early Zionist activities. In addition, he established a good relationship with Rabbi Marx and was respected in the general business community.

The completion of the "Big Shul" in the heart of the Jewish residential neighborhood ushered in an era of increased internal organization and activity as well as the enhancement of the Congregation's leadership in the community.

An important new program was the

Program

Closing Exercises
of the
A. A. Bible Class
Sunday, May 27, 1923

1. Hatikvah...*Assembly*
2. Welcome Address.....................................*A. Rittenbaum*
3. Recitation..*Sarah Pazol*
4. Solo..*Cantor Selsky*
5. Address...*Rabbi A. P. Hirmes*
6. Vocal Solo..*Ida Wachman*
7. Report of Activities....................................*E. Socolov*
8. Violin Solo...*L. Rittenbaum*
9. Address..*J. Dorfan*
10. Solo...*Birdie Eisenberg*
11. Rem rks..*By Teachers*
12. Solo...*Cantor Selsky*
13. Awarding of Prizes....................................*I. Jacobs*
14. Star Spangled Banner

ADMISSION FREE
ALL ARE WELCOME

YOU ARE CORDIALLY INVITED TO ATTEND

A MUSICAL

GIVEN UNDER THE AUSPICES OF THE

AHAVATH ACHIM BIBLE CLASSES

SUNDAY, DECEMBER 12, AT 11:30 A. M. *1926*

AHAVATH ACHIM CONGREGATION

WASHINGTON STREET AND WOODWARD AVENUE

PROGRAM

1—VOCAL SOLO—TRADITIONAL SELECTIONS, BY OSCAR GERSHON.
FOLLOWED BY AN EXPLANATION OF THE ORIGIN OF EACH SONG
ACCOMPANIED AT THE PIANO BY MISS BESSIE SEGAL
2—VIOLIN SOLO—MASTER MENDEL SEGAL.

A. A. Bible Class

This is to Certify that ___SARAH PAZOL___

is an enrolled student of the ___A. A.___ Bible Class
and is entitled to all of it's privileges.

_____ RABBI

SProger
SECRETARY

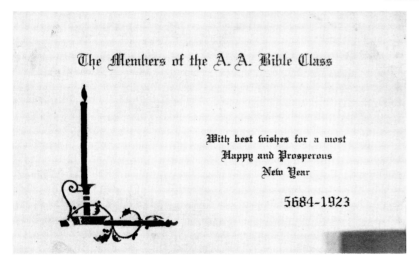

The Members of the A. A. Bible Class

With best wishes for a most
Happy and Prosperous
New Year

5684—1923

Varied social and educational activities of the
A.A. Bible Class.

CLASS BANQUET.

An event of interest will be the banquet to be given by the Bible Class Wednesday at 8 o'clock, at the Synagogue, Washington Street and Woodward Avenue.

The banquet is to celebrate the holiday "Chamisho-Ossor."

Songs, recitations, addresses and readings will constitute the program.

A supper will be served and all members are urged to attend.

Dance Will Be Given By A. A. Bible Class

The A. A. Bible Class will give an entertainment and masque dance in commemoration of Purim on the night of March 6 at the Jewish Education Alliance.

Purim lends a significant advent to spring in Biblical history, which is a preservation of Jewish life and ideals.

The Elder Council has secured the valued services of Max Rose and Ben Coleman to render a number of allegorical tableaus to recapture the color and spirit of Biblical days. These will be interspersed with the dance.

A well known orchestra will furnish the music.

Admission by card only. *23*

✿ ✿ ✿ ✿

The Bible Class of Atlanta, Ga.

Dear Aunt Ray:—

The new scholastic terms for all branches of knowledge have reopened for another year of active work, and so has the Ohaveth Achim Bible Class of Atlanta, Ga. The formal "Installation of Officers" was held Thursday evening, October 19, at the shul, and a very beautiful program was arranged for the occasion.

Sunday morning, October 22, marked the opening day of the second term of this Bible class and over 200 Jewish boys and girls were present. The classes were divided and the courses of study for each grade outlined.

Our Rabbi A. P. Hirmes and his never failing wife, are both a great credit to this class and are both active workers in anything for the betterment and promotion of the class. We have some very excellent teachers and a large class of enthusiastic workers and with all these assets there is no earthly reason why, in time, this Bible class should not be the pride of the Jews of Atlanta.

With all best wishes to you, Aunt Ray and all my cousins, I am,

SARAH PAZOL.

Atlanta, Ga.

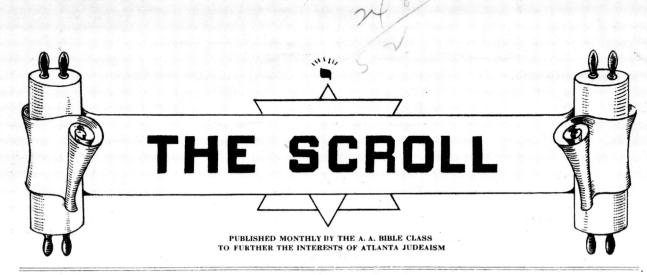

THE SCROLL

PUBLISHED MONTHLY BY THE A. A. BIBLE CLASS
TO FURTHER THE INTERESTS OF ATLANTA JUDEAISM

Volume 1   Atlanta, Georgia, February, 1924   Number 3

Mid-Year Report of A. A. Bible Class

Sunday, Feb. 10, marks the closing of a most successful term for the A. A. Bible Class. In a short period of only four months the members of the Elders Council have worked diligently for the Bible Class, with only one purpose in view, namely, to make this a banner term. This they did beyond question.

The most outstanding achievement, according to many, is the publishing of three issues of the "Scroll", a copy of which you are now reading. Through hard conscientious labor, the "Scroll" has been run on a self-supporting basis, looking only to its advertisers for support. Your chairman of the Elders Council hopes that the new officers will continue its publication for we believe its need has been felt in the city. Your retiring editor, being also your chairman, found it rather difficult to divide his time justly between these two important positions, and therefore suggests that the editorship be given to one who has sufficient time to devote his time to it solely.

Your Council did very little towards increasing the membership of the Bible Class. The reason being that we deemed it wisest to first assimilate those 225 members which we have already in our midst and teach them to appreciate the true meaning of our Bible Class. We believe this plan in the near future will bring noteworthy results, for when these 225 members get to know the Bible Class, they will boost it, hence increasing its membership.

During our term of office, an interesting program was presented every Sunday morning after class study. These programs were in the form of debates on Jewish topics, musical numbers, dialogues, etc. Various prominent speakers were obtained to address the Bible Class, which proved very helpful. At the present time we are in the midst of an Essay Contest on the subject "What I Think of a Bible Class." Many have enthusiastically responded. The winning essay will be printed in the next issue of the "Scroll." A five-dollar gold piece will be given to the winner.

We have tried to mix the study of the Bible with clean recreation in order to keep it interesting. In this we believe we have succeeded. Two of the most outstanding affairs of the Bible Class proper, were the Chanukah program and the Arbor Day Banquet.

During our term of office, class social clubs were begun and perfected. These clubs have a social gathering every other Sunday afternoon. One-fourth of the dues collected go towards the support of the Bible Class. These Class clubs gave some very successful entertainments, most outstanding of which were the "A" class dinner-dance and the "B" class leap year dance. These affairs have done much towards instilling class spirit among the members.

Due to the untiring efforts of Mr. Isador Jacobs, the Music Club has been reorganized and perfected. This club at present has a membership of 25 enthusiastic singers, who meet every Wednesday under the direction of Prof. Watters. In the near future they will give you a performance that will be well worth hearing.

Financially, the Bible Class has never been in a better position. Your chairman with the aid of an efficient committee has obtained from the Ahavath Achim Synagogue a check sufficient to cover all old debts, most of which were carried over from the previous year.

Much praise is due to our honorable Rabbi. A. P. Hermes, and the officers of the Ahavath Achim Congregation for their co-operation. If they would only double their efforts for the next term, much more could be accomplished. The various class teachers should be highly complimented for their splendid success in teaching the Bible. Their lectures are always not only beneficial but also enjoyable.

Your retiring chairman wishes to thank every member of the Elders Council for their untiring co-operation for the past term, for without them little could be accomplished. Much thanks is due every member of the staff of the "Scroll," especially the advertising managers, Mr. Dave Barnett and Mr. I. M. Galanty. They have been wizards in collecting ads. Your President, Mr. Alex Rittenbaum, deserves much praise for he

A. A. Bible Class Nominates Officers

On Sunday, Feb. 3rd, new officers were nominated at the A. A. Bible Class as the mid-year term expires Feb. 10. Mr. Alex Rittenbaum has a clear field for chairman of the Elders Council, while running for President are Mr. Max Rose, Mr. M. Berger and Mr. Chas. Bergman. For Vice-President are Mr. David Speilberger and Mr. Wolfe Lefcoff. For Secretary and Treasurer both Miss Ruth Mendleson and Miss Rebecca Golden are running for re-election. The retiring officers of the Bible Class are Max M. Cuba, Chairman of the Elders Council; Alex Rittenbaum, President; Ben Coleman, Vice-President; Ruth Mendelson, Secretary and Mr. Isador Jacobs and Miss Rebecca Golden, Treasurers.

From what we can gather from the nominating speeches, a phenomenal term can be expected.

"A" CLASS ELECTS OFFICERS.

The "A" Class of the A. A. Bible Class elected the following officers at their regular meeting Sunday afternoon, Feb. 3rd:

Mr. Dave Barnett, President.
Mr. Dave Speilberger, Vice-President.
Miss Sarah Gordon, Secretary.
Mr. Chas. Bergman, Recording Secretary.
Miss Esther Siegal, Treasurer.

It was indeed a very heated election for much campaigning had been done. The newly elected officers are planning big things which they will bring up at their next meeting, Sunday afternoon, February 17. At this meeting new committees will be appointed and refreshments served.

has been a partner to me in this work, laboring side by side in the harness. I feel sure he will make you a splendid chairman of a splendid Elders Council, for the coming term.

A great future stands before the A. A. Bible Class.

Respectfully submitted,

MAX M. CUBA,
Chairman Elders Council A. A. Bible Class, and Editor of the "Scroll."

An early edition of The Scroll published monthly by the A.A. Bible Class, Max Cuba, editor, Alex Rittenbaum, business manager.

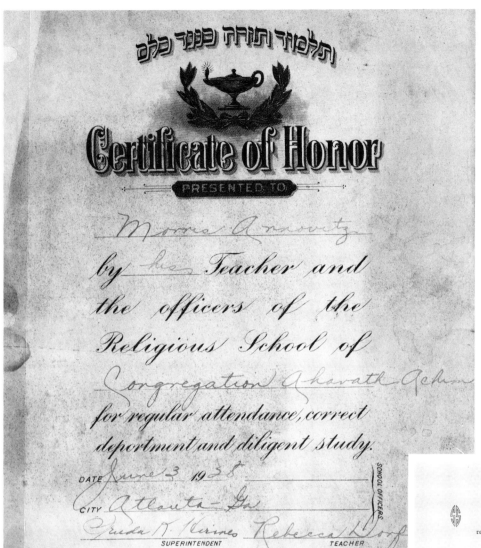

והגדת לבנך ביום ההוא לאמר

Certificate of Honor

PRESENTED TO

Morris Arnovitz

by *his* Teacher and
the officers of the
Religious School of
Congregation Ahavath Achim
for regular attendance, correct
deportment and diligent study.

DATE *June 3 1928*

CITY *Atlanta Ga.*

Freda K. Hirmes   *Rebecca Dorf*
SUPERINTENDENT   TEACHER

SCHOOL OFFICERS

*Religious School certificate awarded to Morris Arnovitz signed by
Mrs. Hirmes, superintendent and Rebecca Dorfan, teacher. 1928*

Mr. and Mrs. S. Sisselman

cordially invite you to be present at the Confirmation Services
of their son

Sidney

on Saturday Morning, April the 17th, 1926, at 9:00 o'clock

at the Congregation Ahavath Achim
Washington Street and Woodward Avenue, Atlanta, Georgia

*Invitation to the Confirmation of Sidney
Sisselman. 1926*

Ahavath Achim Bible School, the predecessor of the High School. The impetus for the creation of the school originated with Isidor Jacobs who, with Joseph H. Goldberg and Rabbi Hirmes, recruited boys of high school age who would continue their Jewish education after Bar Mitzvah. The first meeting of the class was attended by Harry Cohen, Eddie Berger, Sanford Saperstein, Jake Robinson, Charles Bergman and Abe Nissenbaum.

Soon girls were invited to join and the Bible School became an important activity in the life of Jewish teenagers. In addition to the two hours they spent on Sunday mornings, there were picnics and other social events. Each class had a secretary who managed the organizational affairs of the school. Serving in that capacity in the formative years were Sarah Pazol, Pauline Spielberger, Gladys Shulman, Jenny Berchenko and Celie Bergman.

The teachers were laymen dedicated to passing their knowledge and love of Judaism to the next generation. Joseph Goldberg, Charles Bergman and Max Cuba, all of whom became president of the congregation, served as teachers for many years and became role models to the students.

A year after its own formation, the Sisterhood accepted the Sunday School as its principal concern and adopted its motto from the sixth verse of the Book of Deuteronomy — "V'shenantan L'vanacha…And teach them to your children." The School had been in existence for many years but attendance was small and the curriculum limited.

The first Junior Congregation was formed during the early years on Washington St. Its primary purpose was to assist in conducting the *Mincha* and *Maariv* services every Sunday evening. From this group of 20 post-Bar Mitzvah boys, an ushering committee was formed for the High Holidays and first functioned in the fall of 1924. Isidore Siegel and Abe Lewis were co-chairmen of the first group; synagogue members have served in this capacity ever since.

An important activity of the community founded and supported by Ahavath Achim.

Morris Baum, long time secretary of the Free Loan Society.

The late Friday night service was also instituted at this time. It was conducted by members of the Junior Congregation who not only led the prayers but also delivered a sermon on a topic of Jewish interest. Rabbi Hirmes met with the participants and attended the services.

In the time-honored tradition of synagogues all over the world, Ahavath Achim became a *Beit Migdash*…a House of Study. Downstairs, after the daily minyan, the men gathered around long tables to pore over Talmudic texts and ardently champion one point or view or another.

Washington St. was also well-known to numerous *"meshullim"* — traveling messengers sent all over the world to solicit funds for a wide variety of Jewish institutions and organizations. They would appear either early in the morning or late in the afternoon, just in time for one of the two daily services. Often a member would bring the stranger home or walk with him up and down Decatur St. pointing out the Jewish businesses.

P. S. (Philip Shalom) Clein became *shammes* in 1926 after the death of Rev. Solomon. A native of Ireland, Clein came to Atlanta at the turn of the century to join his brother William.

Beginning as a peddler and eventually opening a dry goods store, P. S. Clein married and moved to Charleston, his wife's home. He remained there for several years and then returned to Atlanta where he found the position of *shammes* vacant.

A deeply religious and pious man, Clein loved the business of running the synagogue. For many years he appeared on the first day of Rosh Hashanah and Passover in a top hat, cutaway coat and grey striped pants. His daughter (Esther Silver) remembers him driving up and down Washington St. on many occasions collecting enough people for the afternoon *minyan*. Many members fondly remember him arranging the details of their Bar Mitzvah or wedding ceremony.

Ahavath Achim was not his only interest; the entire Jewish community was important to him. He devoted countless hours to Zionist activities and other communal endeavors. One of his favorite remarks when ending a conversation was, "I'll see you at my place of business."

For all its beauty, the sanctuary during the High Holiday season could be an oven. Only the lower part of the stained glass windows could be opened and there were no fans. During Yom Kippur the distinctive aura of smelling salts hung in the air. The selling of the holiday honors was a boisterous affair, and the spittoons from Gilmer St. were still in use. The cadence of Rabbi Hirmes' Yiddish speeches gave an Old World ambience to the service — and drove the younger generation into the streets.

The internal organization remained virtually unchanged. Still modeled on fraternal orders, a system of investigation of potential members and a black-ball procedure for rejection were in effect. Membership meetings were described by one observer as "hot and fiery" and dominated by Joel Dorfan and Morris Lichtenstein. Unfortunately, no minutes of these years survived.

Subtle changes had gradually occurred in the psyche of the leadership of the Congregation. In the process of their accommodation to America, they found themselves on the one hand clinging to the old and familiar while on the other understanding the need to provide a new version of Judaism in order to retain the loyalty of their children.

Most of the merchants opened their stores on Shabbat but refused to ride on Rosh Hashana or Yom Kippur, often "camping out" at a relative's house if they lived too far from Washington St. to walk. The new synagogue organizations of the era, the Bible School and Junior Congregation, were innovative ways of involving their American-born children in what was still the center of their lives.

While Rabbi Hirmes was perfectly acceptable to Joel Dorfan and Morris Lichtenstein, he was too remote from the teenagers and young adults to be effective. The leadership recognized what had happened and came to the conclusion that they must search for a new rabbi.

Official Program

WELCOME TO

THE DISTINGUISHED ZIONIST DELEGATION

Colonel John Henry Patterson
Dr. Alexander Goldstein

✛

AT

AHAVATH ACHIM CONGREGATION
WASHINGTON ST. AND WOODWARD AVE.

Tuesday Evening, May 23rd, 1922
AT 7:30 P. M.
ATLANTA, GA.

Under the Auspices of

KEREN HAYESOD
J. SAUL, Chairman

A. D. G. COHN
Campaign Director

L. J. LEVITAS
Chmn. Arrangement Comm.

Community wide activities in support of Zionist causes were often held at Ahavath Achim whose members were also the leaders. An example is this program which raised funds for Keren Hayesod, now known as the Jewish National Fund.

Rev. P.S. Clein, shammes.

Wedding banquet celebrating the marriage of Charney Bressler and Jake Abelson. 1923

Not Deformed or Reformed but Informed

"I arrived six weeks before the first day of Rosh Hashanna. So I told the congregation that I would be doing the sermon on the first day of Rosh Hashanna and Yom Kippur in English."

Rabbi Harry H. Epstein
Southern Israelite, March, 1978

Downtown Atlanta, 1920's.

Atlanta Historical Society

His father, Rabbi Ephraim Epstein, was ordained in Lithuania and brought his family to Chicago in 1911 after accepting the pulpit of Congregation Anshe Knesset Israel. Harry the eldest son, was then eight years old.

The father imposed a strict discipline on his son to insure that he would develop a lifetime commitment to Jewish study. As a teenager, he attended the Beth Midrash L'Rabonim, founded by his father and which ultimately became the Hebrew Theological College, a leading rabbinic institution in the U.S.

In 1921, Harry Epstein, 18, was in the graduating class at Yeshiva College in New York. Because of his youth, he was advised to pursue his rabbinical studies in Europe. Early in 1922 he left for Slobodka, Lithuania, location of one of the leading centers of learning in the world. His uncle, Rabbi Moshe Epstein, was one of the *illuminati* of the school.

The Slobodka Yeshiva, founded in 1882 and dedicated to the teachings of the Musar movement, was an institution of over 500 students when Harry Epstein arrived in 1922.

He remained there until 1924 when a decision to open a branch in Palestine was precipitated by the Lith-

Rabbi Harry H. Epstein arrived in Atlanta Aug. 15, 1928, via a route which began in Lithuania, with stops in Chicago, New York, Slobodka, Palestine, and Tulsa.

He was born into a distinguished rabbinic family which included Rabbi Zvi Hirsch Chaim Epstein, the chief rabbinic judge of Bakst, Lithuania, and Rabbi Moshe Mordecai Epstein, known in rabbinic circles as the Prodigy of Bakst.

Joseph Goldberg
1928-1929

Hyman Jacobs
1929-1930

Joel Dorfan
1931-1932

Hyman Mendel
1933-1934

Oscar Gershon
1935-1937

I.J. Paradies
1937-1939

uanian government's discontinuance of its practice of exempting all yeshiva students from military service.

In August, 1924, he traveled with his uncle and nine other classmates from Slobodka to Palestine to be among the first students at the new yeshiva, located in Hebron.

The following year Harry Epstein became *Rabbi* Harry Epstein. Ordained first in Hebron, he remained in Palestine and received *smicha* from five recognized rabbinic personalities including Rav Abraham Isaac Kook, Chief Rabbi of Palestine.

Returning to America to complete his secular education and begin his career in 1926, Rabbi Epstein re-enrolled in the University of Chicago. After a short time, his uncle Rabbi Moshe Epstein, arrived in the United States to begin a fund-raising tour for the Slobodka Yeshiva.

The young Rabbi Epstein became his uncle's interpreter and traveling companion. The travels of so well-known a personality as Rabbi Moshe Epstein were followed in the American Yiddish press, which also noted his articulate nephew.

One of the stops was Tulsa, OK., where the leaders of Congregation B'nai Emunah, impressed with this young man's vigor and erudition, asked him to fill their pulpit. Rabbi Harry H. Epstein's career as rabbi, counselor, spokesman for Jewish life in the American idiom, and community leader had begun.

Meanwhile, the acculturation of Ahavath Achim founders and their first generation sons and daughters continued unabated and a serious search had begun to find a new spiritual leader. Charles Glazer, a man fluent in both Yiddish and Hebrew, remembered reading about the dynamic young Rabbi Epstein in the Yiddish press. In the name of the Congregation, he wrote Rabbi Epstein in Hebrew, asking that he consider the pulpit of Ahavath Achim.

The Rabbi visited Atlanta for the

first time in July, 1928, and in addition to conducting Shabbat services and officiating at the funeral of a prominent member, spoke at the annual meeting of the Jewish Progressive Club.

The younger members welcomed enthusiastically the handsome, beardless rabbi who interspersed his flawless English with literary allusions as well as Talmudic references.

The men who sat around the long tables in the basement of the synagogue studying a tractate of the Talmud eyed him warily, doubting his knowledge and perhaps his piety. A few weeks later he was elected unanimously to the position at the munificent annual salary of $6,000.

Returning to Chicago the Rabbi discussed the offer with his family and the lady who was soon to become his lifelong companion, Reva Chashesman.

Born into a rabbinic family in a small Russian village near the German border, Reva Chashesman received an extensive education, Judaic and secular. In addition to Yiddish, which was spoken at home, and Hebrew, which she was taught in order to study *Chumash*, Reva learned Russian, German and Polish before she was 20. She joined her brother in Berlin who was studying medicine, and then went to Paris and attended the Sorbonne.

Emigrating to America in 1927, she was reunited with her parents in Chicago where her father, Rabbi Judah Chashesman, had assumed the pulpit of Anshe Tiktin. She completed her education at the University of Chicago.

She met her future husband when he came to her house unannounced to borrow a book from her father. After a brief courtship which included Rabbi Epstein's father sending a nephew *sub rosa* to meet her and bring him a report, they became engaged and made plans for their wedding. It was to be celebrated as soon as Reva graduated.

Rabbi Epstein's first weeks in

Harry H. Epstein, a young graduate of Yeshiva College. 1922

Rae Meyer
1930-1933

Rose Klotz
1933-1935

Zelda Berman
1935-1937

Annabelle Samet
1937-1939

Harry H. Epstein

Scion of a distinguished rabbinic family in Lithuania educated to carry on their tradition of scholarship and leadership.

Rabbi Ephraim Epstein

Hannah Epstein

Rabbi Epstein in Tulsa, OK. 1927

Yeshiva student Harry Epstein (standing) and friend pose in traditional Arab dress, Jerusalem. 1925

Rabbi Epstein (right) with friend who later became a judge in the Religious Court in Tel Aviv.

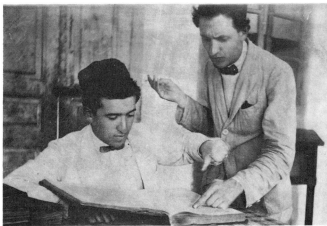

Studying Talmud with a 'chavruta' (study partner) in Hebron.

Classroom scene, Hebron Yeshiva. 1924

Lithuanian visa. 1922

Reva Chashesman

Only daughter of a revered rabbi in a small Russian village received an extensive Judaic and general education, rare for a woman in that day and place.

Reva (2nd from rt. on back row), the only Jewish student in the Suvalki, Poland gymnasium (high school).

Rabbi Judah Chashesman   Rachel Chashesman

An excellent student and accomplished linguist.

Reva becomes Mrs. Harry Epstein. Jan. 13, 1929

Graduation from the Un. of Chicago with high honors. 1928

61

Jeshivath Merkas Harav
of Rabbi
A. I. KOOK
Chief Rabbi of Eretz Israel.
JERUSALEM

*Letter of congratulations from Rav Kook, Chief
Rabbi of Palestine upon appointment to pulpit in
Tulsa, OK. 1927*

NEW SERVICE TIME TO BE INAUGURATED BY AHAVATH ACHIM

Featured by the weekly appearance of a trained choir of 13 voices and

RABBI HARRY EPSTEIN

a sermon by Rabbi Harry H. Epstein, the Ahavath Achim synagogue

corner Washington street and Woodward avenue, will inaugurate a series of religious hours starting at 8 o'clock Friday night.

Designed primarily for the younger element of Atlanta Jewry who find it impossible to attend the twilight Sabbath services, the 8 o'clock program has been successfully carried out by the congregation for the last six years. Unusual interest centers in the opening of this season's services because of the induction of the choir, the first of its kind to participate in orthodox services here.

Rehearsals have been held for six weeks under the direction of Emilio Volpi, local voice teacher, and a special feature of the program will be the rendition of the tradition al "Kaddish," or memorial prayer by the rabbi, together with the choir. Members of the group, several of whom are talented vocalists, include Lew Kaufman, cantor; Harry Siegel, Eli Cherkas and John Cohen, first tenors; Harold Wilensky, Irving Cohen, and Leon Berman, second tenors; Morris Amato, Meyer Morris and Constantine Galfas, baritones; Al Singer, Abe Berman and Marvin Goldstein, bass singers.

Will Lead Festivities at Purim Ball

Leaders of the annual Purim ball, to be given here Wednesday night, are shown in the above photograph. In the front row are Mrs. G. Brodkin and Rabbi Harry H. Epstein. In the back row are Harry Lahman and Henry A. Alexander.

RABBI EPSTEIN AWARDED LIFETIME PULPIT HERE

A lifetime position as religious leader of one of the largest synagogues in the South!

That was the honor bestowed upon Rabbi Harry H. Epstein last Sunday by the unanimous action of the members of Congregation Ahavath Achim. To Rabbi Epstein the distinction of a lifetime appointment to a pulpit came on the occasion of his tenth anniversary as spiritual leader of the Ahavath Achim Synagogue. In the case of his congregation, the honor was an expression of its gratitude to the man who in the space of a single decade has guided the religious organization to prominence in the Southeast.

The unusual tribute was inspired at a meeting of the board of trustees of the congregation, when a resolution was adopted to submit Rabbi Epstein's name as permanent religious leader to the entire congregation. Last Sunday, at a general meeting, congregation members overwhelmingly approved the idea.

Rabbi Harry H. Epstein became religious leader of Congregation Ahavath Achim in 1928. The son of Rabbi Ephraim Epstein, who has been rabbi of the largest Orthodox synagogue in Chicago for 27 year, he was among the first 8 students of the Hebrew Theological College, founded by his father. In 1921, Harry H. Epstein was graduated from Yeshiva College in New York, and continued his studies in Slabodka with his uncle, the famous Rabbi Moshe Mordecai Epstein. With nine other students of the Slabodka Yeshiva, the young American sailed for Palestine to found a Seminary to carry on the work of his uncle in the Holy Land. In ancient Hebron, at the transplanted Yeshiva, he continued his studies and at the age of 22 was ordained Rabbi. A year later, in 1926, he received his Doctor of Hebrew Literature Degree, making a total of six rabbinical degrees that he had received from Palestine and European institutions. Following a tour of the United States and Canada with his uncle, Rabbi Epstein was elected to the pulpit of the Orthodox community in Tulsa, Okla., later coming to Atlanta.

The author of "Judaism and Progress" and other works, Rabbi Epstein has increased the membership of Congregation Ahavath Achim here to the total of 800, and his progressive educational methods have resulted in a membership of 425 children in the Sunday School, and 150 young men and women in the Bible

RABBI HARRY H. EPSTEIN

school. With Mrs. Epstein, who is active in the Ahavath Achim Sisterhood, Atlanta Senior Hadassah and congregational work, he is a leader in Zionist endeavor here.

Rabbi Epstein with his young daughters, Renana and Davida.

Rabbi and Cantor at WSB

RABBI HARRY H. EPSTEIN (right) and Cantor Aaron Lipitz, of the Congregation Ahavath Achim, Atlanta, one of the most representative synagogues in America, who will present an impressive program at WSB Sunday afternoon at 4:30.

SISTERHOOD HONORS MRS. HARRY H. EPSTEIN

Monday, December 6th, at a Sisterhood Torah Fund lunch, an overflow audience showed their affection and admiration for Mrs. Harry H. Epstein (Reva), wife of our Rabbi, who was presented with a beautiful plaque from the Jewish Theological Seminary in recognition of the Mathilde Schecter Residence dormitory room which Ahavath Achim Sisterhood has dedicated in Mrs. Epstein's honor.

Mrs. Sidney Cavalier, Co-Chairman of the Mathilde Schecter Residence Hall Campaign, presented this award to Mrs. Epstein and in glowing terms described Reva's many years of guiding counsel and patient, diligent concern for Sisterhood and its many activities. Therefore, Mrs. Cavalier declared, that the members of Sisterhood eager to honor its First Lady, chose to do so by endowing a room at the Mathilde Schecter Residence Hall of the Jewish Theological Seminary thus perpetually linking Mrs. Epstein's name to this great institution of Jewish learning.

In her emotion charged response, Mrs. Epstein warmly and beautifully thanked the women for their praises and for the high honor they bestowed upon her. She spoke of loyalty to the ideals of Torah as a necessary prerequisite to perpetuate our tradition. In moving words, tenderly she recalled the image of her dear departed mother and affectionately she spoke of the influence she exerted on her life and the example she set for her to follow.

Typically characteristic of her concern for others, Mrs. Epstein closed with the heart-warming words of prayer that this day be an example and an inspiration to all who seek to achieve ever higher goals as exemplified by the teachings of our Torah.

Dedication of a room in the Mathilde Schechter Residence Hall, Jewish Theological Seminary, in honor of Mrs. Epstein. 1965

The Amazing Rebbitzen

Reva Epstein quickly became an important member of not only Ahavath Achim but also the entire Jewish community. Her leadership and knowledge in many areas earned the respect of everyone she met. Through the years, her accomplishments were recognized by Sisterhood, Hadassah, Israel Bonds and the Epstein School.

Reva Epstein. 1953

Honoree of first annual Epstein School Founders Dinner. 1976

PLANING EDUCATION DAY

Mrs. E. Morris Manning, left, chairman of the Study Club or the Senior Hadassah, and Mrs. H. H. Epstein, region education chairman, who are making plans for the National Hadassah Education Day, which is to take place February 14.—Journal Photo.

Hadassah was a special interest. Mrs. Epstein was SE Region Education Chairman in 1940's.

A Tribute To A Gracious Lady

Reva Epstein

To Be Honored At

Epstein School Dinner December 8

Ahavath Achim

A PROFILE

VOLUME II   KISLEV 5737   NOVEMBER, 1976   NUMBER 3

FROM LIFE TO ETERNITY

YIDDISH IS ALIVE AND WELL

A TRAVELING

Reva Epstein to be Honored at Epstein School Dinner

On Wednesday evening, December 8th, our gracious Rebbitzen, Reva Epstein, will be the guest of honor at a community wide dinner in behalf of the Rabbi Harry H. Epstein-Solomon Schechter School. Mrs. Epstein will be recognized for her nearly fifty years of devoted service and dedication to all forms of Jewish education.

Born in Poland, she studied in the Gymnasium in Suvalki. Studied at the University of Berlin, Germany, and at the Sorbonne in Paris, France, majoring in philology and languages. Coming to Chicago, Illinois in 1927, with English a strange language, she graduated from the University of Chicago in 1928 with highest honors. Having her B. A. degree, the University offered her an Instructorship in languages (she being proficient in English, German, French, Polish, Russian, Hebrew and Yiddish). She declined this honor in favor of marrying Rabbi Epstein in January 1929.

Mrs. Epstein has been active in all and varied women's organizations, concentrating in areas of education and programming. She is past educational chairman of southeastern region of Hadassah.

To our Sisterhood, Reva has been its guiding light and because of her widespread perspectives and generating force the Ahavath Achim Sisterhood is today one of the outstanding organizations in our movement.

A personality of the highest caliber, with unusually high standards plus a profound love of learning and genuine piety, her wisdom and innate charm have fashioned her as a sterling "woman of valor" in its truest sense.

"She walks in beauty and learning" sums up the nobility and sincerity which have endeared her to all who know her. A perfect companion to Rabbi Epstein, she has continuously challenged all of us to ever higher standards of personal growth and organizational development.

PROFILE would like to join in urging everyone to join in honoring Mrs. Epstein and supporting the School by attending the Dinner on December 8th.

Mayor William B. Hartsfield congratulates the Epsteins on the completion of 25 years at Ahavath Achim.

Visiting Mrs. Epstein's parents, Rabbi & Mrs. Chashesman.

Celebration of Rabbi Epstein's birthday with children and grandchildren. 1982

Rabbi and Mrs. Epstein on vacation in Chicago. 1933

Redesigned pulpit minus the wooden lions. Funds for the project donated by Borochoff family.

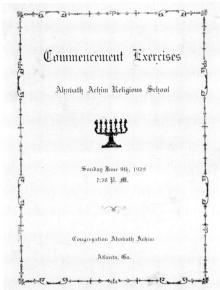

Religious School graduation program. 1929

Atlanta were hectic. From his previous visit he knew there were two distinct groups whose needs and expectations were very different.

The founding generation wanted their familiar Yiddish sermons, noisy services and afternoon Talmud classes while their children, now young adults with families of their own, wanted spiritual messages they could relate to and prayers which they could understand as well as recite by rote.

There were compromises to be made on all sides. Rabbi Epstein's insight and his astute handling of a potentially impossible situation was masterful. He gained the confidence of the older generation by teaching their Talmud class and proving to them that a beardless, American rabbi could also have a command of the ancient texts.

Before making any significant changes, he met with influential people and told them what he was planning to do. He remembers telling them, "I'm not making these changes for myself or for you but for your children and grandchildren."

Without family or friends and with so many difficult situations to resolve, the first weeks and months at Ahavath Achim could have been extremely lonely were it not for the kindness and hospitality of Mrs. Joseph Goldberg (Lena), the wife of the president of the congregation.

Lena understood the young rabbi's needs not only for meals but for emotional support and encouragement. Many years later, when Lena Goldberg died, Rabbi Epstein cut short a vacation in Chicago to return to Atlanta and officiate at her funeral.

The Rabbi and Reva were married in Chicago Jan. 13, 1929, and, after a wedding trip to Miami and Havana, came to Atlanta. They were met at the Terminal Station by Lizzie Jacobs (Scheinbaum) and Nessie Rich, two of the Sisterhood pioneers.

These two ladies had spent the entire morning cleaning the Rabbi's apartment on Washington Terrace in anticipation of the arrival of the newlyweds. When the stylish Mrs. Epstein stepped off the train they were amazed. Who had ever seen a *rebbitzen* who looked like Reva Epstein?

Lizzie and Nessie and all the Sisterhood women who followed them quickly learned that there was more to Reva than a beautiful face and fashionable clothes. She shared the Rabbi's passion for Judaism and the desire to educate a generation, who in their rush to become real Americans, had left their traditions behind.

Her extensive secular education and thorough Jewish knowledge was a rare combination and her friendship and wise counsel quickly endeared her to the Congregation. She organized and taught study groups and became the unofficial program chairman for the Sisterhood, always stressing the need for activities which would deepen their knowledge of the Jewish heritage. The depth of the widespread ignorance of the majority of the congregation is personified by a woman who once asked her during a study group meeting, "How many miles is it from Diaspora to Jerusalem?"

The Rabbi and Reva were an unbeatable team!

Improvement of the Synagogue's educational system was a major priority. Rabbi Epstein involved himself actively in the revamping and strengthning of the Sunday School, Bible School and the United Hebrew School. Requirements for Bar Mitzvah were upgraded and a regular Junior Congregation established which met each Shabbat. Both daily attendance and enrollment increased.

By 1930 the Sunday School needed a miniumum of 11 classrooms and the Sisterhood provided the funds to partition the large vestry room on the main floor into four sections.

The faculty was upgraded by recruiting men and women who were professional teachers in the public school system. Those listed at the beginning of the school year in 1930 were David Meyer, Ben Sherman, Sidney Rose, Eva Boss, Mrs. Sarah Piassick, Fannie Heiman, Matilda Shapiro, Bertha Wachman, Celia Bergman, Esther Finerowsky and Lillian Reisman. Max Cuba was the superintendent, Isidor Jacobs the registrar, and Ida Mae Goldstein the school secretary.

While some changes caused only minor ripples, others created major waves of protest. One was the rebuilding of the Ark and pulpit.

Rabbi Epstein found the two lions with the red lights in their eyes especially offensive. He remembers thinking he was in a "Buddhist temple" the first time he saw them. After some effort he convinced Mr. Borochoff to donate $2,500, a very significant sum as the Great Depression engulfed the nation. The redesign of the Ark did not cause a stir; it was the

Above left: Mary Heiman marries Harry Dwoskin. 1927
Above right: Mary Taratoot, high school graduation
Left: Isadore Jacobs, wife Lizzie and children Joseph and Ragolda. 1930

Children of Mr. & Mrs. Charles Goldstein

67

The A. A. Synagogue

VOLUME 1.   ATLANTA, GA., SEPTEMBER, 1930.   NUMBER 1

לשנה טובה תכתבו

In making our bow to the members of the A. A. Synagogue, we wish to extend best wishes for a "Happy, Bright and Prosperous New Year."

In publishing this Bulletin, we feel that a long-felt need will be filled and an interest awakened in the various activities of our Synagogue.

Our aim and purpose is to keep you fully informed and posted of the daily doings of the Synagogue. To remind you of all Jewish holidays, festivities, services and sermons. To keep you in close touch with the activities of The Sunday School, their work and progress. The Bible Classes and their accomplishments, the Hebrew School, the A. A. Sisterhood, and concerning the various individual members of the "Shool" generally and their families.

The task for those who have undertaken the regular publication of this Bulletin is not an easy one. Their success can only be accomplished by the interest and co-operation displayed by the entire membership of our Congregation. The officers and various boards, together with the several organizations within the "Shool", have rallied in great style and are enthusiastic in giving their aid and support. It is most gratifying to know that such wonderful harmony exists.

In order that the "Bulletin" might be of interest to both young and old, a Yiddish column is to appear regularly, and it is sincerely hoped that you will eagerly await each subsequent issue.

Co-operate with us by mailing or sending in promptly anything which should appear in this "Bulletin" and realize that you are part and parcel of this publication.

"L'Shono Tovo Tekosevu," We Greet You!!

The Rabbi's Column

L'Shono Tovo Tikosevu!

Again we are standing on the arbitrary and peremptory threshold of Time, bidding farewell to the outgoing year and greeting an incoming one. Rosh Hashono of the year 5691 is beckoning its imposing approach with a fair promise of enriching our lives with a new cargo of twelve lunar months, laden with varied human emotions and experiences. New Year's Day is invested with such a mystic spell that it grips the very heart of even the most callous and frivolous Jew. We are awe-stricken at its solemnity and seriousness, and stand aghast before the throne of God, in anticipation of His divine judgment meted out to us.

At this turning point of the seasons, we ask: "What will the New Year hold for us? Will it truly be a New Year?"

The old year is dead and a new year is born. A good time to begin with greater resolve to carry through to fruition the hopes, aims and resolves of our Jewish community. With utter disregard of the past, let us benefit by the experiences it taught us, and make the future better because of the past.

Many people waste their time talking about past mistakes. They dwell on their weakness, and constantly repeating their acknowledgment of weakness adds to their handicaps. On the contrary, positive and successful thinking generates a constant flow of creative, constructive ideas and has a powerful influence for success. No one welcomes your weakness, neither will it help you when you talk about it.

Let us begin the New Year aright. Let us do things! Oh, yes, some day you will do "Something big." But every day this "something big" is put off, and each day the thing gets harder and harder to do. Do that "big thing" today, at the opening of a New Year, and enjoy the fruits of the love and admiration of your fellow-men while you are here.

The need of Atlanta Jewry is co-ordination in their communal work; therein lies success in all their undertakings. The need of Atlanta Jewry is conscientious men and women, aware of their duties, and possessed by a willingness to serve. Only they who serve deserve! Let us be deserving men and women.

Let us enter the New Year with a full realization of our duties and responsibilities to ourselves, to our community and to our fellow-men, and may it bring us all Happiness and Contentment in full measure.

א פאר ווערטער אין אידיש

מיר ווינשען אונזערע מיטגליע־
דער א גוטען און געזונטען יאהר.
מיר האפען אז דער קומענדער
יאהר וועט אונז בריינגען דאם
וואם יעדערער וואונשט זיך אליין.

מיר גלויבען אז יעדער פון אונ־
זערע מיטגלידער איז א גלייכער
שותף אין אונזער שוהל, און אלם
א שותף דארף ער נעמען א גלייכן
חלק אין דער ארבייט און דארף
נעוויס וויסען וואם עם קומט פאר
אין אונזער שוהל, אין אללע צוויי־
גען פון אקטיוויטעם. אבער צום
באדוירערן איז פאראן זייער פיל,
מען מען זאגען, אז די מערהייט
פון אונזערע מיטגלידער קומען אין
אונזער שוהל נאר צוויי מאל איאר
און דאן נאר אויף אקורצע וויילע.
דערפאר איז גייטיג דיזער בולע־
מען וואם וועט ערשיינען
מאנאטליך. דער צוועק פון
בולעטין וועט זיין צו געבען
אונזערע מיטגלידער אללע נייעם
פון אונזער שוהל: וואם מיר טוען
פאר אונזער יונגענט אין תלמוד
תורה, און די זונטאג קלאסעם,
און די ביבעל קלאסעם, וואם עם
קומט פאר אנאנצע וואך און שבת
אין אונזער שוהל; נייעם וועגען
יעדען בר־מצוה, וואם אונזער
ווירדיגער רב וועט ריידען יעדען
פרייטאג צונאכט, בכלל וועט
דער בולעטין וועקען די שלאפענ־
דע מיטגלידער צו די ארבייט
און ערמוטיגען די שאפענדע און
בויענדע כחות פון אונזער שול.
דער אמת איז אונזער שוהל ליידעט
זייער שטארק פון דער קראנקהייט
וואם רופט זיך גלייכגילטיגקייט.
מיר אללע זיינען צו קאלט צו
אונזער שוהל, אבער עם גייט
אנייער יאר און מיר ווילען אז ווען
מיר וועלען זיך קלאפען ,,על חטא"
זאלען מיר ניט פארגעסען די זינד
פון זיין נאכלעסיג צו אונזער שוהל
און מקבל זיין צום טאן ארבייט
פאר אונזער שוהל דעם קומענדען
יאהר.
י. ב.

First publication of the Congregation, predecessor of The Bulletin, Harry Wengrow, editor. Note Yiddish column. 1930

Ahavath Achim members were always leaders of the Zionist cause in Atlanta. Joel Dorfan, Ralph Willner, and Oscar Gershon led a fund drive to raise $4,000 to purchase land in Palestine. 1935

To Aid Jews in Palestine

REPRESENTATIVES OF THE LEADING JEWISH ORGANIZATIONS discussing plans for the Jewish National Fund drive to be inaugurated in Atlanta May 21 for the purpose of raising $4,000 to buy land for Jewish people in Palestine. Left to right, Joel Dorfan, of the Free Loan Association of the Ahavath Achim Congregation; Major Ralph L. Willner, of the Jewish War Veterans, and Oscar Gershon, president of the Ahavath Achim Congregation.—Staff photo by Wynn.

removal of the lions.

"It was such a fight that I had to sneak them out in the middle of the night and hide them in the attic," Rabbi Epstein remembers.

The publication of the first Bulletin, on the other hand, was welcomed by all. The first edition is dated September, 1930. Some features were a Yiddish column, social items such as the marriage of Mollie Bressler and Hyman Bergman, Sisterhood News (Rae Meyer was the newly elected president), school activities, an editorial, and a front page column written by the Rabbi. An interesting paragraph read:

"Much progress is being made in Atlanta towards stricter observance of the Sabbath. It is learned with a great deal of pleasure that the Jewish grocers and bakers are closed on Saturday."

THE ATLANTA JOURNAL

e Dew   WEDNESDAY, JUNE 8, 1938   Tune In

Atlanta Zionists Vote to Honor Rabbi Epstein for Services

A tree will be planted in Palestine as a tribute to Rabbi Harry H. Epstein for ten years of unflagging service in behalf of the Zionist movement.

A resolution honoring the spiritual leader of the Ahavath Achim Congregation for his service to Zionism was unanimously adopted at a meeting of the Atlanta Zionist District Monday night. Rabbi Epstein delivered an address on the present status of the movement to build a Jewish homeland in Palestine.

Delegates were named to represent Atlanta at the annual convention of the Zionist Organization of America, to open July 2 in Detroit. Those named were Robert Travis, Meyer Rich, Sol P. Benamy and Sam Berman. Alternates are Rabbi Epstein, Sam Eplan, David Gershon and Charles Bergman.

Committee chairmen were named as follows: Mr. Bergman, executive; Rabbi Epstein, cultural; Mr. Gershon, program; Mr. Benamy, membership, assisted by Mr. Berman, and Barney Medintz, publicity.

The membership chairman reported 185 active members here. Martin Hershberg reported on the national Masada convention held in Cleveland.

RABBI HARRY EPSTEIN

Rabbi Epstein not only led Zionist activities but also inspired others to take active roles.

Graduating Bible Class 1932

Soon after his arrival Rabbi Epstein completely revamped the Bible Class. The students were divided into four levels, a standard curriculum was developed, and regular attendance required for

graduation. The teachers were: Rabbi Epstein, Charles Bergman, Harry Wengrow, and Joseph H. Goldstein.

Atlanta's City Hall, costing $1 million; completed in March, 1930.

There were two issues published in 1930 and one in 1931; then the project was abandoned for lack of funds. It was not resumed until Sept. 11, 1939, when the Brotherhood took the Bulletin as their project.

Since its founding, Ahavath Achim was in the forefront of Zionism in Atlanta. Both the rabbinic and lay leadership endorsed the dream of Theodore Herzl for the return to Zion. Early in the century, the Ahavath Zion Association had been founded by leaders of the congregation.

In 1904 Jacob deHass, the leading spokesman for the Federation of American Zionists, visited Atlanta and spoke to an enthusiastic audience at the Gilmer St. *shul.* Rabbis Mayerowitz, Levin and Hirmes spoke at Zionist-sponsored events and encouraged support from the congregation. Lay leaders

of the movement were J. Smullian, Hyman Mendel, N.A. Kaplan, Leon Eplan and, of course, Joel Dorfan and Morris Lichtenstein.

Rabbi Epstein, from the beginning of his career, personally assumed leadership for the cause and also inspired others to become the foundation for Zionist activity in Atlanta. The tragic death of his brother, Aaron David Epstein, a yeshiva student in Hebron, as the result of Arab riots in August, 1929, made events in Palestine very personal to Atlantans. That unhappy incident was reported extensively and gave Rabbi Epstein high visibility which he used to stir the community.

He organized the Atlanta chapter of the Zionist Organization of America and served as its president. He was continually called on to speak throughout the Southeast for the

Pazol family Seder, 575 Capitol Ave., S.E. 1935

United Palestine Appeal and other related causes. Just as important as his own involvement was the motivation he gave others.

This group of young men provided the leadership for the Zionist movement for the next four decades. They were Robert Travis, Sol Benamy, Meyer Rich, Sam Eplan, David Gershon and Sam Berman.

Another vital activity of the era was the Chevrah Tehilim and Free Loan Society which was officially chartered in 1930. Although the concept of granting interest-free loans had been in existence within the community since before the turn of the century, it was not highly organized until 1923 when a group of men began to meet regularly on Sunday afternoon.

At each meeting, a chapter of Tehilim (Psalms) was read and inter-preted by members or specially invited guests. The purpose of the group was expanded to include hearing petitions for the loans and generating the money necessary to grant them.

After the selection from Psalms was studied, the loan applicants appeared before the committee. The amounts granted depended on the available funds but were usually between $25 and $100. The request could be purely personal or business related and were rarely turned down. Throughout the Depression years the Free Loan Society was a vital community institution and sustained many families who faced difficult times. It was relied upon again after World War II to help a new generation of Europeans who had survived the Holocaust.

Although yearly dues were collected, the principal means of fund-

Eastern Airlines began regular service between Atlanta and New York in Dec., 1930. Five stewardesses wearing first uniform introduced by Eastern.

THE BROTHERHOOD

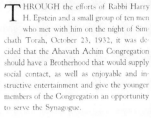

THROUGH the efforts of Rabbi Harry H. Epstein and a small group of ten men who met with him on the night of Simchath Torah, October 23, 1932, it was decided that the Ahavath Achim Congregation should have a Brotherhood that would supply social contact, as well as enjoyable and instructive entertainment and give the younger members of the Congregation an opportunity to serve the Synagogue.

The first meeting of the members of the Congregation was called on October 31, 1932 and at that time The Synagogue Brotherhood was officially organized amidst great enthusiasm. The officers elected at that meeting were: Simon Mendel, President; Sam H. Hirsh, Vice President; Jos. M. Brown, Secretary; Dr. Irving H. Goldstein, Treasurer.

Since the organization meeting the Brotherhood has functioned exceedingly well, serving the Synagogue and providing strength of Brotherhood amongst its members. It has served the Synagogue by sponsoring Friday evening services, furnishing a Choir for those services; ushering during High Holidays and all other occasions; publication of the Synagogue Monthly Bulletin and, on behalf of the social, religious and cultural entertainment of its members it has sponsored Annual Banquets or Get-Togethers, to which the entire membership of the Congregation have been invited; sponsored prominent Lecturers such as Pierre van Paassen, Rabbi Barnett R. Brickner, Dr. Ludwig Lewisohn, Dr. Edward L. Israel and many others.

Simon I. Mendel,

Sam. H. Hirsh,

Jos. M. Brown

Dr. Irving H. Goldstein,

Sol D. Morgan

Joseph L. Goldberg,

Abe Goldstein

Mendel Romm

Sol O. Klotz

Sam Eplan

THE BROTHERHOOD

The following have ably served as Presidents of the Brotherhood:

1932-1933	*Simon I. Mendel*
1933-1934	*Sam H. Hirsh*
1934-1935	*Jos. M. Brown*
1935-1936	*Dr. Irving H. Goldstein*
1936-1937	*Jos. L. Goldberg*
1937-1938	*Abe Goldstein*
1938-1939	*Sol D. Morgan*
1939-1940	*Sol O. Klotz*

Realizing the great need of the Synagogue Center, the Brotherhood undertook the sponsorship of the Center Ball which was held at the Shrine Mosque on the evening of April 16, 1940, and arranged the issuance of this Souvenir Program. Through their efforts a considerable sum of money has been raised to assist in the building of the Synagogue Center and the membership of the Brotherhood are among the most active of those engaged in that magnificent Building Program.

As occasions arise in the future where the progress of the Synagogue is concerned, the members of the Brotherhood will be found in the forefront carrying on their work as an integral part of Atlanta Jewry.

The Synagogue Brotherhood was an important organization for two decades. Several of its leaders later served as president of the Congregation.

Program book, Brotherhood Banquet, Nov. 25, 1935.

raising was an annual concert which brought famous *hazzonim* to perform in Atlanta. If a renown personality like Yossele Rosenblatt was scheduled to appear, the concert was **the** event of the year.

Joe Glazer remembers Rosenblatt, the star of the cantorial world, accompanying Ahavath Achim's cantor, Aaron Lipitz, at an old upright piano when, out of courtesy, he gave the local man the podium for a short selection. Lipitz seized the opportunity and, to the consternation of the audience, almost monopolized the evening.

An interesting tradition of the Free Loan Association was the celebration of the *Yahrzeit* of King David on the afternoon of the first day of Shavout. This date, according to tradition, is the annivesary of the writing of the Book of Psalms, and King David is the acknowledged author of many of its verses.

One of Rabbi Epstein's methods of involving the younger element of the congregation and preparing them for

Sisterhood activity to raise funds to purchase dishes for the synagogue kitchen. 1936

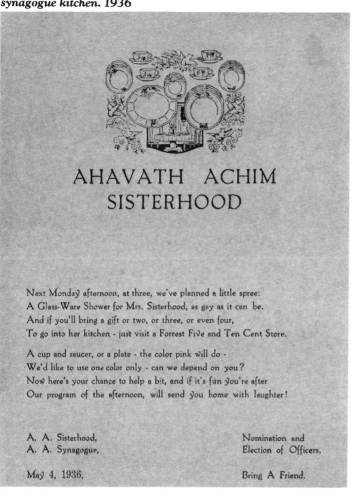

AHAVATH ACHIM
SISTERHOOD

Next Monday afternoon, at three, we've planned a little spree:
A Glass-Ware Shower for Mrs. Sisterhood, as gay as it can be.
And if you'll bring a gift or two, or three, or even four,
To go into her kitchen - just visit a Forrest Five and Ten Cent Store.

A cup and saucer, or a plate - the color pink will do -
We'd like to use one color only - can we depend on you?
Now here's your chance to help a bit, and if it's fun you're after
Our program of the afternoon, will send you home with laughter!

A. A. Sisterhood,	Nomination and
A. A. Synagogue,	Election of Officers.
May 4, 1936,	Bring A Friend.

Annual Chanukah Dance

Sponsored by

Ahavath Achim Sisterhood

Egyptian Ball Room   Shrine Mosque

Tuesday Evening, December 13th, 1938

Sisterhood Chanukah Ball ad journal, proceeds earmarked for proposed Northside facility. 1938

Mr. and Mrs. Ben Kaplan
cordially invite you to the
Bar Mitzvah בר מצוה
of their son
Sidney Jack
Saturday Morning, October 14th, 1939
at 9:00 o'clock
at Congregation Ahavath Achim
Washington Street and Woodward Ave.
Atlanta, Georgia

AT HOME
SUNDAY, OCTOBER 15TH, 1939
3 TO 6 P. M
708 WASHINGTON ST., S. W.

Bar Mitzvah invitation, Sidney Kaplan. 1939

leadership was the formation of the Brotherhood. In the fall of 1932 he met with 10 men who became the nucleus of an important organization which functioned for many years. Its first president was Simon Mendel (the son of Hyman Mendel) who became president of the congregation in 1933. The Brotherhood represented a significant milestone in the maturing of the synagogue as the second generation of members began to assume leadership roles.

As the Congregation began to respond and was infused with enthusiasm by the dynamic leadership of Rabbi Epstein, the effects of the Depression were felt throughout the community.

Bankruptcy and business closings were everyday occurrences, throwing potential customers of Jewish merchants out of work. The city and state coffers were also empty, and by 1932 Georgia owed four million dollars in back pay to the state's teachers alone. Atlanta circulated script in lieu of wages to employees, and Mayor I. N. Ragsdale appealed to the unemployed to spend their time repairing their homes.

The collection of yearly congregational and school fees became increasingly difficult. Many statements mailed in 1933 had special notations typed in red pleading for payment of the $12 membership charge. These fees were waived time and again as families struggled to maintain themselves. Rabbi Epstein volunteered a reduction of his salary; Charles Glazer taught all the classes of the United Hebrew School for $35 per week.

In spite of the times, the number of children enrolled in Sunday School necessitated additional classroom

Charles Glazer taught all classes of the United Hebrew School for $35 per week during the Depression.

space. Initally, a house on Woodward Ave. was rented; when that became inadequate, arrangements were made with the city to use the Crew St. public school building.

The Sisterhood, led by a sucession of dedicated women, continued to raise funds for all the expenses. Records kept by Zelda Berman (Mrs. Sam) during her presidency, 1935-37, show income from the annual Chanukah Ball and other activities of $2,740 and expenses of $2,106, leaving a surplus of more than $600.

A new synagogue Constitution and By-Laws was adopted at a special meeting Mar. 9, 1936. Dues were raised to $28 per year, payable quarterly. Regular membership meetings were to be held on the first Sunday of March, June, September and December, the last being the time for the election and installation of officers.

Candidates for membership were still subject to exclusion by black ball, and all applications were to be posted on the bulletin board two weeks prior to the general meeting.

An interesting standing committee was the Traveling Solicitors Committee. Its function was to advise the president as to the distribution of funds for traveling rabbis, cantors and *magiddim*. Oscar Gershon was president, and Rabbi Epstein was assisted by Cantor M. Landman.

As the severe financial pressures of the Depression ended, the Congregation attended to the need for a separate school building to house its burgeoning enrollment.

After a number of locations were discussed and rejected, property was bought on 10th St. near Piedmont Ave. for $9,500 on Nov. 16, 1939.

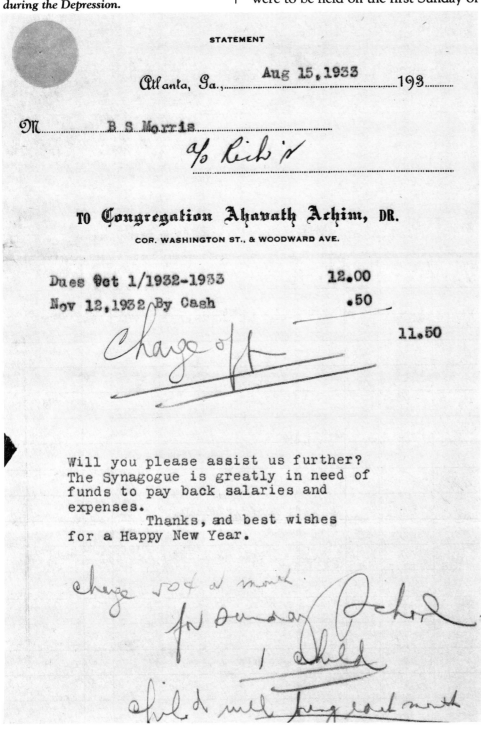

STATEMENT

Atlanta, Ga., Aug 15, 1933 193......

M...... B S Morris ....

a/o Rich's

TO Congregation Ahavath Achim, DR.

COR. WASHINGTON ST., & WOODWARD AVE.

Dues Oct 1/1932-1933	12.00
Nov 12,1932 By Cash	.50
	11.50

Charge off

Will you please assist us further? The Synagogue is greatly in need of funds to pay back salaries and expenses.
Thanks, and best wishes for a Happy New Year.

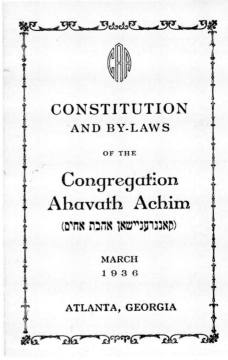

CONSTITUTION
AND BY-LAWS
OF THE

Congregation
Ahavath Achim
(אַנגרעניישאן אהבת אחים)

MARCH
1936

ATLANTA, GEORGIA

Publication of new Constitution and By-Laws. March, 1936

Dues statement with urgent request for payment. 1933

From Southside to Northside . . . A Turning Point

"TENTH STREET LOCATION PURCHASED FOR SYNAGOGUE CENTER!
CAMPAIGN TO RAISE $100,000 NOW IN PROGRESS!!
Our Own School Building By Rosh Hashono, 1940!!!"

Synagogue Bulletin, Jan. 10, 1940

Hitler's invasion of Poland on Sept. 1, 1939, plunged Europe into war two decades after the end of World War I. The enormous Jewish community of Eastern Europe would soon experience the unrelenting anti-semitism and deprivation their German brethren had been subjected to since the enactment of the first Nuremberg Laws in 1935.

No one, however, envisioned so early in the war the ultimate physical destruction of two-thirds of European Jewry. This tragedy and its aftermath reached every corner of the Jewish world and touched every man, woman and child.

Atlanta and indeed all America, which so recently struggled with the possibility of economic collapse, was not overly concerned with events so far away.

The city was approaching a population of 300,000; small, diverse factories produced more than 1,500 commodities, and more than 2,500 nationally known companies had established division offices, branch factories or warehouses in the area.

In addition to steadily growing rail traffic, Atlanta Airport in 1940 had 33 regularly scheduled flights every day. Hurt Park had been built just a

Peachtree St., looking north toward Marietta St. intersection. Peachtree Arcade, present site of First National Tower, left foreground. 1938

Meyer Rich
1940-1941

Abe Goldstein
1942-1943

Thomas Makover
1944-1945

Charles Bergman
1946-1947

Simon Bressler
1948

Max Cuba
1949-1950

75

World Premiere of "Gone With the Wind" at Lowe's Grand Theatre. Dec. 15, 1939

few blocks from Five Points, and the world premiere of *Gone With The Wind* in December, 1939, had bathed the city momentarily in floodlights.

The Jewish community, estimated between 6,000 and 7,000, had experienced moderate numerical growth. There were four congregations in addition to Ahavath Achim: Anshe S'fard, Or VeShalom, Shearith Israel and The Temple.

A wide range of social, fraternal, Zionist, Socialist and welfare organizations (35 in all) had been organized in addition to the Atlanta Jewish Welfare Fund, which had its first campaign in 1936. Proceeds from early drives were allocated to a variety of *yeshivot* in Europe and Palestine as well as numerous social service and educational institutions in America. By 1940 the emphasis had shifted to refugee relief coordinated by the Joint Distribution Committee.

In addition to growth and maturity, a gradual shift in the housing pattern of Atlanta Jewry had been occurring for many years. First to vacate the Southside for the new northern suburbs were the more established German Jews who began leaving the area in the 1920's.

By 1930 The Temple had acquired property on Peachtree Rd., and dedicated its new building in 1931. A beautiful example of neo-Classic architecture in the Southern colonial tradition, the structure remains an Atlanta landmark and is listed on the National Register of Historic Places.

Ahavath Achim members had also moved north. Their numbers increased enough to warrant a request to the Congregation for the establishment of a "northside *minyan*." An

Hurt Park with City Auditorium in the background. 1940

Dr. Nathan Blass
1951-1952

Rubye Goldstein
1939-1941

Gertie Bressler
1941-1943

Esther Friedman
1943-1946

Frances Bressler
1946-1947

Doris Levin
1947-1949

Front page of The Bulletin *urging participation in fundraising for Northside building.*

Ark, Sefer Torah, prayer books and furnishings were supplied, and soon those involved in the *minyan* broke away from Ahavath Achim and founded Congregation Adas Yeshurun.

They remained independent for a few years but in 1936 merged back into the parent synagogue as a branch of Ahavath Achim. A house at 526 Boulevard, N.E., was obtained for their use. This location was also the northside branch of the United Hebrew School.

While the initial venture away from the familiar southside was problematic, the need to be where more members were locating was overwhelming. Coupled to that new reality was the fact that the City had notified the Board that it could no longer lease the facilities of the Crew St. school.

As soon as suitable property was found and the building permit acquired, a campaign was launched to raise an additional $45,000 to add to the $55,000 already pledged. The Brotherhood organized a gala Center Ball under the leadership of Abe Goldstein; it raised approximately $5,000. Four Bible School classes collected $265. The 760 members were urged to contribute.

Preparation of the site began Feb. 15, 1940, and a year later the school moved. The two-story red brick structure was built to accommodate 1,000 students. It had 22 classrooms, a library, auditorium, secretary's office and Rabbi's study.

The inaugural event held in the Educational Center (as it was called) was the first Sisterhood Donor Luncheon, Feb. 4, 1941. Chaired by Mary Dwoskin and Helen Cavalier, the event's slogan was "Buy Your Child A

Sylvia Parks
1949-1951

Synagogue Bulletin

PUBLISHED BY THE SYNAGOGUE BROTHERHOOD IN THE
INTEREST OF THE CONGREGATION AHAVATH ACHIM

VOLUME 2.   ATLANTA, GA., MARCH 20, 1940   NUMBER 6

GRADING WORK NEARING COMPLETION ON NEW SYNAGOGUE CENTER LOT!!

Plans For Building Awaiting Sufficient Financial Aid
★ ★ ★ ★ *of Membership* ★ ★ ★ ★

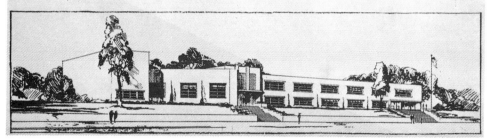

Without the blast of trumpets, but with the determination to see the work started and pushed through to a successful conclusion, the officers and committees in charge of the work of erecting the new Sunday School Center have progressed so far with the task of grading the new site that the construction of the building awaits only the financial response of the membership. The spirit and enthusiasm of a great majority of our congregation has been dormant.

AWAKE AND DO YOUR SHARE. THIS IS ONCE-IN-A-LIFETIME OPPORTUNITY TO HELP IN A PROJECT WORTHY OF ATLANTA JEWRY.

Atlanta Airport, control tower in foreground

Atlanta Historical Society

The Educational Center

The completion of the 10th St. Center was a major accomplishment. For the first time, all 650 students of the Religious School could be housed in a single synagogue facility. In addition to adequate classrooms, there was an auditorium, kitchen, library, and administrative offices.

Dedication Program

of AHAVATH ACHIM

Educational Center

★ ★

——————EVENTS——————

1. Welcome..Meyer Rich, President

2. Vocal Selections....................................Cantor Joseph Schwartzman

3. Greetings from Affiliated Organizations

4. Tableau—"Contribution of Jewish Women to Education"
   —presented by Sisterhood Cast

5. Dedication..Rabbi Harry H. Epstein

★ ★

Delicious Supper Will Be Served Promptly at 7:30 P.M.

★ ★

Remember the date . . .

TUESDAY, FEBRUARY 18, 1941

Dedication program. Feb. 18, 1941

The completion of classes is a happy time for children everywhere. Students leaving the new center. 1943

Sisterhood Plans Donors Luncheon At Center

The regular meeting of the A. A. Sisterhood was held Monday, January 6th, in the Vestry Room of the Ahavath Achim Synagogue at 3 o'clock.

Preceding the meeting Rabbi Harry H. Epstein met with the cultural group. An interesting and instructive hour was in store for those attending.

Mrs. Louis Rosenbaum, Sunday School Chairman, was in charge of the Program at the meeting. Many of the Sunday School children participated in a most interesting skit.

Mrs. Harry Dwoskin made a detailed report of the Donors Luncheon to take the place of the regular February meeting.

This Donors Luncheon, given to raise money to buy desks and other equipment for the Center, will take place at the Center on February 4th at 12:30 o'clock. Five dollars or more entitles anyone to become a Donor and be present at the Luncheon. The meal will be strictly kosher and a very beautiful program has been planned.

Members and friends of the Sisterhood and the Congregation are cordially invited to attend and are urged to make their reservations as early as possible with Mrs. Harry Dwoskin at Vernon 7042, or Mrs. Sidney Goldstein, co-chairman, at Vernon 5342.

Ahavath Achim Educational Center, soon after completion. 1941

First annual Donor Luncheon announced to be held in new building. 1941

Desk," and more than 300 women responded by paying $5 per person.

Reva Epstein was toastmistress, and a tableau, "Contributions of Women to Religious Education," was presented. It was the beginning of a continuing event of the Sisterhood. The proceeds from the Donor Luncheon and Chanukah Ball totaled $3,200, which bought furnishings for the building.

From that day the Center was a mecca of activity. In addition to classes of all kinds and weekly Shabbat services, Jewish youth groups, women's organizations and families used the facility daily. The leadership was quite generous in allowing groups not affiliated with the Synagogue to use the building for meetings free of charge.

All administrative functions were moved to the new building and the Board of Trustees met in the new library. Morris Srochi bought all the chairs and other furnishings for the auditorium and dedicated the room in memory of his wife, Dora. He also gave the first large collection of books — 2500 — for the library.

The completion of the 10th St. Educational Center was another milestone in the life of the Congregation, a tangible result of the energy and leadership which marked Rabbi Epstein's several years of service. At one of the early meetings in the Center, a congratulatory resolution was drafted. It read (in part):

"WHEREAS, Rabbi Epstein has served the Congregation Ahavath Achim for more than thirteen years as its spiritual leader and during that period of time has performed his service without thought of mental or physical impairment; and NOW THEREFORE, the Board of Trustees of the Congregation Ahavath Achim, in meeting assembled, do hereby extend to our beloved Rabbi Harry H. Epstein, our heartfelt thanks for his

A. A. EDUCATIONAL CENTER
Institute of Jewish Studies

Registration: Monday, October 27th
7:30-10 P. M.

SESSIONS: MONDAY NIGHTS, 8-10 P. M.

SEMESTER: NOVEMBER 1941, through JANUARY, 1942
FEBRUARY, 1942, through APRIL, 1942

SUBJECTS, HOUR, INSTRUCTOR

1. JEWISH HISTORY, 8-9 P. M., RABBI EPSTEIN.
2. HEBREW, 8-9 P. M., RABBI SCHWARTZ.
3. CONTEMPORARY JEWISH PROBLEMS, 9-10 P. M., RABBI EPSTEIN.
4. JEWISH RELIGION, 9-10 P. M., RABBI SCHWARTZ.

Any other course will be offered on request of a minimum of 10 persons.

Teachers' Training must include the following subjects over a period of two years:

1 course in Bible
1 course in Religion
2 courses in Hebrew
3 courses in Jewish History
1 course in Applied Educational Principles

Morris Srochi was probably the most significant donor of the Center. A native of Austria, he came to Atlanta after a short stay in New York before the turn of the century. (His name appears in handwritten list of 1900 spelled 'Serochy'.) After some experience working in a bakery, he opened his own business which was known as The Atlanta Baking Company. His three sons eventually joined him and together they built a substantial enterprise which prospered. They manufactured a loaf called 'Betsy Ross' and later changed its name to 'Miss Sunbeam.' Throughout his life, Morris Srochi was generous to the Congregation and other communal causes.

An early class of the Nursery School. Standing on back row, (left to right), Mary Dwoskin, Rabbi Epstein, and teachers. 1947

Announcement of the opening of the Nursery School. Nov. 3, 1941

Four-year olds. 1949

Synagogue Bulletin

OF CONGREGATION AHAVATH ACHIM

SYNAGOGUE
Washington St. and Woodward Ave., S. W.
JAckson 6310

PUBLISHED BY SYNAGOGUE BROTHERHOOD

EDUCATIONAL CENTER AND OFFICES
250 Tenth Street, N. E.
VErnon 2764

VOLUME 3	ATLANTA, GA., DECEMBER 18, 1941	NUMBER 4

Abe Goldstein Elected Congregation's President

At the Annual Membership Meeting held last Sunday, December 14th, the following officers were unanimously elected to head the Congregation for the coming year:

Abe Goldstein, President.
Chas. W. Bergman, Vice-President.
Simon I. Mendel, Treasurer.
Berry Rittenbaum, Recording Secretary.
Max M. Cuba, Financial Secretary.

Rabbi Epstein, speaking in behalf of the Board of Trustees, praised the splendid administration of the out-going President, Meyer Rich, and paid tribute to their leadership which brought to a reality the Educational Center. As a token of appreciation, a beautiful traveling bag was presented to Mr. Meyer Rich in behalf of the members

First Bas Mitzvah Ceremony This Friday Evening At The Synagogue

Joyce Jacobs, daughter of Mr. and Mrs. Jake Jacobs, will become the first Bas Mitzvah in the history of the Atlanta Jewish Community, Friday evening, December 19th, at 8:15 at the Synagogue.

Joyce will read from the Prophets in Hebrew and English and will render an oration on the significance of Bas Mitzvah. She will then receive a charge and blessing from the Rabbi.

To our mind, there is not among all our innovations any one more important than this Bas Mitzvah ceremony. Just as our boys, when they reach the age of 13, become Bar Mitzvah, "sons of duty," so should our girls,

Redesigned front of **The Bulletin** *depicting both buildings.*

many years of service to the Congregation and to the manner in which he has so shaped the destinies of our Congregation so that it has attained the pinnacle upon which it now so nobly rests;

"BE IT FURTHER RESOLVED that the Trustees wish to express to Rabbi Epstein our warmest congratulations upon his conceiving and bringing about the realization of the Educational Center of the Congregation, for we fully realize that without his efforts the project was doomed to failure, and only through his inspiration and refusal to turn back in face of disappointment and tribulations has he practically single handed established an institution unsurpassed in our Country."

A new addition to the educational activities was the Nursery School, which opened in November, 1941, and was the first program of pre-school education under Jewish auspices in the city. The idea was born when Mary Dwoskin began looking

for a school for her oldest daughter, Jean. Finding only church-related facilities, Mary went to Rabbi Epstein who enthusiastically endorsed the idea. For over 20 years, Mary Dwoskin nurtured the school. Serving in every capacity except teacher, she ordered supplies, recruited students, and hired staff. The first teachers were Annette Lashner and Ina Marash, both of whom had degrees in preschool education. Classes met each morning at the Center from 9 to noon; tuition was $5 per month for members and $6 for non-members.

A fortuitous event for the school was the hiring in 1951 of Miriam Belger, who came to Atlanta from New York in 1942 with her husband, who was transferred by Lerner Shops. Mrs. Belger, a graduate of Hunter College, began to teach in the weekly Religious School three years before joining the Nursery School faculty. Then, there were two classes of approximately 20 students each.

Mary Dwoskin, chairman of the Center Nursery School for 20 years. Her tireless devotion to the Sisterhood was recognized by being elected Honorary President.

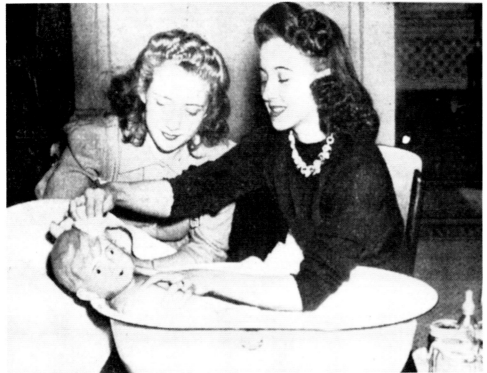

Girl Scouts Betty Cohen (left) and Shirley Brucker of Center Troop 49 practice child care. 1942

Boy Scout sash from Center troop.

Girl Scout sash with badges earned by Mildred Morris.

Bernie Kahn receiving Eagle Scout award from his mother.

Other innovations directly associated with the opening of the Center were the formation of the Girl Scout and Boy Scout troops sponsored by the Synagogue, and the first Purim Carnival, held in 1941 and organized by the Brotherhood.

Several key individuals joined the Ahavath Achim staff during this time. Their collective talents, dedication and personal appeal augmented the attraction of Ahavath Achim as new Jewish families came to Atlanta during and after World War II.

Cantor Joseph Schwartzman came to Atlanta in the fall of 1940. As a young boy in Bender, Bessarabia, he fell in love with the music of the synagogue. At eight, Schwartzman became the alto soloist in the choir of the largest *shul* in Bender. In addition to studying at the local yeshiva, he trained with some of Europe's well-known cantors.

Cantor Schwartzman migrated to America as a teenager and officiated for the first time in Hartford, CT., soon after his arrival. Living in New York with relatives, he continued his musical and *chazzanut* training with a well-known composer and teacher, Zavel Zilberts. After a position at a congregation in the Bronx, where he met his wife, Cantor Schwartzman went to the oldest and largest synagogue in Pittsburgh, Beth Hamedrash Hagadol.

In Pittsburgh, at a national Zionist Organization of America convention, Atlanta delegates heard him sing during the opening ceremonies. Ahavath Achim had employed two cantors since financial pressures of the Depression years had forced the release of Cantor Lipitz. After an audition, Cantor Schwartzman accepted the Atlanta position and arrived in time for Selihot, 1940.

The new *chazan* worked enthusiastically with Rabbi Epstein to introduce congregational singing into the Shabbat morning services. His knowledge and skill in training choirs attracted able men and boys who developed a deep affection for him. His lovely tenor voice and meaningful renditions of the prayers were hallmarks of services on Washington St. and in the present building. He remained with the Congregation until his retirement in 1965.

All male choir on Washington St.

Cantor Joseph Schwartzman

Cantor Schwartzman came to Ahavath Achim in Sept., 1940 and remained until his retirement 25 years later.

Cantor Schwartzman early in his career.

Dr. Louis Finkelstein, Chancellor of the Jewish Theological Seminary, installs Cantor Schwartzman as Honorary Fellow in Cantors Assembly. 1960

Women join the choir

Choir positioned on the Bimah in Peachtree Battle shul.

Leon Steinberg, loved by students young and old.

Leon Steinberg came to Atlanta to teach in the United Hebrew School on Apr. 1, 1941, at age 24. Born in a small village in Poland, he left Europe with his family to live in Palestine while a young boy. His scholarly father imbued him with a deep love of the Hebrew language which remained with him throughout his lifetime. He attended the Tach KiMoneh Secondary School and Hebrew University in Jerusalem. Arriving in New York in 1938, Steinberg attended Cooper Union College and taught Hebrew.

His career at Ahavath Achim was a 37-year love affair with two generations of students, Rabbi Epstein and humanity at large. A short, stocky man whose black hair was combed straight back, Steinberg's warmth and genuine interest in every person he met made him an immediate favorite.

He rarely spoke of himself but never missed an opportunity to find out what was happening in the lives of others. When children came into his class, he first captured their hearts and then tried to involve them in his circle of learning. As one youngster expressed it, "Mr. Steinberg loves everyone in his class. You don't even have to be a good student."

Steinberg's scholarship was as impressive as his personal traits. His vast knowledge of Jewish personalities, especially those associated with the Zionist movement and Israel, and his admiration for the Hebrew poet Chaim Nachman Bialik were natural elements of his casual conversation.

His understanding of the nuances of Hebrew earned him a Certificate of Outstanding Excellence in the Knowledge of Hebrew, *summa cum laude*, from Hebrew University. For many years he wrote a summary of the weekly *sedra* which appeared in the synagogue *Bulletin*.

His command of English was also extraordinary. He wrote well and spoke without the slightest accent. In personal correspondence he often used flowery phrases in expressing appreciation for some small favor. He continued his secular education and earned an M.A. degree from Ohio Christian College.

His students included the young and old. Adults interested in increasing their knowledge of Hebrew found an

Betsy Mendel greets her teacher at her Bat Mitzvah reception.

Mr. Steinberg practices with Bar Mitzvah student Miton Jacobson. 1949

enthusiastic teacher who went to great lengths to accommodate their schedules. Boys and girls preparing for Bar and Bat Mitzvah loved the special time they spent with Mr. Steinberg. He also had non-Jews among his students, especially men studying for the ministry in local seminaries.

In the fall of 1943 another devoted and talented teacher joined the staff of the United Hebrew School. Joseph Meir Zelman was born in 1915 in Biala-Podlaska, Poland (the birthplace of Leon Steinberg). His family background included Rabbi Yom Tov Lipmann Heller, a liturgical poet.

He received a traditional Jewish education in Poland and at 18 joined Betar, the youth movement of the Zionist Revisionists. In 1933, under the leadership of Menachem Begin, he left for Israel to join students and young workers who declared themselves "part of the Jewish Legion to be established in Eretz Israel."

Traveling to New York in 1940 he accidently met his boyhood friend Leon at a Zionist gathering and later visited him in Atlanta. Coincidentally, the steady increase in students enrolled in the Hebrew School required another fulltime teacher. Zelman was hired; another outstanding individual who influenced a generation of students. A few months after beginning his teaching duties, he became the Director of the Educational Center.

A man of average build behind whose blue eyes always seemed to be a joke or witticism, Zelman's patience and understanding were in sharp contrast to the old fashioned *melamed* who rapped knuckles when he was displeased. Zelman's ability to evaluate the potential of each student enabled him to tailor individualized study programs so each could savor the joy of success.

A boyish enthusiasm and ready smile were hallmarks of his teaching and his other activities. His Bar and Bat Mitzvah students developed a closeness with him during their intensive study, a closeness which became lifelong friendships. As adults his former students sought him out at synagogue functions to share events in their lives. His genuine interest in each one created a special place for Zelman in the hearts of all who knew him.

Joseph Meir Zelman

Participating in Bar Mitzvah festivities with Kenny Schatten.

Mr. Zelman with Mildred Rosenbaum, school secretary for many years.

Joe Zelman and Leon Steinberg, life long friends and colleagues.

85

Newlyweds Rose and Elliott Berman on steps of synagogue. July 26, 1942

BOY CANTOR HERSHELE AT FREE LOAN BANQUET

SUNDAY, FEBRUARY 20, AT CENTER

Next Sunday evening, February 20th, at 7 P. M. at the Educational Center the Free Loan Association of our Congregation will hold its Annual Banquet.

HERSHELE, the 11-year-old Wonder Boy Cantor with the golden voice,

Fund raising activity of Free Loan Association. 1944

A **milestone** for Ahavath Achim and the Jewish community occurred when Joyce Jacobs became the first Bat Mitzvah on Dec. 19, 1941. The following month Inge Sultan observed her Bat Mitzvah, followed by Renana Epstein.

A rite of passage whose roots are found in the philosophy of Dr. Mordecai Kaplan, Bat Mitzvah was a means of bringing girls into the serious study of Hebrew and Jewish texts. Writing in the *Bulletin* published the week of Joyce's Bat Mitzvah, Rabbi Epstein explained his reason for instituting the ceremony.

"To our mind, there is not among all our innovations any one more important than this Bat Mitzvah ceremony...This ceremony will inspire our girls to a better understanding and a more significant appreciation of Jewish life."

Any girl over 12 was eligible provided she knew Hebrew. Special classes were offered on Friday afternoon and Sunday morning to prepare the girls. Until the retirement of Rabbi Epstein, the ceremony was held on Friday night and consisted of the chanting of the Haftorah and a short reflection.

Father-Son dinner sponsored by the Brotherhood. (L to R) Abe Lewis, Charlie Trippi (football hero), Rabbi Epstein, and Mayor Hartsfield. Circa 1950

Ahavath Achim Religious School

לדעת

This Certifies That

Sherry Elaine King

having completed the **High School Department** Course of Study prescribed by the Ahavath Achim Religious School and having satisfactorily passed all required examinations is awarded this

DIPLOMA

In Witness Whereof, our signatures are hereunto affixed at Atlanta, Georgia, this twenty-first day of May, 1948. Corresponding with the twelfth day of Iyar, 5708.

Simon M. Bernstein
President of Congregation

Harry H. Epstein
Rabbi

Chas. W. Bergman
Chairman, Educational System

Mrs. Oscar Levin
President of Sisterhood

Graduating Class

Religious School diploma. 1948

Rosalind Balser, left, and Frances Bressler, co-chairmen of Sisterhood's Chanukah Ball. 1944

Religious School picnic. (L to R) Anita Schwartzman, Hazel Berman, Joyce Spielberger, Betty Cohen, and Virginia Diamond.

"... and thou shalt teach thy children diligently."

1921   1946

Ahavath Achim Sisterhood cordially invites you to attend its Twenty-Fifth Anniversary at the Ahavath Achim Synagogue on Friday Evening the Twenty-Second Day of November at Eight Thirty in the Evening

Sisterhood's Silver Anniversary celebration. Nov. 22, 1946

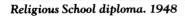

AHAVATH ACHIM SUNDAY SCHOOL
REPORT TO PARENTS
"The Home and the School should work together for the good of the child"

Name Helen Goldman

Grade 9   Promoted to Grade Bible Class

STUDIES	1ST TERM CHANUKAH	2ND TERM PURIM	3RD TERM SHAVUOS
BIBLICAL LITERATURE		a	a-
BIBLICAL HISTORY			
POST BIBLICAL HISTORY			
CUSTOMS AND CEREMONIES		a	a
CURRENT EVENTS		a-	
HEBREW		a	
CONDUCT			a
EFFORT			a
NO. DAYS ABSENT			
NO. TIMES LATE			

A—Excellent   B—Good   C—Fair   D—Poor
E—Passed on Condition   F—Failure

Report Card, Religious School. 1941

Installation of Sisterhood officers. 1941

5711 - AHAVATH ACHIM - 1951

HEBREW SCHOOL -- GRADUATING CLASS

RABBI HARRY H. EPSTEIN

FREDRIC BENAMY

MR. LEON STEINBERG

DEWALD COHEN

LARRY GLASSMAN

BENARD GOLDSTEIN

DARRYL LEITER

BARRY SIMMONS

DOROTHY TILLEM

IRA TILLEM

JEROME TILLEM

Hebrew School Graduation. 1951

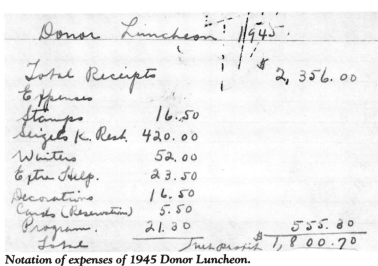

Notation of expenses of 1945 Donor Luncheon.
Profit: $1,800.70.

AHAVATH ACHIM

Confirmation Service

First Day of Shavuos, 5703
Wednesday Morning, June 9, 1943
Ten O'clock

at

The Synagogue
Atlanta, Georgia

*The Congregation will please remain in their places during
the entire Service*

Program, Confirmation Service. 1943

Jacob Butler well known for his interest in photography.

Announcement of the discontinuance of the sale of High Holiday honors. 1942

Bat Mitzvah was just one of the changes Rabbi Epstein introduced. Reading the mood of the times with great clarity, he understood what the synagogue had to do to retain the loyalty of the second generation. In addition to streamlining the services, he instituted the use of a uniform prayer book and responsive reading in English.

Decorum and dignity replaced the one time loosely organized, noisy atmosphere. He stressed adult education to do away with the layers of superstition and practices based on the folkways of Europe.

Another radical departure was the discontinuance of the sale of High Holiday honors from the pulpit, in September, 1942.

Even though Rabbi Epstein had given all sermons in English from his arrival in Atlanta, he continued for many years to deliver a Yiddish sermon late in the afternoon on Rosh Hashanah.

Bernath family

Ahavath Achim responds to World War II

The Nazi Flag, along with those of other countries, appears on Peachtree St. during the meeting of the Baptist World Alliance. It was hardly noticed. July, 1939

V-E DAY

The Synagogue Council of America is requesting all Rabbis to advise their congregation and communities that they are to gather in their Synagogues for special thanksgiving services at 8 P. M. on V-E Day, the day on which cessation of hostilities in Europe will be officially announced.

If the welcome word comes in the night, the Service will be held at 8 o'clock on the following evening.

Our Congregation will join all Synagogues and Churches in planning for such a Thanksgiving Service to be held at the Synagogue at 8 P. M. on the announced V-E Day.

Notice in The Bulletin. April, 1945

Corporal Norman Diamond, U.S. Army.

HELP WITH FURNITURE FOR NEWCOMERS!

D. P. families continue to arrive in Atlanta. But they are only half-way home — they need to be settled in places they can call their own — only then will they have completed their long journey.

You can help with the following — We need:

BEDS without mattresses	SOFAS	REFRIGERATORS	HIGH CHAIRS
CHESTS	CHAIRS	KITCHEN CABINETS	PLAY PENS
BUFFETS	RUGS	KITCHEN TABLES	LAMPS
DRESSERS	MIRRORS	KITCHEN CHAIRS	SMALL TABLES
PILLOWS & BLANKETS	STOVES	CRIBS	TAYLOR-TOTS

ACT NOW! Let's Finish the Job! Call ALpine 2985!

Plea for home furnishing for Holocaust survivors arriving in Atlanta.

Alterman brothers in the U.S. Navy.

OUR MEN AND WOMEN IN THE ARMED FORCES

Private Norman Cohen
Staff Sgt. Sidney Weinstock
A. C. Morton H. Srochi
Ensign Sylvan H. Meyer, U. S. N. R.
Private Leonard A. Meyer
Private Marshall Klein
Private Max Shapiro
Teddy Levitas, A. S.
Captain Arthur Garson
Private Dan Garson
Captain Marvin C. Goldstein
Staff Sgt. Leon Goldstein
Private Edwin Feldman
Private Jack W. Berner
Sgt. David Sims
First Lt. Harold C. Rosenberg
Staff Sgt. Lawrence C. Danneman
P.F.C. Donald Lee Danneman
Lt. Maurice Rich
T. Sgt. Louis Minsk
Private Max Bernstein
Private Sidney Isenberg
First Lt. Marvin W. Blumberg
Harold Ellman
Spencer Carl
Morris Boss
Lt. Herman Barnett
Major William A. Levin
David Macarev
Private First Class Edward Kessler
Dave Kaplan
Ensign Herbert J. Kanter
Tech Sgt. Leonard Seligman
Sgt. Berney Scheenberg

Aaron L. Rose
Private Gilbert Rinzler
Cadet Stanford I. Makover
Lt. Robert W. Ney
Pvt. Stanley M. Ney
Clinton Smullyan, Lt., U. S. N. R.
Lt. Seymour Hirsch
O. C. Robert J. Lipshutz
Julian J. Raynes, Ens.
Lt. Maurice Krieger
Stephen H. Gorski, Warrant Officer
Pvt. Danny Parker
Capt. Allan Marcus
Lt. Ed Kessler
Sgt. Joe Blass
Sgt. Irving Stone
Staff Sgt. Arthur Streve
Lt. Seymour Cohen
Cdt. Morris Arnovitz
P. F. C. Lamar Krieger
Barrow Levin, B-M-2/C
Lt. (j.g.) Joshua Jacobs
P. F. C. Louis Sloan
Lt. Jack J. Wallen, U. S. M. C.
Cpl. Max Kauffman
Lt. Louis Kell
Staff Sgt. Buster Gold
Lt. Perry Gold
P. F. C. Eric P. Sommers
Sgt. Louis Schever
Arthur Marvin Kaplan, S 2/c
Private Rose Berchenko
Freda Bizinsky, A. S.
Ruth Shapiro, A. S.

 ☆ ☆

In Memoriam
Abraham Seitz
Jos. I. Cohen
Raymond Ney

☆ ☆

BUY WAR BONDS AND STAMPS 5

List of men and women serving in the Armed Forces appearing in Chanukah Ball program. 1943

Celebrating the end of World War II on Peachtree St.
Aug. 14, 1945

Golda Meir visits Atlanta to solicit support for the new State of Israel.

Front page The Southern Israelite, *May 21, 1948.*

MOURNING A VALIANT SON

Ari Lashner, age 30, American who had sailed with Haggadah refugee ship was killed March 16th by sniper fire at Kfar Blum, Jewish settlement in Galilee. He went to Palestine as a pioneer two years ago. During the last war Lashner served as Radio man in the U. S. Merchant Marines. He leaves a wife and child at Kfar Blum.

"His Memory Is Everlastingly Blessed"

Announcement of the death of Ari Lashner in
The Bulletin.

Community-wide celebration of the proclamation of the founding of the State of Israel. Progressive Club, 1948

Throughout World War II the Congregation joined other patriotic Americans in encouraging the sale of War Bonds, collecting clothes for refugees, supporting the work of the USO, and mourning those who fell in battle.

Servicemen stationed in the area were invited into members' homes for major holidays. Rabbi Epstein sent Rosh Hashana messages to all members serving in the Armed Forces. Ahavath Achim, along with other religious groups, conducted special services on occasions such as V-E Day (Victory in Europe) and the death of Franklin Roosevelt.

The ongoing Jewish tragedy in Europe reverberated throughout the community. Many members still had family members overseas whom they tried desperately to save. As the concentration camps were slowly liberated by the Allied armies, the awful truth and magnitude of the "Final Solution" became stark reality. A worldwide Fast Day was observed Mar. 14, 1945, for the martyred dead and the living dead.

A group of orphaned children came to Atlanta soon after the war followed by a number of Holocaust survivors. Herte Sanders, a refugee from Vienna, spearheaded the resettlement effort. Rabbi Epstein publicized the project in the *Bulletin* and made calls to secure apartments, furnishings and jobs. He also outfitted a recreation room at the Educational Center so the children could come together on Sunday afternoon.

The Free Loan Society made money available to those who wanted to start businesses of their own. The Congregation has a proud record of service to this group and has been rewarded by their continuing membership in Ahavath Achim.

The founding of the State of Israel on May 15, 1948, was marked by a midnight service sponsored by the four Zionist youth groups in the city — Masada, Junior Hadassah, I.Z.Y.F. and Young Judea. Rabbi Epstein and Rev. Stanley Grauel, minister on the refugee ship Exodus, spoke.

It was fitting for this event to be held at Ahavath Achim. Since its founding both the rabbinic and lay leadership had been in the forefront of the cause of Zionism in Atlanta. The proclamation of the State was the realization of efforts by these men and women in concert with Jews all over the world.

Joining the Conservative Movement

" . . . The Jewish Theological Seminary of America . . . located in the City of New York, for the purpose of establishing and maintaining a theological seminary for the perpetuation of the Jewish religion . . . the integration of Jewish and general philosophy and learning . . . "

Charter, Jewish Theological Seminary

Evening view on Peachtree St. with theatre marquees and spectacular Coca Cola sign flashing. 1950

Atlanta Historical Society

Ahavath Achim was not the first Conservative congregation in Atlanta. Organized in 1905, Beth Israel Synagogue was affiliated with the emerging Conservative Movement which had been infused with new vigor by the appointment of Dr. Solomon Schechter as Chancellor.

Announcing the formation of Beth Israel, the press noted that the new congregation was "not to represent either the Christian Jew organization or the old-line Jewish organization. It is to strike out on middle ground."

Within a few months of its founding, the congregation broke ground for its building on the corner of Washington and Clark Streets. Among the leaders of Beth Israel were pioneer members of Ahavath Achim. Exactly what prompted Leon Eplan, Philip Elson, Joseph Saul and others to organize a new *shul* cannot be determined. For 15 years Beth Israel represented Conservative Judaism in Atlanta. But in 1920 the congregation disbanded.

Officially, Ahavath Achim was an Orthodox synagogue. Many of Rabbi Epstein's innovations were, however, very much in step with the philosophy and practices which Dr. Schechter recommended in 1913 when he founded United Synagogue of Amer-

Joseph Zaglin
1953-1954

Joseph Cuba
1955-1957

Abe Goldstein
1958-1959

Elizabeth Berchenko
1951-1953

Rose Morris
1953-1955

Dorothy Rosenblum
1955-1957

Congregational meeting, Srochi Hall, 10th St. Center. Circa 1950

ica. In a speech delivered by Dr. Schechter to the initial meeting of United Synagogue, the following were among his goals:

"Order and decorum in the synagogue

"The English sermon

"Selection of rabbis and teachers who are scientifically trained

"Religious education for women and their adequate participation in the work of the congregation"

By the time Ahavath Achim joined the Conservative Movement in 1952, these practices had already been instituted by Rabbi Epstein and were firmly established. The most noticeable shift from Orthodoxy was the gradual change to mixed seating. This occurred more out of necessity than ideology.

As the membership grew immediately after World War II, there were not enough seats in the balcony to accommodate the women. In response, a portion of the main floor was roped off and reserved for the overflow. Gradually the separation disappeared and wives were joining their

Charter, United Synagogue of America. June 15, 1952

Lois Makover
1957-1958

Many nervous brides fondly remember Irving Galanty attending last minute details.

Irving Galanty, Executive Director, 1955-1977.

Irving was well known for adding artistic touches when preparing Srochi Auditorium for festive occasions.

Irving with Rabbi Epstein and congregational leaders Sylvan Makover and Dave Alterman.

husbands and sisters were sitting with their brothers. Some of the ladies, like Mrs. Epstein, chose not to come downstairs, and remained in the balcony.

Soon after the affiliation with United Synagogue, a chapter of USY (United Synagogue Youth) was organized. Its first major activity was attending a regional convention in Savannah. Accompanied by Rabbi DeKoven, the Educational Director, high school teacher Dave Alterman and Irving Galanty, supervisor of the high school, six teenagers represented the Synagogue. They were Phyllis Alterman, Howard Burnham, Larry Glassman, Milton Goldman, Lillian Lander and Charles Rosenberg.

The Fifties were years of growth and maturity. With the influx of new members came the challenge of meeting the needs of a complex constituency. The Hebrew School bus service began in 1951 as families moved into many different sections of the city. Leo, the bus driver, is remembered with affection by a generation of students. New personnel were added to the staff, and new programs initiated.

One of the most important new positions created during this period was that of Executive Secretary. The first person appointed was Harry Barkin, a member of the congregation and former U.S. government accountant. He was to handle all financial matters, a job previously done on a volunteer basis by the financial secretary. Now it demanded continuous attention. Barkin was followed by Gerhard Spies, who joined the staff in the fall of 1953 and held the position two years.

Irving Galanty became Executive Secretary in November, 1955, and worked tirelessly in that position for 22 years. Coming to Atlanta as a very young child from Brooklyn, Galanty's family was first associated with Beth Israel (Atlanta's early Conservative synagogue) where he attended Sunday School. They eventually joined Ahavath Achim and became involved with many phases of synagogue life. He recalled attending services in the Gilmer St. building and his Bar Mitzvah in the Washington St. *shul.* It was there he met

Blass family celebrating Michael's Bar Mitzvah, 1954

his wife, Fannye Heiman, whose parents had come to Atlanta shortly after the turn of the century.

As a teenager, Galanty was a student in the Bible School, organized in 1920. He was also involved in early publications of the Synagogue and as a young man was active on the Ushering Committee. When the High School Department was moved to Grady High School, Galanty became the supervisor there. He was called on by Rabbi Epstein to help organize the first chapter of U.S.Y. shortly after Ahavath Achim became affiliated with the United Synagogue.

After serving as director of the Building Fund in 1955 for six months, Galanty was appointed to the fulltime position of Executive Secretary (later changed to Executive Director). His intimate knowledge of the institution and its members was a great asset.

His job necessitated his presence and advice at times of tragedy and joy. Organizations using the synagogue's facilities relied on his expertise. Functions planned by Jewish groups in local hotels called him for assistance in arranging kosher meals. He became active in the National Association of Synagogue Administrators and served on its board.

Numerous groups and individuals both within and outside Ahavath Achim wrote to express their apprecia-

Bulletin notice announcing the formation of Minyonaires. 1951

Rabbi Epstein and Reva enter the sanctuary to celebrate their 25 years with Ahavath Achim. 1953

Cantor Schwartzman and the choir perform for the festivities. Washington St., 1953

tion for his assistance. He was the leader of the administrative staff which was called on to manage an ever-larger and complicated institution.

He worked very closely with Rabbi Epstein, and the two men developed a warm affection and admiration for each other. When time permitted, they had lunch together at the Howard Johnson's Restaurant on the corner of Northside Dr. and the Expressway. Looking back on his career, Irving said, "Working with Rabbi Epstein…has really been something I have enjoyed and an association I have treasured."

Amidst great celebration, Rabbi and Reva celebrated their 25th year with the Congregation in 1953. A gala reception expressed the appreciation and loyalty the membership felt for the man whose leadership had bridged the generations and brought them into the modern world. Reva shared the day with her husband as she also had become a vital component of the mystique of Ahavath Achim.

Rev. Jacob Friend joined the fulltime staff in the fall of 1956. His extraordi-

Rev. Friend serves as official interpreter for Russian prelates visiting
Atlanta.

Rev. Jacob Friend

Rev. Friend was also a sofer (scribe).

nary background included rabbinic ordination in Europe, considerable scholarship in astronomy and mathematics,
musical studies at the Conservatory of
Music in Vilna, and escape from Hitler
via Shanghai and Manila.

He was employed as the *B'al Koreh*
(Torah reader), Hebrew teacher and
occasional leader of the service. He loved
his involvement with the children of the
school and held the adults spellbound

Under Rabbi Epstein's guidance
the Adult Education activities continued to expand. Study groups were
organized on Sunday mornings as well
as educational programs presented
at Sisterhood meetings. Throughout
the 1950's outstanding personalities
were brought to Atlanta by the Synagogue, including Maurice Samuels,
author and lecturer; Cantor Moshe
Koussevitsky; Dr. Stephen Kayser,
curator, Jewish Museum; Ellis Arnall,
former governor of Georgia; Rabbi

Irving Miller, Zionist leader; Richard
Tucker, opera star; Rabbis Max Arzt
and Ben Zion Bokser, leaders of the
Conservative rabbinate; Ralph McGill,
Atlanta Constitution editor, and many
others.

Sisterhood became an affiliate of
National Women's League, later known
as Women's League for Conservative
Judaism, in 1958. The question of joining
the national group generated considerable
discussion among the membership.

Many felt there were few advantages for
a group as well organized and successful as
the Ahavath Achim Sisterhood. A small
delegation, led by Dorothy Rosenblum
(president from 1955-57), attended a
national convention as observers and
came home convinced that Sisterhood
should affiliate.

The following year, at a special meeting
held in the Mayfair Club, the group voted
to join. Since then the Sisterhood has
participated actively on a regional and

Hebrew School students in Chanukah play.

Leaders of the Brotherhood (l to r): David Meyer, Sidney Cavalier,
Abe Lewis, Louis Rittenbaum, Mendel Romm, Sr., Dr. David
Kahn, Dr. Irving Goldstein, Dr. Theodore Levitas, Sam Eplan,
Sidney Goldberg, and Jake Friedman.

A. A. SISTERHOOD

presents

In Concert

RICHARD TUCKER

Leading Tenor, Metropolitan Opera

at the

Tower Theatre

March 19th   8:30 P. M.

Advance sale of tickets for members — March 2nd, 3rd, 4th
Box Office — Tower Theatre
Weekdays — 10:30 A. M. 'til 5:30 P. M.

Sisterhood fund raising activity. 1955

national level in the affairs of Women's
League. Rae Alice Cohen served as president of Southern Branch from 1972-74
and as a national vice-president.

Undoubtedly, the most important
event of the period was the building of the
new synagogue on the corner of Northside Dr. and Peachtree Battle Avenue. The
need for more space for the ever-
expanding membership and activities had
become increasingly apparent.

As early as the summer of 1944 the
leadership recognized the need to build a
larger facility on the north side. The
fund- raising began in earnest and by
September, 1944, $55,000 of a goal of
$300,000 had been pledged. Five years
later, in January, 1949, a brochure was
sent to the Congregation announcing a
goal of $750,000 of which $275,000
had been raised.

There were then more than 1300
families affiliated with Ahavath
Achim. Not only was the synagogue
building inadequate but the Educational Center was also too small to
house the entire Religious School on
Sunday. Nearby Grady High School
was leased for that purpose.

A number of possible sites
were investigated and a few purchased. The most promising of those
bought was on Monroe Drive adja-

Confirmation class in front of Washington St. shul. 1950

cent to I-85. The project would have proceeded had it not been for the strenuous objection of A.D. Srochi, chairman of the Lot Committee. He pointed out numerous disadvantages, such as the proximity of industrial and fertilizer plants.

The location Srochi favored was a 10-acre northwest site in the center of one of the best residential areas of the city and convenient to major transportation arteries. In addition, the topography of the land was such that minimal grading was required; that would result in considerable savings.

At a special membership meeting Oct. 4, 1954, it was decided to purchase the lot on the southwest corner of Northside Dr. and Peachtree Battle Avenue for $125,000. The vote was 350 to 7.

Planning and fund raising for the new building continued; on Apr. 18, 1955, an official groundbreaking was held and construction begun. During the spring and summer, as the skeleton of the multi-use building took shape, curious members would drive miles out of the way to observe the progress and marvel at the size.

Some still had vivid memories of the 90′ x 40′ Ahavath Achim on Gilmer Street and many had their

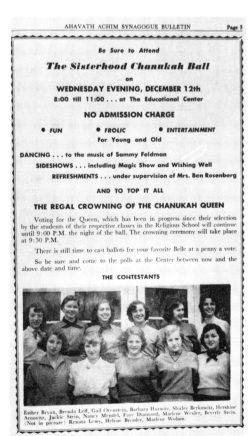

Notice of Sisterhood Chanukah Ball.

Sisterhood adult education. 1953

The New Building

After years of fund raising and numerous proposed locations, the dream of a new facility located in the northern quadrant of the city was ready to become a reality.

SIGNING OF THE CONTRACT FOR OUR NEW BUILDING
Signing: Mr. Joseph Cuba, President; Mr. Max Rittenbaum, Recording Secretary
Witnessed by Co-Chairmen Building Fund: Mr. Abe Goldstein; Mr. Max M. Cuba

Seated: Mr. Max Rittenbaum; Mr. Joseph Cuba
Standing: Mrs. Harry Dwoskin, Mr. Irving M. Galanty, Dr. Nathan Blass, Mr. Simon Mendel, Mrs. Si Rosenblum, Dr. Irving H. Goldstein, Mr. Hyman B. Meltz, Rabbi Harry H. Epstein, Mr. Charles W. Bergman, Mr. Abe Goldstein, Mr. Max M. Cuba, Mr. Harry Dwoskin, Mr. I. J. Paradies and Mr. Alex Kaminetsky

Synagogue leaders sign contract for the new building. 1955

Discussing the architect's drawing (l to r): Ed Saul, Dr. Nathan Blass, and Mel Brown.

Examining a proposed model for the building (l to r): Sylvia Parks, Dora Smith, Charles Aftergut, and Norman Diamond.

Groundbreaking, Feb. 18, 1957.

Construction begins.

Architect's rendering of entire complex.

Sisterhood leaders serve as hostesses for a congregational picnic held in the shell of the new building.

Families enjoy outing held amidst the construction.

103

The Next Generations

Synagogue membership continued to grow and now included scores of newcomers to Atlanta as well as the children and grandchildren of many original families.

25th Wedding Anniversary of Zelda and Sam Berman. Children, Jerry, Hazel Berman Karp, and Herbert Karp.

Elaine and Marilyn Greenbaum, first twin B'not Mitzvah. May 13, 1955.

Bar Mitzvah, Marshall Solomon.

Lewis Alterman and his grandchildren.

Helen and Sidney Cavalier.

Taratoot family Seder.

City-wide service celebrating 300 years of Jewish Settlement in America held at Ahavath Achim on Washington St. 1954

Testimonial dinner given for Rev. Clein when he retired as Shamos. 1954

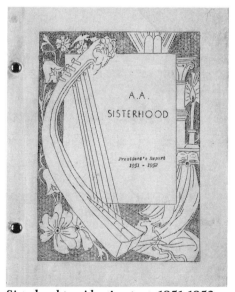

Sisterhood president's report. 1951-1952

earliest memories of Jewish communal life rooted in the grand, yellow brick structure on Washington St.

Fortunately, the Washington St. home for 37 years lay in the path of the slowly evolving expressway system so a purchaser for the property was not a problem. The problem lay in the amount of compensation offered by the City. After much negotiation, the Synagogue accepted $155,000 for the property, considerably less than its appraised value.

A poignant Farewell Service was held Feb. 16, 1958. The Torah scrolls were carried out of the building in solemn procession and the Eternal Light was extinguished. The last vestige of the Jewish community's early presence in Atlanta would become a right-of-way for a super highway. A whole generation of immigrants and their children had become Americans in this southwest neighborhood and had moved on. It was a bittersweet moment.

The sale of the Educational Center brought $185,000 from the purchaser, the Atlanta Labor Temple, and an exit from the building by Mar. 10, 1958.

Now the Congregation was homeless. Services were held in the newly completed Jewish Community Center, and the Religious School moved to Samuel Inman School. A house

was rented for Rabbi Epstein's office and administrative space.

In spite of upheavals, Synagogue activities continued without interruption. In his annual report in June, 1958, President Abe Goldstein (and president in 1942) listed the accomplishments of the past year and complimented the entire Congregation. He noted the spirit of cooperation demonstrated by all elements of Ahavath Achim, and the exceptional leadership of Rabbi Epstein during that difficult time.

There were now 1,582 families associated with the Congregation, 83 of whom had joined during the preceding year. The operating budget showed a year-end surplus of more than $9,000 in spite of numerous, unexpected expenses associated with the two moves. A Congregational Seder had been held for the first time and a Mr. & Mrs. Club organized with Pauline and Herschel Isaacson serving as presidents. The educational and youth programs continued to grow and involved 1,350 children.

The highlight of the evening was the report of Joe Cuba, immediate past president and chairman of the Construction Committee. The building was now 75% complete and was scheduled for partial occupancy by Rosh Hashana, 5719 (1958).

Farewell to Washington Street

After weeks of negotiations with the City, the 37 year old building was sold to become right-of-way for the emerging expressway system. Closing the doors and removing the sacred objects was a bittersweet moment.

Ahavath Achim
Synagogue BULLETIN

Atlanta, Georgia

Affiliated with the
United Synagogue of America

SYNAGOGUE
Washington St. and Woodward Ave. S.W.
JA. 4-9359

EDUCATIONAL CENTER and OFFICES
250 Tenth Street, N.E.
TR. 4-4427

VOL. 28, NO. 23   SHEVAT 22, 5718   FEBRUARY 12, 1958

OUR LAST WEEK-END IN OUR WASHINGTON STREET SYNAGOGUE

"I love the habitation of Thy House, the place where Thy Glory dwelleth."—Psalm 26:7

COME! LET US WORSHIP TOGETHER ON THESE LAST DAYS IN OUR "SHULE"!

"The soul of Judaism lived indestructibly in its House of Prayer, Assembly and Learning."

THE LAST FRIDAY EVENING SERVICE
FEBRUARY 14th— 8:15 TO 9:15 P.M.

Mr. I. Borochoff, who donated the present Synagogue Ark, will be honored with the Pessicha

Blessing the New Month Adar — Rosh Hodesh:
Thursday and Friday, February 20-21

* * * *

THE LAST SATURDAY MORNING SERVICE
FEBRUARY 15th — Shacharis at 9:00 A.M.

"Shabbat Shekalim"

Sedra: "Mishpatim" — Exodus 21-24 and 30:11-16
Haftorah: II Kings 11:17-12:17

Beginning with Next Sabbath, February 21-22
Our Adult Sabbath and Holiday Services
(Until September, When Our New Synagogue
Will Be Completed)
Will Be Held at The Jewish Community Center

All Other Synagogue Activities Will Continue
at Our Educational Center on Tenth Street

You Are Invited To Attend
THE FAREWELL SERVICE
TO OUR WASHINGTON STREET
SYNAGOGUE WHICH WILL BE HELD
ON SUNDAY AFTERNOON,
FEBRUARY 16th
AT 3:00 O'CLOCK

AT THIS SERVICE WE SHALL ACTUALLY
MOVE OUT OF OUR SYNAGOGUE

All Ritual Objects Will Be Removed
and the Synagogue Will Be Closed as a House
of Worship—After 38 Years
of Spiritual Guidance

We Know That Every Man, Woman and Child
Within Our Congregation Will Want
to Be Present to Take Respectful and Final
Leave of the Synagogue That Has
Meant Very Much to All of Us

Schedule for the last weekend on Washington St.

Ahavath Achim
Farewell Service
to its Synagogue

Shevat 26, 5718
Sunday, February 16, 1958 — 3:00 P. M.

"Whenever the Cloud (the Divine Presence) was taken up from over the Sanctuary . . . the children of Israel journeyed; and in the place where the Cloud abode, there the children of Israel encamped . . . At the commandment of the Lord they encamped, and at the commandment of the Lord they journeyed."

—Numbers 9:17 and 23

Program from the Farewell Service and Dismantling.

Past presidents remove Torah scrolls from the Ark.

Menorahs are carried from the pulpit.

Removal of the cornerstones, Max Cuba (left) and Abe Goldstein.

NEW BUSINESS HOME OF ATLANTA LABOR TEMPLE ASSOCIATION
Modern Two-Story Structure Is at 250 Tenth Street, NE, Near Piedmont Park

Sale of the Educational Center.

Labor Temple Buys Center At Tenth Street

The Atlanta Labor Temple Assn. has purchased the Ahavath Achim Congregation Educational Center at 250 Tenth St., NE, for a price reported to be approximately $200,000.

Negotiations were handled by George Kennedy of Adams-Cates Co., realtors.

The Labor Temple Assn. was obliged to move from their old school property at 345 Washington St., SW, to make way for the Expressway Interchange, W. J. Beacham, secretary-treasurer, said.

* * *

THE EDUCATIONAL Center is to be combined with the new Jewish Temple now under construction at Northside drive and Peachtree Battle avenue, NW.

The Tenth street structure bought by the Labor Temple Assn. is a modern, two-story brick building. It has 23,000 square feet of space, including a large auditorium. It fronts 557 feet on Tenth, and has a depth of 158 feet. It is located between Piedmont avenue and Piedmont Park, on a tract of approximately two acres.

The labor association was represented at the closing of the sale by W. M. Crim, president, and Henry T. Mathews, attorney. The Congregation was represented by Abe Goldstein, president, and Charles Bergman, attorney.

Staff Photo—Bill Wilson

CONGREGATION PRESIDENTS REMOVE SCROLLS FROM THE BIG SHULE
(Left to Right) Abe Goldstein, Hyman S. Jacobs, I. J. Paradies

TEARS FLOW IN SYNAGOGUE

Big Shule Closes Doors, Yields to Expressway Work

By LAURA McGREGOR

The Big Shule has gathered her people together for the last time. The Ahavath Achim Synagogue, known to her congregation as the Big Shule, is in the path of the expressway. And like some other buildings on Washington street, the 38-year-old house of worship must yield to the growth and development of the city.

The rambling synagogue was filled to capacity Sunday as members of the congregation took part in a farewell service to the building.

With much emotion members took the ritual objects — the kiddush cup, menorahs, sacred books, the ark cover and others — from the building in solemn procession.

* * *

A WAVE of sadness swept over the older members of the synagogue as the Ner Tamid, the perpetual light suspended above the ark, was lowered and the eternal flame was extinguished. Many wept as the light went out for the first time in Big Shule's history.

The congregation presidents, led by Abe Goldstein, incumbent president, took the satin and gold-covered Torah scrolls from the ark.

With the sounding of the shofar, the Big Shule, now stripped of all her ritual objects, became silent as her people departed. Morris Freedman symbolically locked the door with the original key that opened the synagogue in April, 1920.

Rabbi Harry H. Epstein, who has been the congregation's spiritual leader since 1928, said this is the first time a congregation has moved out of its building without moving into another synagogue.

* * *

AHAVATH ACHIM is one of the largest congregations in the United States. There are about 1,600 families in its membership. At present a new $2,500,000 synagogue and educational center is under construction at the corner of Peachtree Battle avenue and Northside drive. The new facilities are expected to be ready for occupancy in September.

With the end of the Washington street synagogue goes the last of Atlanta's southside synagogues. The Temple moved to its present location on Peachtree street in 1929. Other southside congregations followed later.

Until September, Ahavath Achim will hold worship services in the Jewish Community Center.

5719 ... A Year of Promise, Fulfillment and Commitment

"With Rosh Hashono of this year we inaugurate the 72nd year in the career of our Synagogue. Ahavath Achim is dedicated to the Service of the God of our Fathers and .to the continuity of the heritage of our Jewish people . . . "

Rabbi Harry H. Epstein
Ahavath Achim Bulletin, Aug. 27, 1958

Skyline viewed from the vicinity of the future site of Atlanta Stadium. Old synagogue would have been located somewhere in lower right foreground. 1960

For weeks prior to Rosh Hashanah, 1958, the Synagogue staff worked at fever pitch. The balcony pews were not yet installed, workmen were everywhere, and members and prospective members making arrangements for the holidays clogged the office whose only furnishings were folding chairs lining the walls.

A prayer book cost $3 and men were urged to cover their heads with a *"yarmulke"* instead of a hat. Jerre Freidman Ashkenazie left the building *erev* Rosh Hashanah and spent the following week in the hospital suffering from exhaustion.

As the Congregation streamed into the sanctuary Monday morning, Sept. 15, 1958, members feasted their eyes on the grandeur and relished the accomplishment. It had been years since the entire membership could gather for a High Holiday service under the same roof. Children's services were held in Ellman Chapel and Paradies Hall.

The clean, unadorned lines of this new "modern architecture" were startling; for many the image of what a synagogue building should be was exemplified in the classic curves and decoration of Washington Street. Some felt it was too modern but everyone gradually learned to appreciate the simplicity and spaciousness of their new spiritual home.

Harry Dwoskin, vice chairman of the Construction Committee, was largely responsible for the planning of the interior design just as his father, Morris Dwoskin, had been instrumental in the decoration of the previous building. The time-honored tradi-

Hyman Meltz
1959-1961

Dr. Irving Goldstein
1961-1963

Max Rittenbaum
1963-1965

Michael Kraft
1965

Harry Lane Siegel
1965-1968

Sylvan Makover
1968-1970

tion of passing communal responsibility from generation to generation was enacted again.

Because the design stressed strong, square spaces, the interior provided the perfect foil for outstanding artwork. The focal point of every synagogue is the *bimah* (altar) where the Aron HaKodesh (Holy Ark which contains the Torah scrolls) is located. Special attention is given to the decoration of this cabinet.

In the new Ahavath Achim a magnificent set of doors, featuring a geometric interpretation of the Star of David, was designed by New York artist James Sumer. Executed in a progression of wood blocks, each finished in gold leaf and highlighted in paint, the Ark doors and the marble facing framing the Ark immediately capture attention.

The great expanse behind the Ark is covered by a modern screen of oak highlighted at regular intervals with carved wooden protrusions covered in gold leaf. The screen reaches the ceiling some 50 feet above the floor.

Most of the artwork for the building was designed by Perle Pelzig, a noted Israeli artist. His work includes the stained glass windows in the main sanctuary and Ellman Chapel, the metal sculpture, Procession of the Torahs in the foyer, and the Ark and *Ner Tamid* (Everlasting Light) in Ellman Chapel.

While the general membership delighted in celebrating the High Holiday season in such beautiful surroundings, the lay leaders grappled with mundane matters. Another $500,000 in Building Fund pledges was needed to complete the building, and cash collections on former pledges was essential to meet the construction payroll.

Exterior of new building shortly after completion. 1958

View of the building from the lower parking lot. 1958

Dave Alterman
1970-1972

Janet Meyer
1958-1960

Betty Levitt
1960-1962

Betty Ann Shusterman
1962-1963

Doris Koplin
1963-1965

Sherry Halpern
1965-1967

Bimah and Aaron HaKodesh

Stained glass windows in northeast wall

View of the Sanctuary from the rabbi's pulpit

Perspective from the balcony

Phyllis Cohen
1967-1969

Phyllis Levine
1969-1971

Helene Cohen
1971-1973

110

Sanctuary decorated for a wedding

Covered walkway to Orkin Educational Wing

Srochi Auditorium prepared to accommodate a dinner meeting of over 500 people.

Close-up of Ark doors, executed in a progression of wood blocks finished in gold leaf.

Bimah in Ellman Chapel

Ellman Chapel from the foyer

Lenox Square Mall before it was enclosed. 1959

Bell Bomber plant (now Lockheed of Georgia) producing B-29's during World War II.

It had been determined that a minimum of $20,000 per month was needed for operating costs; items like utilities, taxes, insurance and maintenance supplies doubled and tripled. The anticipated 1958-59 budget was $224,238, an increase of $40,000 from the previous year's operating expense.

Consequently, a 33 1/3% dues increase was proposed and passed in October, 1958. The new dues structure:

Male member — $100
Female member — $50
Junior member — $50

The total cost of the new synagogue was estimated to be $2,600,000. This included land, design expense and construction. A loan of $1,000,000 was negotiated with the C&S National Bank to cover building costs while efforts were made to collect on pledges and secure new ones.

Max Cuba, a past president, served throughout this crucial period as co-chairman (with Abe Goldstein) of the Building Committee. It was an enormous undertaking but one which the leadership faced with confidence in their ability to succeed.

Addressing remarks to 107 new families in December, 1958, President Abe Goldstein enumerated the activities of Congregation on all levels and urged their full participation. It was an impressive program which required a dedicated staff headed by Rabbi Epstein and an equally dedicated laity. As in the past, there were men and women ready to accept the challenge.

The self-confidence of the leadership was in no small measure tied to the mood of the city which was still enjoying the postwar boom of the 1950's and early '60's. Buckhead and sections of northwest Atlanta were finally incorporated into the city in 1952, and the wartime Bell Bomber Plant in nearby Marietta was converted to civilian purposes and renamed Lockheed of Georgia.

Lenox Square, the first of Atlanta's regional shopping malls, opened in 1959 attracting new business and creating new opportunities for creative merchandisers.

Ivan Allen Jr. was elected mayor in 1961 following William B. Hartsfield who had overseen the construction of a new $20 million terminal building at the airport. Architect John Portman's dramatic ideas for a revitalized downtown became the Merchandise Mart and Peachtree Center. Innovative concepts like Executive Park, the nation's first suburban office park, appeared on the pages of the national press.

In spite of general prosperity, an era of social upheaval and racial revolution was storming the country. The long history of northern *de facto* and southern *de jure* racial segregation was soon to erupt in a series of inner city riots, massive demonstrations and violence. Fortunately for Atlanta, the bitterness and destruction which plagued cities like Detroit, Los Angeles and New York did not occur mainly because of the leadership of both the black and white communities.* While there was some unrest and a crises in the public schools, the city escaped relatively unscathed.

*Rabbi Jacob Rothschild of The Temple was especially active in the local civil rights struggle.

A new constitution and by-laws for the synagogue had been discussed for many years; the last complete revision had been finished in 1936. In the interim, numerous sections of the old code had been rewritten but there was a definite need for a new document. A completely new constitution was presented and passed by the membership in February, 1960.

Some of the enormous changes of the intervening years were clearly reflected. The stated affiliation with United Synagogue of America and the mention of permanent staff members such as assistant rabbi, executive director and educational director immediately emphasized the shift from orthodoxy and the physical growth of the institution. The inclusion of Sisterhood women as permanent members of the Board of Trustees was another dramatic change.

While the deletion of the blackball provision was a leap into the modern world, it is interesting to note that a married woman could vote only if her husband was not present.

The tremendous growth of the school population had long ago necessitated professional help for Rabbi Epstein; some of the early educational directors/assistant rabbis were Rabbi

Janet Meyer, Sisterhood president, welcomes Phyllis Weinstein of Birmingham, president of Southern Branch, Women's League for Conservative Judaism.

Mrs. Belger and students enjoy the spacious Nursery School rooms of the new building.

Rabbi Jacob Rothschild presents commemorative bowl to Dr. Martin Luther King, winner of the Nobel Peace Prize. 1965

113

Administrative staff: (standing) Jerre Friedman Ashkenazie, (seated) Sylvia Friedberg and Edith Waronker.

Jerrold Leeson, first full-time Youth Director. 1961

Rabbi Raphael Gold, Educational Director, 1960-1970.

DeKoven, Mr. Kaminetsky and Rabbi Langer.

Rabbi Raphael Gold became Educational Director in September, 1960, and remained with the congregation for 10 years. A 1952 graduate of the Jewish Theological Seminary of America, Rabbi Gold was the first product of the Conservative Movement to serve.

A native of New York City and a graduate of Brooklyn College, Rabbi Gold occupied a pulpit in Washington, D.C. and was Educational Director of Temple Israel in Wilkes-Barre, PA, before coming to Atlanta.

During his tenure, uniform standards for Bar and Bat Mitzvah, Confirmation and Religious School were developed and the instructional hours in the Hebrew School were increased. A student conducted Junior Congregation on Shabbat morning became an important element of the school program and was attended weekly by as many as 250 girls and boys.

The Sunday morning Minyonaire service and breakfast for fathers and sons which had begun in the early '50's continued to grow. A group of dedicated mothers headed by Helen Cavalier have prepared and served the breakfast for many years. Some of the women continue to participate long after their children no longer attended the service.

In 1970 Rabbi Gold assumed the pulpit of Congregation Agudath Israel in Montgomery, AL, with Rabbi Epstein officiating at his installation.

The activities of the synagogue's pre-teen and teenage programs, United Synagogue Youth and Kadimah, continued to attract the young people of the Congregation. Originally supervised by laymen (Dave Cowan, Dave Alterman and Bernard Gordon were especially active), a fulltime Youth Activities Director was hired in the fall of 1961.

Jerrold Leeson joined the staff in that position after completion of military service. A native of Minneapolis and graduate of the University of Minnesota, Leeson was fluent in Hebrew and had served in administrative capacities as well as Youth Director in synagogues in Minneapolis. He brought a special talent for writing and directing dramatic presentations which created increased interest in the youth program.

A stable office staff headed by Jerre Freidman Ashkenazie and consisting of Mildred Rosenbaum, Edith Waronker and Sylvia Friedberg was developed, enabling an increasingly complex institution to function efficiently.

The 76th Annual Meeting was held June 5, 1963, at which time Rabbi Epstein's 35th year of service was celebrated. Six hundred fifty persons attended the dinner meeting, including

Youth Activities

A wide range of cultural, religious, and social activities were developed for the young people of the Congregation.

USY members rehearse a cantata to be presented at a regional convention.

Junior Congregation Officers. 1956

Regional USY Convention held at Ahavath Achim. 1965

Congregation receives Solomon Schechter Award for Youth Activities. 1968

Newspaper published by students of the Religious and Hebrew Schools, Jerry Udinsky, editor. 1962

Religious School Faculty. Circa 1965

Religious School Consecration. 1966

Hebrew School graduates. 1959

members of the Rabbi's family and past presidents who had served since his arrival: Hyman Jacobs, I. J. Paradies, Abe Goldstein, Charles Bregman, Thomas Makover, Simon Bressler, Max Cuba, Dr. Nathan Blass, Joseph Zaglin, Joseph Cuba and Hyman Meltz. Deceased past presidents who had served with Rabbi Epstein were also remembered: Joseph Goldberg, Joel Dorfan, Hyman Mendel and Oscar Gershon. Dr. Irving Goldstein presided as he completed his term as president. The guest speaker was Rabbi Isaac Klein, past president of the Rabbinical Assembly.

As always, Reva Epstein was recognized for her own contribution to the Congregation and community. In tribute to her special place in the hearts of the women of Sisterhood, $10,000 was raised to dedicate a room in her honor in a new residence hall for women planned at the Jewish Theological Seminary.

Rabbi Epstein continued his vigorous leadership, his dedication and involvement in all aspects of the Congregation being evident in every program and new idea. Israel and every legitimate cause of the Jewish people were also part of his daily agenda. His tireless devotion not only enriched many organizations but also inspired others to assume leadership roles.

Cantor Isaac Goodfriend and his family were officially welcomed to Ahavath Achim at a special Oneg Shabbat, Mar. 11, 1966. Born in Lodz, Poland, into an Hasidic family, Cantor Goodfriend received a traditional Jewish education, and began

singing in his synagogue choir at age five. A teenager at the time of the Nazi invasion of Poland, he spent three years in a forced labor camp. He subsequently escaped and was given refuge by a Polish farmer.

After the war, he went to Berlin and worked as a tailor. While there he became a *B'al Tefillah* and eventually a cantor. He began his formal musical studies at the Berlin Conservatory of Music and continued to develop his rich baritone voice at the McGill Conservatory of Music after his migration to Canada in 1952.

Before coming to Atlanta, Cantor Goodfriend served congregations in Montreal, Boston and Cleveland. His clear enunciation and sensitive phrasing of the traditional liturgy established a standard of musical excellence recognized by the entire Jewish community.

Cantor Goodfriend and his wife Betty quickly became involved in Sisterhood programs and taught Adult Education courses; the Cantor enriched the school curriculum with Jewish music programs, and was featured in USY productions. Their warmth and gregarious style endeared them to young and old.

In addition to his official duties at Ahavath Achim, Cantor Goodfriend has served as president of the Jewish National Fund in Atlanta, and is a member of the U.S. Holocaust Commission.

He was invited to sing the national anthem at the inauguration of President Jimmy Carter (Jan. 20, 1977) and participated in the centennial celebration of the Statue of Liberty (October, 1986).

Cantor Goodfriend singing the national anthem at the inauguration of Pres. Jimmy Carter. Jan. 20, 1977

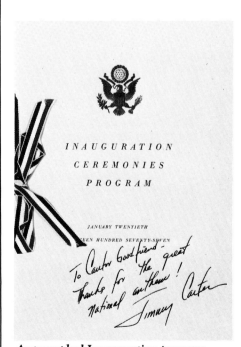

Autographed Inauguration program

Cantor Isaac Goodfriend and Betty

Both survivors of the Holocaust, Betty and Isaac met after the war, married and came to America to build a new life.

Betty and Isaac Goodfriend

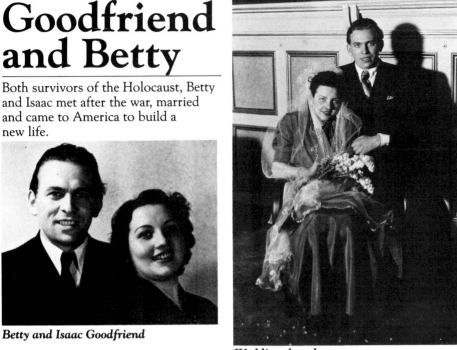

Wedding day photo

Mr. & Mrs. Isaac Goodfriend. Berlin, 1945

Cantor Goodfriend at the wedding of relatives in South America

Interned in a Nazi labor camp as a teenager, Isaac (back row on left) escaped after three years.

First appearance as a cantor. Berlin, 1951

Polish farmer who saved his life is visited by Cantor Goodfriend. 1979

Establishment of the Isaac Goodfriend Collection of Holocaust Literature at Emory University.

Singing at a ZOA convention in Israel. It was the last public appearance of Golda Meir before her death.

Cantor and Betty with mayor of Jerusalem, Teddy Kollek. 1970

Leading Mourner's Kaddish at Birkenau Concentration Camp. 1979

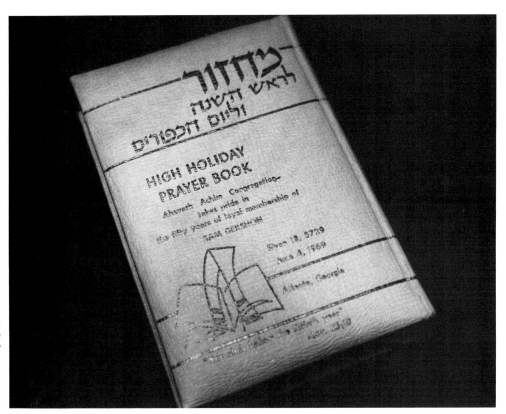

Inscription on special prayerbook: "Ahavath Achim Cong. takes pride in the fifty years of loyal membership of ____."

A group of 74 individuals were honored as 50-Year Members at the annual meeting in June, 1969. Among them were past president Abe Goldstein, past Sisterhood presidents Lizzie Jacobs Scheinbaum, Anabelle Samet and Rose Klotz, and numerous men and women who had served in leadership roles over the years. Rabbi Epstein presented a High Holiday prayer book to the honorees and recognized their contributions to the Synagogue.

THE 50-YEAR MEMBERS
(IN 1969)

Charles Abelman	Mrs. B. Levine
Mrs. B. A. Arnold	Mrs. Abe Levitt
Mr. and Mrs. J. Arnovitz	Mrs. Sara Lipman
Mr. and Mrs. Oscar Bartell	Mr. and Mrs. Hyman Mendel
Mrs. Joseph Berger	Mr. and Mrs. Perry Mendel
Mrs. Morris M. Berger	Mr. and Mrs. Dave Miller
Mrs. A. Borochoff	Mrs. Morris Nissenbaum
Mr. and Mrs. Hyman Cohen	Mr. and Mrs. Max Pamarance
Mr. and Mrs. Jake Cohen	Mrs. Pearl Pfeffer
Mr. and Mrs. Louis Cohen	Mrs. A. G. Reisman
Mrs. Michael Ellman	Mr. and Mrs. Willie Reisman
Mr. and Mrs. Ed Fagelson	Mrs. Mary Russ
Mr. and Mrs. Max Fagelson	Mr. and Mrs. Louis Samet
Joseph A. Freedman	Mrs. H. R. Saul
Mr. and Mrs. Morris Freedman	Mrs. J. L. Saul
Mr. and Mrs. Sam Gershon	Mrs. Lizzie Scheinbaum
Mr. and Mrs. Joseph Goldberg	Mrs. B. F. Shainker
Mrs. Sarah Goldberg	Harry B. Siegel
Abe Goldstein	Mrs. Sam Silverman
Mr. and Mrs. Abner Hirsch	Mrs. Julius Solomon
Mr. and Mrs. Ike Hirsh	Mr. and Mrs. A. R. Spielberger
Mrs. Michael Horwitz	Mr. and Mrs. A. D. Srochi
Mrs. Hyman Jacobs	Mr. and Mrs. Sam Sugarman
Mrs. Sarah Jacobs	Julius Tenenbaum
Mrs. Minnie Kessler	Jake Turetsky
Mr. and Mrs. Sol Klotz	Abe Wolbe
Mrs. Pincus Koplin	Mrs. Ida Wolkin

Sisterhood Publishes Kosher Recipes

By GRACE HARTLEY
Atlanta Journal Food Editor

"Our cook book is DIFFERENT," Mrs. Martin Goldstein, the editor proudly pointed out.

"All the recipes are Kosher —that is, there is no mixture of meat and milk or any milk products, in the same recipe. No ingredient in any recipe is contrary to Jewish dietary laws and some of the recipes have been in certain families for several generations — and never written down before."

The book "Mind over Platter" contains authentic Jewish dishes plus recipes from several foreign countries. Then, too, there is a nice balance between fancy, gourmet dishes and everyday type family meals.

"OH, MY, the problems we had to pull this book together" Mrs. Goldstein went on to relate. Getting together so many from so many people and keeping after them until they turned up was a major problem."

"After that we had to standardize each recipe and check for accuracy. Then came the proofreading which was a real chore. In fact, every step was so time consuming and tedious that it has taken one and a half years to finish."

Why did they publish the book? First to provide the members of the Ahavath Achim Sisterhood a book of interesting ideas for meals relating to centuries old traditions.

Next was to raise funds for the Sisterhood which supports and maintains the religious school connected to the synagogue.

THERE ARE some 1400 children enrolled in all divisions of the school starting at the kindergarten level and going through high school.

The price of the book is $3.50 and is available at Ahavath Achim Sisterhood Gift Shop, 600 Peachtree Battle Ave. NW.

Members prepared two meals from the cook book for us, a meat meal and a dairy meal. For the meat meal there was chopped liver salad, Challah (bread), Chinese custard soup, chicken ambassador, Yom Tov (Carrot Ring) and Meringue des poires au chocolate.

Chopped Liver Salad

1 pound liver (or ½-pound chicken and ½-pound beef)
3 large onions, cut up.
4 hard cooked eggs.
3 tablespoons chicken fat.
Salt and pepper.

MRS. EPSTEIN SHOWS CHALLAH FRESH FROM OVEN
To Mrs. Martin Goldstein, Editor of Mind Over Platter

MRS. HOWARD CIGAL GETS HELPING DESSERT
Meringue des Poires From Mrs. Goldstein

Staff Photos—Charles Pugh

Sisterhood's first cookbook, Mind Over Platter. 1967

Ahavath Achim Sisterhood
cordially invites you

Opening meeting
Monday, Oct. 7th
1:00 P.M.
Srochi Auditorium

Our rose is Rose Klotz

presenting

IMPRESSIONS: 1963

accompanied by

Frances Wallace

Opening meeting; speaker, Rose Klotz. 1963

MRS. MICHAEL BLASS ILLUSTRATES NARRATIVE
Chanukah 'One of World's Greatest Sagas'

MRS. GILBERT HALPERN LIGHTS CANDLE
Commemoration of the 'Triumph of Freedom'

MRS. RICHARD FRANCO WROTE THE NARRATIVE
Accompanies the Choir of Singers

Staff Photos—Billy Downs, Robert Connell

Churchwomen Join Hands, Hearts in Chanukah Rites

Church Women United of Atlanta were special guests the other day of the Sisterhood of the Ahavath Achim Synagogue for a "Musical Narrative of the Story of Chanukah."

It was the first time the two groups had joined together here for a Chanukah institute. More than 175 women turned out for the program in Ellman Chapel at the Ahavath Achim Synagogue, 600 Peachtree Battle Ave. NW.

A traditional Chanukah lunch of potato latkes and applesauce, jello and molds and tuna-fish salad was served after the narrative.

"ON THE 25TH day of the Hebrew month of Kislev, on the 18th day of this month of December, in Jewish homes all over the world, Chanukah candles will be lit—for eight consecutive days—beginning with one candle on the first night and adding an additional one on each day," the narrative began.

Today, Dec. 22, is the last day of Chanukah. The festival of lights began here a week ago with the lighting of the first menorah candle in each of Atlanta's synagogues with a symbolic torch flown here from Israel.

"When it comes to tales of dauntless courage in the face of overwhelming odds, of triumph of right over might . . . of religion over paganism . . . of spirit over force . . . Chanukah is one of the world's greatest sagas," the chorus chanted.

THE ISRAELI torch was lit at Modin, the city where Mattathias and his five sons struck the first blow for religious freedom against the Syrians more than 2,000 years ago.

"And there ensued a furious battle . . . Finally, at the town of Emmaus, after a bold and bloody attack, the Syrian commander bowed to mark the victory of Judas Maccabee . . . And it came to pass that in 165 B.C., the Jews returned to Jerusalem . . . the

Mrs. Michael Blass. Mrs. Franco wrote the narrative presented the church women.

"WHEN they reached the city, their joy turned to bitterness . . . Dirt and desolation met the eye everywhere . . . The people braced themselves . . . They cleansed the Temple and scrubbed it . . . On the 25th day of Kislev, the Temple was rededicated. With a little flask of oil—the only holy oil they could find amid the destruction—they relit the great menorah."

The chorus included Mrs. Larry Frank, Mrs. Joel Piassick, Mrs. Randy Moret, Mrs. Macy Moret, Mrs. Ilene Zier, Mrs. Gilbert Halpern, Mrs. Davis Abrams, Mrs. Gerald Blonder and Mrs. Marvin Silver.

Mrs. Halpern lit the menorah candles during the program; Mrs. Blonder and Mrs. Silver narrated portions of the program.

"Exceeding all expectations, the oil miraculously lasted for

SISTERHOOD OF AHAVATH ACHIM CHORUS SANG STORY OF CHANUKAH
Church Women United of Atlanta Are Special Guests

Church Women United joins Sisterhood in Chanukah Workshop. 1968

Rabbi Auerbach served the Congregation from 1970-1980.

Dr. & Mrs. Nathan Blass present portrait of Rabbi Epstein.

Gloria Auerbach with Mrs. Epstein

In 1969 Ahavath Achim had occupied its new home for a decade. The membership had reached 1,749 and the projected budget for the coming year was $597,792, an increase of $33,000 over 1968. The position of assistant rabbi had been created, and was filled by Rabbi Alexander Graubart.

More than 200 pre-teen and teenage boys and girls participated in a most successful youth program which was recognized by a Solomon Schechter Award. The Hebrew School faculty was increased, and for the first time in 10 years all students attended class six hours per week. Sylvan Makover, the son of past president Thomas Makover, was elected president for a second term.

During the summer of 1970 two staff members joined the Ahavath Achim family: Rabbi David Auerbach became Associate Rabbi and S. Hirsch Jacobson was hired to replace Rabbi Raphael Gold as Educational Director.

David Auerbach, a native of Montreal who graduated from McGill University in 1959, entered the Jewish Theological Seminary and was ordained in 1965. While there he received a Master of Hebrew Literature degree and was a distinguished student in Talmud and homiletics. Upon graduation he was elected to the pulpit of Congregation Shaar Shalom in Chomedey, a suburb of Montreal.

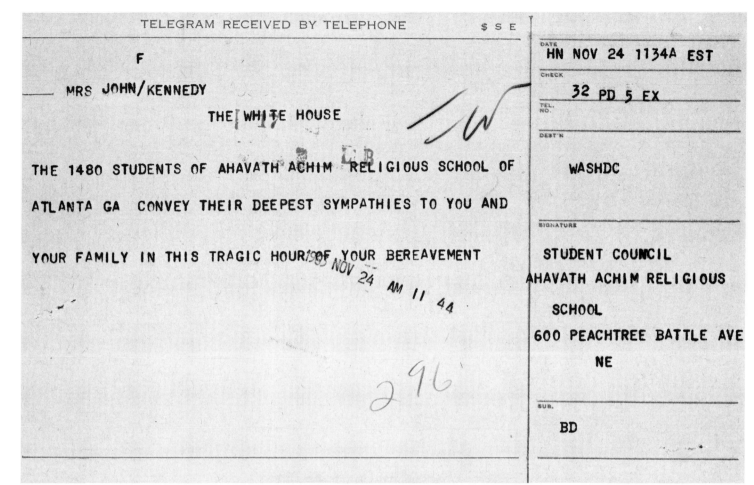

F

MRS JOHN/KENNEDY

THE WHITE HOUSE

THE 1480 STUDENTS OF AHAVATH ACHIM RELIGIOUS SCHOOL OF

ATLANTA GA CONVEY THEIR DEEPEST SYMPATHIES TO YOU AND

YOUR FAMILY IN THIS TRAGIC HOUR OF YOUR BEREAVEMENT

DATE
HN NOV 24 1134A EST

CHECK
32 PD 5 EX

TEL. NO.

DEST'N
WASHDC

SIGNATURE
STUDENT COUNCIL
AHAVATH ACHIM RELIGIOUS
SCHOOL
600 PEACHTREE BATTLE AVE
NE

SUB.
BD

Rabbi Auerbach and his wife Gloria launched a series of informal meetings in their home for the younger members of the Congregation. These encouraged the participation of a segment of the membership who had no family ties to Ahavath Achim.

During the course of their service Gloria became ill and died of cancer. The Congregation mourned her passing with Rabbi Auerbach and his young children. In 1980 he was elected to the pulpit of Beth David Congregation in Miami, FL.

The son of Rabbi Abraham Jacobson, Hirsch Jacobson grew up in Brookline, MA., and was educated at Boston University and Hebrew Teacher's College of Boston. He attended the Jewish Theological Seminary and received a Master of Hebrew Literature degree. Before accepting the position in Atlanta, he served congregations in South Orange, N. J. and New City, N.Y.

Jacobson introduced many innovations to several aspects of the school program. He revised the system of student evaluation and instituted parent-teacher conferences. The old Student Council was reorganized as the "Kenesset" and sparked renewed interest among the students. A "Mechina" (readiness) class for six-and seven-year-olds met four hours per week, and a "Prozdor" class for teenagers was formed to provide instruction in Tal-

Religious School students send condolence message to Mrs. John F. Kennedy. Nov., 1963

Hirsch Jacobson, Educational Director, brought many innovative ideas to the school.

Celebration of Rabbi and Reva's 40th year with Ahavath Achim.

The Mr. & Mrs. Club

Organized in 1958, the Mr. & Mrs. Club encouraged the active involvement of many couples. Their energies and talents added a new dimension to the life of the Congregation.

Janet and Lenny Meyer at a Mr. & Mrs. square dance.

Mr. & Mrs. the club co-wed

Vol. I.   AHAVATH ACHIM SYNAGOGUE   No. 1 July 15, 1963

ACTIVE PROGRAM PLANNED FOR MR. & MRS. CLUB '63-64

FIRST BOARD MEETING HELD JUNE 24

"TERRIFIC SOCIAL AFFAIRS" —ONA AND MARSHALL

"FRESH, NEW, APPROACH TO CULTURAL ACTIVITIES" —ANN AND NORMAN

"WELCOME TO YOU ALL" —MEREDITH AND TED

"KEY TO SERVICE —THROUGH OUR YOUTH" —ELAINE AND MARVIN

"SOUND FINANCIAL PLANNING A MUST" —PHYLLIS AND MORTON

"OUR CONSTITUTION MUST BE BROUGHT UP-TO-DATE." —JANE AND JOEL

HOT OFF THE WIRES... exciting First Board Meeting held at the synagogue with a packed interested attendance of officers and Board members... forthright purposes and goals stated by President Ralph Saul, "It is really very simple. Bigger and better social and recreational activities, fresh approach to culturals and closer motivation of prospective new members. We want to EXPAND on all the ACTIVITIES of the club through new channels giving it more of a real purpose for existing and a closer attachment to the synagogue." Each committee must have a minimum of six couples serving on the committee. Wider PARTICIPATION is an aim for 1963-64... Each committee chairman must submit a budget of any affair or function to the Board for approval... New special committees announced: ADVISORY, Past Presidents with Joel Fryers, chairmen, to look into the re-writing of the Constitution; BUDGET, Morton Levine, chairmen to work on a sound budget; HOSPITALITY, Ted Levye, chairmen, to widen the scope of this committee; YOUTH, Marvin Singers, chairmen, to study how best to use the money from the Purim Carnival and any other fund-raising affairs; PUBLICITY, Sol Steins, chairmen, to enlarge through a Bulletin and other means; and Bowling Secretary, Sylvia Born, to keep things moving in the Bowling world... With much approval a motion was passed to have a SHOW in the spring of '63 - '64(date to be announced) with proceeds to be spent on a worthwhile synagogue cause... SHOW to be written and produced by our own Paul Landis... motion passed that a $2.00 per couple charge as admission for dinner at opening meeting to help pay dinner expenses (further explanations in President's message-Page 3)... 1963-64... OUTLOOK GOOD!!!

"GREATER FUN IN RECREATIONAL ACTIVITIES" —ROSALYN AND JULIAN

"THE BIG SHOW NEEDS YOU" —RHONA AND PAUL

"JOIN IN EVERYTHING —WE'LL PUT YOUR NAME IN PRINT" —BESS AND SOL

"LET'S GROW, GROW, GROW WITH MORE NEW MEMBERS" —HANNAH AND MORRIS

"GET ON THE BOWLING LIST" —SYLVIA BORN

"CHECK WITH US ON DUPLICATE BRIDGE" —ICKY AND DORIS

SOCIAL CHAIRMAN ONA & MARSHALL NERENBAUM have planned a terrific summer Affair for you plus a full social calendar for the coming year. More details in the next CO-WED.

Newsletter, The Co-wed. 1963

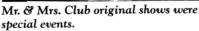

Mr. & Mrs. Club original shows were special events.

mud and other classic texts.

A Men's Club was organized in the fall of 1970 to bring a new generation of young men into active involvement in synagogue affairs. Rabbi Auerbach served as advisor, and Steve Zier was first president. The Club was quite active for several years, sponsoring a Sunday Morning Forum which brought prominent speakers (*e.g.*, Dean Rusk, Andrew Young and others) to the synagogue, a Youth Olympics and the Purim Carnival.

The Mr. & Mrs. Club continued to organize the social life of the Congregation with a wide variety of events which included dances, picnics, a bowling league, bridge club, original shows and a Kosher Food Fair. They were also the originators of the Quarterly Blood Drives which "banks" blood for the use of synagogue members.

Rabbi Epstein was honored in December, 1970, when he received the Abe Goldstein Award for Human Relations from the Anti-Defamation League of B'nai B'rith.

For a number of years the Congregation encouraged attendance at Camp Ramah, a summer experience in Jewish living sponsored by the Conservative movement. A line was added to the budget which provided a stipend for each family sending a child to Camp Ramah. Monies were also budgeted for teenagers spending the summer in Israel.

Past Presidents

Sisterhood Celebrates Its 50th Anniversary

During the weekend of Dec. 3-4, 1971, the Congregation recognized the years of service of Ahavath Achim Sisterhood.

Three generations of Sisterhood women; Lizzie Scheinbaum, her daughter Ragolda Stein, and granddaughter Diane LeRoy.

Gov. Jimmy Carter issues Jubilee proclamation.

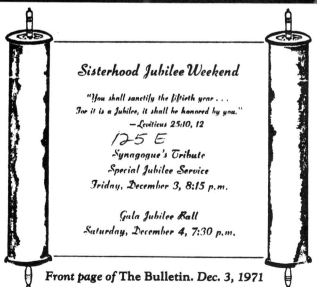

Sisterhood Jubilee Weekend

"You shall sanctify the fiftieth year . . .
For it is a Jubilee, it shall be honored by you."
—Leviticus 25:10, 12

125 E

Synagogue's Tribute
Special Jubilee Service
Friday, December 3, 8:15 p.m.

Gala Jubilee Ball
Saturday, December 4, 7:30 p.m.

Front page of The Bulletin. Dec. 3, 1971

Salute to Sisterhood

This newspaper editor has been variously accused of being a sentimentalist through the years and we hope it is true because the accusation though directed rather derisively means we like people. We can think of no better qualification for the role of sitting in the slot on matters concerning Jewish public opinion.

And few things arouse this sentimentality more than an anniversary, especially such as the forthcoming fiftieth for Ahavath Achim Sisterhood. We're not exactly sure if this makes it the oldest or the biggest but this fact is sheer trivia, since it is not now and has never been in competition or contest with sisterhoods of other congregations. Each sisterhood gains its own integrity and personality in the kind of specific service it renders to its own congregation. In a way there is a similar thread in that all sisterhoods augment the main congregation, leaving to the men the basics of providing a spiritual leader, a building, the cemetery and a welter of problems which require heavy finance, such as we like to feel the men are most capable of handling. Certainly in the traditional Jewish family role.

To the women of the congregation are left such matters as religious education of the children which means aiding and abetting the Sunday school as well as providing subtleties and knick-knacks and in general supervising the kitchen facilities. At Ahavath Achim this has meant the strictest kind of efforts to maintain the proper requirements of Kashrut. In many ways, what the sisterhood does is provide the nitty-gritty of congregational continuity, the performance of what to be frank about it are more aptly described as chores and work. We have yet to hear of a sisterhood shirking responsibility on this score nevertheless.

What is on the record for Ahavath Achim Sisterhood during its first half century is a tribute to the determination, the inspiration, the willingness, the devotion and the loyalty of the members to the cause of Judaism — through years, through the many years. Members have steadfastly risen to the challenges — whether at the Big Shule on the South Side, the Educational Center on Tenth Street or the Peachtree Battle facility.

Editorial tribute from The Southern Israelite.

Moments of Congregational Life

The months and years were filled with events and activities; both special and mundane. Each became a part of our recorded history.

Diane Bernstein presents a tribute to Joe Zelman, beloved teacher, on behalf of Sisterhood. June, 1973

First annual meeting held in Peachtree Battle building. L to R: Dr. Irving Goldstein, Hyman Meltz, incoming president, Abe Goldstein, and Max Rittenbaum. May, 1959

Sisterhood hosts brunch for Gold Book workers. 1964

Planning for the 25th anniversary of the Donor Luncheon. Cecile Waronker with original chairmen, Helen Cavalier and Mary Dwoskin. 1966

Sisterhood women with Nellie Willis, popular cateress.

Estelle Karp and Cantor Schwartzman often performed together.

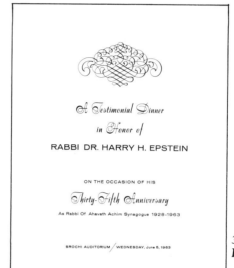

A Testimonial Dinner
in Honor of
RABBI DR. HARRY H. EPSTEIN

ON THE OCCASION OF HIS

Thirty-Fifth Anniversary

As Rabbi Of Ahavath Achim Synagogue 1928-1963

SROCHI AUDITORIUM / WEDNESDAY, June 5, 1963

35th anniversary tribute to Rabbi Epstein. June 5, 1963

"Set aside for jubilation before the Lord"
—Leviticus 19:24

Ahavath Achim's
Historic Double "Simcha"
The Commemoration of its
85th Anniversary Year
1887-1972
and
The Celebration of
Rabbi and Mrs. Harry H. Epstein's
45th Year of Ministry
1928-1972

"Realize that there is nothing better than to rejoice
in one's accomplishments, for that is one's portion"
—Ecclesiastes 3:22

Friday Evening, November 10, 1972
and
Saturday Morning, November 11, 1972

Celebration of Rabbi Epstein's 45th year with the Congregation. Nov., 1972

Recognition of 25 years of service by Cantor Schwartzman. 1966

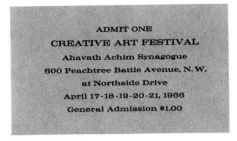

Second Jewish Art Festival. 1967

Art Festival chairman, Sol Singer, his wife Ruth, Harry Lane Siegel, president of the Congregation, and his wife Elsie. 1967

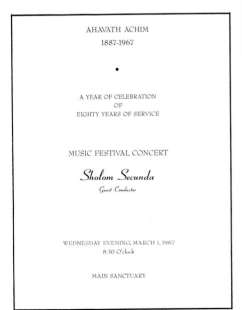

Program for Music Festival Concert, Sholom Secunda, guest conductor. 1967

Sisterhood activities expanded. The now familiar *Gold Book*, first published in 1957 as a weekly calendar and membership list, was the first publication of its kind organized by a Jewish women's group in Atlanta.

Revenue from the sale of advertisements and from the annual Donor Luncheon supported teachers' salaries in the Religious School, holiday celebrations, Camp Ramah and Israel Pilgrimage stipends, and the purchase of pieces of equipment for the school and synagogue. Sisterhood funds had assisted in the furnishing of the Srochi kitchen and the paving of the lower parking lot.

An important service to the Congregation was the organization and maintenance of a Judaica Shop which stocks ceremonial objects and Jewish books. Growing from a single display counter in the foyer of 10th Street to a complete Jewish shopping center in the new building, Sisterhood has made available a wide variety of merchandise to enhance the Jewish home.

Other projects included holiday workshops, the training of women to transcribe textbooks in braille, interfaith gatherings with various church groups, ongoing classes and study groups, and the publication of a kosher cookbook, *Mind Over Platter.*

In 1971 Sisterhood commemorated its Jubilee. Included in the plans was a special Shabbat service scheduled for Dec. 3. A snow storm blanketed Atlanta and forced cancellation of the Friday evening service but was sufficiently melted to allow the Jubilee Ball to be held the following night. Eighteen past presidents attended the celebration.

The synagogue continued to offer an enormous range of activities and events designed to interest a diverse and large membership. The Monday night lecture series, held following adult education classes, presented local and national personalities speaking on an array of timely subjects.

Eli Wiesel, Chaim Potok, Meyer Levin, Milton Himmelfarb, Rabbi Immanuel Jakobovits and Dr. Allen Pollack came to Ahavath Achim. Leading rabbis of the Conservative Movement — Simon Greenberg, Saul Teplitz, Morton Siegel and Wolfe Kelman — presented the philosophy of the movement.

Trends in Jewish art and music were not neglected. Traveling exhibits from the Jewish Museum came to the synagogue. Artist Jossi Stern spoke, and musician Gershon Kingsley presented a concert. Composer Sholom Secunda presented original works, and several cantorial concerts were held. In April, 1966, the first Art Festival opened.

1973 - 1982

"The World's Next Great City"

"We roll a red carpet out for every _____ Yankee who comes in here with two strong hands and some money. We break our necks to sell him."

Mayor William B. Hartsfield

Following the tradition of all the boosters in its history, the Atlanta Chamber of Commerce coined the "The World's Next Great City" slogan in the early Seventies, triggering a new outburst of swagger and unbridled faith in the city's future. And former Mayor Hartsfield's comment explaining the secret of success in attracting new business was still very much operative more than a decade after he had vacated City Hall.

The Chamber's pride, while somewhat overstated, was not all empty boast. Major league sports had come to fill the new stadium built in the general vicinity of the onetime Washington St. *shul.* Another sports palace, The Omni, occupied a former railroad gulch; rising adjacent to it was the Georgia World Congress Center, which sent soaring the number of conventions booked into the city.

MARTA took over the operation of public transportation, and began a subway system. New projects, from subdivisions in "far away" Roswell to downtown hotels and office buildings, continued to rise.

The area's vitality and favorable media image continued to attract new residents from every part of the country. In addition, ethnic groups (*e.g.,*

Projects by Atlanta architect John Portman dramatically changed the shape of the city's skyline.

Dr. Marvin Goldstein
1972-1974

Gerald Cohen
1974-1976

Dr. William Schatten
1976-1978

Norman Diamond
1978-1980

Dr. Herbert Karp
1980-1982

Diane Bernstein
1973-1975

The new facility of The Jewish Home.

The Hebrew Academy, Atlanta's first Jewish day school.

Vietnamese, Cambodian and Cuban) began settling here, creating a rich diversity. The first Jewish mayor, Sam Massell, was elected in 1969, followed by the first black mayor, Maynard Jackson, in 1973.

Nor was activity in the Jewish community stagnant; in its own way, this moderate-sized Jewish enclave was developing a splendid range of institutions and density of population. In a general population of a million plus, Jews were estimated between 35,000 - 40,000.

The newest traditional congregation, Beth Jacob, founded in the 1940's, celebrated Rabbi Feldman's 20th anniversary there while the only other Reform congregation, Temple Sinai, broke ground for its sanctuary just inside the Perimeter Highway (Jan. 28, 1973).

The new Jewish Home opened in 1971, elevating the level of care for the Jewish elderly to a degree unparalleled in the entire community. The Hebrew Academy, Atlanta's first Jewish day school, situated since 1966 on Druid Hills Road, was the first Hebrew day school to be accredited by the Southern Association of College and Schools, and continued to attract students represen-

ting a cross section of the community. Yeshiva High School, the only Jewish high school in Georgia, opened in 1970.

The old barriers and animosity between the "German" and the "Russian" Jews had disappeared in the wake of the Holocaust and the founding of the State of Israel. A central community address began to develop after the merger in 1967 of The Jewish Welfare Fund, the Jewish Community Council and the Jewish Social Service Federation.

Men and women from throughout the community worked side by side to promote the welfare of Jews and Jewish institutions all over the world. The announced goal for the annual campaign in 1973 was $6,350,000.

Ahavath Achim marked its 85th year and honored Rabbi Epstein for his 45 years of service by granting him a year's sabbatical in Israel. He and Reva left Atlanta in the fall of 1972 and returned the following summer.

It had been an extremely busy year. In addition to a full schedule of normal activities, key synagogue personnel were involved in planning for the opening of the Solomon Schechter School in the fall of 1973.

The idea of founding a day school within the Conservative movement had been in the air for several years. Rabbi Epstein and Hirsch Jacobson had discussed the issue when Jacobson first came to the Congregation.

Returning from a United Synagogue of America convention in 1971, Ralph Saul, then the synagogue's financial secretary, included the possibility in his

Doris Goldstein
1975-1977

Miriam Strickman-Levitas
1977-1979

Shirley Minsk
1979-1981

The Epstein School

Founded in 1973 as part of the Solomon Schechter School Association, the school was named in tribute to Rabbi Epstein.

Judge Ernest Tidwell signs the school's incorporation charter in the presence of Rabbi Epstein and Congregation leaders.

Opening day of the Rabbi Harry Epstein/Solomon Schechter School of Atlanta. Aug., 1973

Advertisement in The Southern Israelite. Summer, 1973

Students enjoy Epstein School Carnival, an early project of the PTA.

131

Epstein students help to decorate the Sukkah at the Jewish Home.

Purim fun with Judaics teacher, Michael Allon.

Children of recent immigrants from the Soviet Union join the student body. 1981

Middle school students and their teachers.

Epstein School faculty. 1979-80

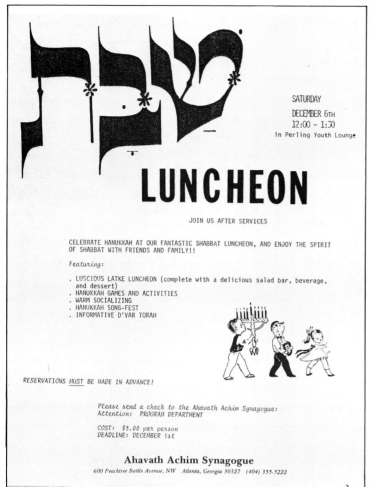

SATURDAY
DECEMBER 6TH
12:00 - 1:30
in Perling Youth Lounge

LUNCHEON

JOIN US AFTER SERVICES

CELEBRATE HANUKKAH AT OUR FANTASTIC SHABBAT LUNCHEON, AND ENJOY THE SPIRIT
OF SHABBAT WITH FRIENDS AND FAMILY!!

Featuring:

. LUSCIOUS LATKE LUNCHEON (complete with a delicious salad bar, beverage,
  and dessert)
. HANUKKAH GAMES AND ACTIVITIES
. WARM SOCIALIZING
. HANUKKAH SONG-FEST
. INFORMATIVE D'VAR TORAH

RESERVATIONS MUST BE MADE IN ADVANCE!

Please send a check to the Ahavath Achim Synagogue:
Attention: PROGRAM DEPARTMENT

COST: $3.00 per person
DEADLINE: December 1st

Ahavath Achim Synagogue
600 Peachtree Battle Avenue, NW   Atlanta, Georgia 30327   (404) 355-5222

Family Involvement Committee activity.

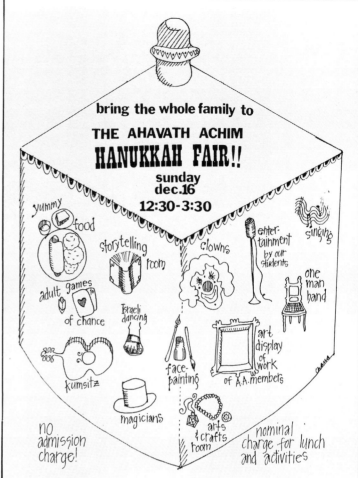

bring the whole family to
THE AHAVATH ACHIM
HANUKKAH FAIR!!
sunday dec.16
12:30-3:30

yummy food · storytelling room · clowns · entertainment by our students · singing

adult games of chance · Israeli dancing · one man band

kumsitz · face-painting · art display of work of A.A. members

magicians · arts & crafts room

no admission charge!

nominal charge for lunch and activities

Chanukah activities for the entire family.

report. After continual urging by Rabbi Epstein, the Board endorsed the establishment of the school, and it was announced to the membership by President Marvin Goldstein. Dave Alterman served as its first chairman. Irving Galanty and Hirsch Jacobson handled the enormous number of educational and logistical details involved in such a massive undertaking.

Before the school opened Aug. 27, 1973, it had been named the Rabbi Harry H. Epstein Solomon Schechter School of Atlanta in honor of the man who had built an institution capable of founding and nurturing a Jewish day school.

Its ultimate success would depend on the constant involvement of Rabbi Epstein, the lay leadership and the Ahavath Achim membership. Aside from the construction of the succession of physical structures, this was indeed the Congregation's most ambitious project.

In the following years the synagogue's program reflected changes in Jewish life occurring all over the country. Young Jewish adults were delaying marriage, which produced a significant group of single adults whose needs were not being met. In addition, many of the singles were not native Atlantans and had no ties to the community. This new phenomenon demanded action, and Ahavath Achim's first single programming began in 1974.

The mobility of American society and the lure of the new Sunbelt brought another group to the city: young Jewish families without an extended family with whom the Jewish life cycle and holidays could be shared. The Family Involvement Committee, formed in 1974, was a means of inviting these families to participate in meaningful Jewish experiences under the auspices of the synagogue. It was the forerunner of the establishment of *Havurot*, an idea developed in California by Rabbi Harold Schulweis.

To encourage interest in the Hebrew School program and continuing adult Jewish education, the Parent Enrichment Program (PEP) was begun in January, 1975. A project of the United Synagogue Commission on Jewish Education, PEP is a program of classes for Hebrew School parents who study, on an adult level, material their children are covering in the first year curriculum.

In addition to the classes, parents and children also participate in an

Each spring, Mr. Rogers planted an array of bright flowers.

The Good Moment

I remember, I remember, before the sun
   gave birth to dawn
A quiet and peaceful moment
   on Ahavath Achim lawn.

A pair of doves with suntipped wings
   settled in the trees
The soft refrain of avian song
   came gently with the breeze
The moth that sought its treasure
   fluttering around the light
Spread its wings across a rose
   to await another night
No sound was at the crossroads
   no cars on Northside hill
For it was the Sabbath morning
   and everything was still

I remember, I remember, when the sun
   gave birth to dawn
That quiet and peaceful moment
   on Ahavath Achim lawn.

L. E. Rogers

Lesley E. Rogers

While Mr. Roger's official title was head of the maintenance staff, he was much more. His sensitivity and warmth, his delight in the accomplishment of each Bar and Bat Mitzvah, his invaluable help in the preparations for all activities, his program of beautification of the grounds, his genuine interest in the staff and active members, and his daily acts of love and kindness made him a personality who captured the hearts of all who knew him. A man of little formal education, Mr. Rogers knew how to regulate the building's furnace and soothe the tears of a distraught 4 year old. He served the Congregation for only eight years before his death in a freak accident on the driveway of the Synagogue.

An accomplished poet who won local and statewide awards, Mr. Rogers included this poem in his last collection.

Atlanta Chai USY officers. 1982

Barbara Kleeber with Mechina class honored by JNF for planting a large number of trees in Israel. 1981

annual Shabbat dinner and select holiday celebrations. Barbara Kleber, who has been a member of the Hebrew School faculty since 1962, has taught the class for the past eight years.

Additional programming for singles and families created the need for a staff member to coordinate and supervise these new activities as well as the ongoing Youth Activities. Allen Teperow, a graduate of the Hornstein Program at Brandeis University which trains Jewish communal professionals, came to Ahavath Achim in the fall of 1976 to fill the new position of Program Director.

Recognizing the need for a means for women involved in synagogue activities throughout the city to come together, Sisterhood leadership meet with their counterparts in other congregations and inaugurated the Joint Sisterhood of Atlanta project. The first program was held at Ahavath Achim in November, 1976.

Rebecca Hoelting and Caren Solomon enjoy USY activities together.

USY president Stacey Joseph and advisor Wayne Goldstein.

Harriet Draluck, editor, and Betsy
Sugarman publicize the new Sisterhood
cookbook, Golden Soup.

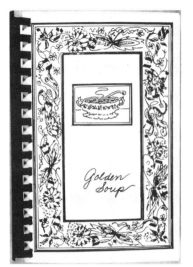

*Sisterhood publishes a second
kosher cookbook. Sept., 1975*

"Thou art One, Thy name One,
and who is like Thy people
Israel, one people on earth."

(a Sabbath prayer)

*Invitation to first city-wide Joint
Sisterhood program. Nov., 1976*

*Dr. Philip Wendkos, Educational
Director, 1977-1983.*

Staff Photo - Hugh Stovall

Mrs. G. Sugarman, Mrs. S. W. Draluck Prepare Latkes

Rabbi Zvi Shapiro became the second headmaster of the Epstein School in 1976. A graduate of Antioch College (B.A.) and Northwestern University (M.A.), Rabbi Shapiro was ordained at the Jewish Theological Seminary in 1970. Before coming to Atlanta, he was the Assistant Principal of the Solomon Schechter High School of Brooklyn.

Among other important events of this era were the first synagogue-sponsored trip to Israel (led by Rabbi Epstein and Reva), the official adoption of the Sephardic pronunciation of Hebrew throughout the synagogue, and the establishment at Emory University of the Isaac Goodfriend Collection of Holocaust Literature.

Dr. Philip Wendkos joined the staff in June, 1977, as Educational Director. His background included an undergraduate degree from Yeshiva University, graduate studies at Hunter College, and a PhD. from Dropsie College in Philadelphia. His previous positions were in Rochester, NY, at the Bureau of Jewish Education, and in Baltimore, MD., at Chizuk Amuno Congregation.

In the fall of 1977 a joint milestone was marked — the 50th year of Rabbi

Epstein's leadership of Ahavath Achim and the 90th anniversary of the founding of the synagogue. The man and the institution had been intertwined for half a century; together they had participated in the global events of the Jewish people, and helped shape the Jewish community of Atlanta.

A year-long series of Jubilee Events was launched with a lecture by noted writer Irving Howe, author of *World of Our Fathers*. On the evening of March 31 a Jubilee Service was held during which Mrs. Meyer Rich, past president of Sisterhood, and Abe Goldstein, past president of the Congregation, participated.

The following morning, April 1, Rabbi Epstein's birthday, the Congregation gathered for a very special Shabbat, and heard an address by Rabbi Stanley Rabinowitz, President of the Rabbinical Assembly. The Jubliee Weekend was concluded with a Testimonial Banquet attended by an overflow crowd who had come to express their love and appreciation for both Rabbi Epstein and Reva. Together they had devotedly guided and influenced the lives of three generations of members.

As a permanent reminder of these events, a history was published tracing the career of Rabbi Epstein and

"The authority of the Rabbi is derived from the Torah: he is its servant, not its master." "To urge the love an adherence to the Torah upon your community in all its force and all its significance seems to me the mission of the Rabbi of the present generation"

ABRAHAM SCHECHTER, "THE RABBI AS A PERSONAL ENTITY"

The United Synagogue of America

In convention assembled notes with pride the service for 50 years of

Dr. Harry H. Epstein

As the Rabbi of Ahavath Achim Congregation
Atlanta-Georgia

His inspired leadership, his eloquence of speech and his skill in the knowledge of the Torah fulfilled the hopes of Solomon Schechter when he established the Conservative Movement in this land. We pray that Rabbi Epstein celebrating now his 50th Anniversary as Rabbi of Ahavath Achim Congregation, a Congregation which marks now its 90th Anniversary, may continue on to serve God, Torah and Israel.

Dated the fourth day of Kislev, 5738 corresponding to the 13th day of November 1977

Recognition of Rabbi Epstein's 50 years of service by United Synagogue of America. Nov., 1977

Ahavath Achim Bulletin

VOL. 48, NO. 23 — II ADAR 22, 5738 — MARCH 31, 1978

Special Jubilee Issue
Our Golden Jubilee Weekend Paying Tribute To
Rabbi and Mrs. Harry H. Epstein
For Fifty Years of Illustrious Leadership
Friday, March 31, through Sunday, April 2, 1978

JUBILEE SABBATH SERVICES
FRIDAY, MARCH 31, 8:15 P.M.
Followed by a Gala Oneg Shabbat

SATURDAY, APRIL 1, 9:00 A.M.
Followed by a Gala Kiddush
Celebrating Rabbi Epstein's Birthday
Guest Speaker:
RABBI STANLEY RABINOWITZ
President, Rabbinical Assembly

GOLDEN JUBILEE TESTIMONIAL BANQUET
SUNDAY, APRIL 2, 6:30 P.M.
Guest Speaker:
DR. GERSON D. COHEN
Chancellor, Jewish Theological Seminary

Please See Page 2 for Program Highlights

*Jubilee issue of **The Bulletin** in honor of Rabbi Epstein and Reva.*

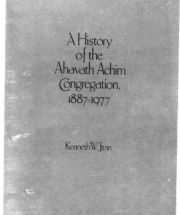

A History of the Ahavath Achim Congregation, 1887-1977

Kenneth W. Stein

History published in conjunction with Rabbi Epstein's Jubilee and the 90th year of the Congregation.

Rabbi Epstein's Academic Career Religious and Secular

Yeshiva College, New York
Slobodka Yeshiva, Lithuania
Hebron Yeshiva, Palestine
Rabbinic S'mecha, Palestine
Master of Hebrew Letters
BA & MA, Emory University, Atlanta
Phd., University of Illinois System
Doctor of Theology (Honorary), Central School of Religion,
Indianapolis, Indiana
Doctor of Divinity (Honorary),
Jewish Theological Seminary, New York

Rabbi and Reva on sabbatical in Jerusalem. 1973

Nursery School 4 year olds pose for class picture. 1978

the evolution of Ahavath Achim. It was written by Dr. Kenneth Stein, associate professor of history at Emory University, and mailed to each member of the Congregation.

It was an appropriate juncture at which to gather accurate data on the membership. The Long Range Planning Committee designed a questionnaire and developed a profile.

Total Membership: 1,835 families, 4,300 individuals including children.

Median age: 50 years

Number of children: 1,950

Location of membership: 69.9% in N.W., N.E.; 9.7% in Sandy Springs; 3.9% in Chamblee and Doraville; 2.4% in Cobb County; 1.5% in Decatur and Stone Mountain; and 7% outside Metro area.

Over the years one of the original functions of the synagogue, the traditional preparation of the dead for burial by the Chevra Kaddisha, had gradually slipped away. A small, unheralded group of men and women had performed this *mitzvah* for many years but their numbers had been dissipated by age and death.

It became a crisis in the mid-1970s and attempts were made to interest new people to become involved. During those years Irene Becker and her father, Abe Fraidlin, were the mainstays of the group and functioned as best they could under the circumstances.

With the encouragement of Rabbi Epstein and diligent work by Sunny Stern, a new group was formed and began functioning early in 1981. The new Chevra Kaddisha consisted of about 40 men and women. Their willingness to serve illustrates the regenerative power of Jewish tradition and the continual dedication of Ahavath Achim to the basic practices of Judaism.

The emphasis on increased involvement continued. Opportunities to participate in such activities as family retreats, Shabbat luncheons, festival

Certificate of Achievement

"Happy is the person who has found wisdom"

We most proudly recognize the
outstanding achievement of,
commend and congratulate

Mrs. Gloria Benamy

for having successfully completed
the prescribed course of study

Hebrew Literacy I

Presented Friday Evening January 30, 1981

Rabbi   President

Educational Director   Chairman

תעודת הצלחה

"אשרי אדם מצא חכמה"

אנו מכירים את ההישגים
ומביעים שבחות של

הנ"ל

להשלמת למודים

בקריאת עברית (א)

הוענק ליל שבת כ"ו שבט תשמ"א

נשיא   הרב

יו"ר הועדה   מ"ח

Hebrew Literacy certificate. 1981

celebrations, and special programs for young couples, singles and single parent families grew. A group was formed to visit members in area hospitals.

Involvement in a different realm of synagogue affairs was demonstrated when 850 people filled the sanctuary the evening of May 28, 1980, to vote in a contested election over rabbinic succession. This was a unique occurrence in Ahavath Achim's 92-year-history.

In a way it was reminiscent of the earliest days of the Congregation when differences of opinion roused the membership and sent them to their rented hall to vigorously debate an issue. In 1980 the members spoke through their votes, and Dr. Herbert Karp and the rest of the official slate was elected.

Over the years Adult Education took many forms; it ranged from a group of elderly men poring for hours over a single page of the Talmud in the basement of Gilmer St. to 600 people sitting spellbound in Srochi Auditorium listening to Eli Wiesel.

One of the most successful in a long continuum of classes, lectures, movies and weekend *kallot* was Hebrew Literacy. Launched by Rabbi Epstein during the High Holidays, 1981, and chaired by Sidney Kaplan, Hebrew Literacy offered classes at practically every hour of the day in reading the Hebrew found in the Friday evening service.

More than 300 people signed up for the 12-week course taught exclusively by lay members. The students were young, old and middle-aged, male and female, fourth generation Atlantan and newcomer…a wonderful cross section of the entire Congregation.

The Hebrew and Religious School programs continued. An evaluation conducted January-February, 1980, by the Atlanta Bureau of Jewish Education stated that the school "…is well administered, and functions in an efficient and orderly fashion." Of special note was the high academic level observed in a special class attended by contestants in the National Bible Contest. David Kleber placed first in the city and represented Atlanta in the finals in New York.

As young families moved further into the northern suburbs, the need for a satellite location for the Hebrew School became obvious. A group of parents in Sandy Springs petitioned the Board to establish an alternative location. After

Adult Bar Mitzvah, Harry Axelrod, congratulated by Rabbi Epstein. Dec., 1982

Sisterhood Events and Personalities

Invitation, anniversary celebration.

Cast of show celebrating Sisterhood's 60th anniversary. 1982

Ida Levitas, lifelong community leader and supporter of every Sisterhood and Synagogue activity.

Helen Cavalier, reservation chairman for all Sisterhood and Congregational dinners as well as major domo of the Morning Minyon and Minyonaires breakfast.

Betty Goodfriend lends her charm and knowledge to Sisterhood Jewish Family Living workshop.

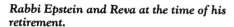
Rabbi Epstein and Reva at the time of his retirement.

Shabbat of
Attainment
שבת השלמה

Saturday Morning
December 11, 1982
Shabbat Hanukkah, 5743
at Nine O'Clock

services will include

Dedication of the
Sanctuary to
Rabbi Harry H.
and Reva Epstein
חנוכת בית הכנסת

Special Kiddush Following Services

Dedication of the Sanctuary program.
Dec., 1982

Rabbi Leonard Lifshen

much study by the Education Committee and discussion by the Board, an arrangement was made with Underwood Hills Elementary School and classes two afternoons a week began during the 1981-82 year.

Rabbi Leonard Lifshen came to the Congregation as Associate Rabbi in the fall of 1981. A graduate of the City College of New York and the Jewish Theological Seminary, Rabbi Lifshen was also a certified *mohel*. He had served congregations in Oklahoma City and Dallas.

As a result of a tedious process drawn out over several years, a new Constitution and By-Laws was written, studied by the Board, and ratified by the membership.

Once again, as with previous documents, societal changes are reflected. Married women with or without their husbands were given the right to vote in Congregational meetings. Expanded participation was invited by mandatory rotation after six years of board members and the inclusion of a cross section of the membership on the nominating committee. There was also a provision for the formation of a Rabbinic Selection Committee, a group unnecessary for the past half century.

Synagogue activity expanded into a new area with the establishment of the Cultural Arts Committee. Utilizing the exceptional acoustics of Ellman Chapel, a series of free Chamber Concerts was begun. Works utilizing Jewish themes were played as well as music from the general literature. A beautiful Steinway Grand piano was donated in memory of Morton Srochi for this activity. Harriet and Sam Draluck were the first chairmen of the committee.

In a letter dated Dec. 14, 1981, Rabbi Epstein announced his intention to retire, effective Aug. 15, 1982. That date would mark the conclusion of his 55 years in the active rabbinate, 54 of which were at Ahavath Achim — a remarkable record of a remarkable man.

141

Welcome Rabbi Arnold M. Goodman

" . . . I wish you well as your assume your new responsibilities in Atlanta.
Warmest personal regards. Sincerely
(Former Vice-President) Walter F. Mondale"

Telegram, September 2, 1982

Downtown Atlanta, 1984: Some of the newest prominent structures are: Georgia Pacific Bldg. (stepped structure in middle), Marriott Marquis Hotel (left of Georgia Pacific), and Trust Company Bank (lower right). Central City Park is seen in front of Georgia Pacific.

For the vast majority of congregants it was extraordinary not to see Rabbi Epstein's familiar figure occupying the pulpit as they entered the sanctuary for Rosh Hashanah, 5743 (Sept. 18, 1982). Instead, they saw a tall (6'3"), angular man resplendent in his white *kittle* and flowing *tallit*.

His energy and commanding *persona* captured the attention of the worshippers. There was an air of anticipation as they waited to see how "the new rabbi" would conduct their familiar service.

Many had never attended a High Holiday service anywhere else or known a religious leader other than Rabbi Epstein. It was the same disquietude felt by their forebears a half century earlier when Rabbi Epstein first stepped into the pulpit on Washington St.

Arnold Goodman was born in New York and grew up in the Williamsburg section. The only child of Eastern European parents who came to America as young children, Rabbi Goodman attended a very traditional yeshiva, Torah Vodaath, throughout elementary and high school.

Judaic studies were conducted in Yiddish until approximately 3 p.m., after which teachers from the public schools

Joel Lobel
1982-1984

Marshall Solomon
1984-1986

Franceen Tillem
1981-1983

Donna Smith
1983-1986

Gail Levitt
1986-1988

Rabbi Goodman holding Torah with the special mantle used by the President of the Rabbinical Assembly.

Arnold Goodman as a young child in Williamsburg.

came to the yeshiva to teach secular subjects. The school day ended in the early evening. This traditional, Old World education gave him a thorough grounding in Talmud and Midrash and a good secular education, but little knowledge of the outside world. Living in that section of Brooklyn was more like living in a small town in Eastern Europe than in an American metropolis.

While his education was extremely Orthodox, his family was not. Kashrut was observed and major holidays celebrated but his father, a pharmacist, was often required to work on Shabbat. The future Rabbi's maternal grandparents lived with the Goodmans, and it was his grandfather who urged his parents to send him to Torah Vodaath, and paid the tuition.

He entered City College at 16, intending to be a math teacher. There, for the first time, he met Jews of all stripes and varieties as well as a smattering of non-Jews. Rabbi Goodman now describes this experience as "culture shock."

He had never known Jews who ate "*treif*" and didn't understand Yiddish. His own English had been so corrupted by the constant use of Yiddish at school and at home that City College suggested he enter a speech class designed for foreign-born students.

His first year at City College was a time of tremendous adjustment socially and intellectually. While taking advanced math during his sophomore year, he decided that a career in that discipline was not for him and changed his major to psychology. He also realized he missed his involvement in Jewish studies.

On the recommendation of a friend, he began courses in the evening and on Sunday at the Jewish Theological Seminary in what was known as Seminary College, continuing throughout his college career. Upon graduation from City College in 1948, he entered Rabbinic School at the Seminary.

His parents were not thrilled at his choice of a profession. His father was especially disappointed as he had envisioned a law career for his son, a goal he himself had wanted but could not pursue because of economic restraints.

After the completion of his first year at the Seminary, Arnold Goodman married Rae Parnes whom he had met while an undergraduate at City College.

The future rabbi as a chubby pre-teen with his maternal grandfather who financed his yeshiva education.

Rabbi Goodman's first position, Chaplin, U.S. Army.

Posing with Rae and his sons Ariel (left) and Daniel after receiving his law degree from DePaul Un. 1962

A tall, lean undergraduate at City College, New York.

Rae Parnes marries Arnold Goodman. 1949.

Chancellor of the JTS, Dr. Gershon Cohen, greets Rabbi Goodman and Rae at Rabbinic Assembly Convention. 1983

Her very traditional family was not overly enthusastic about welcoming a non-Orthodox son-in-law even though he was "*shomrei mitzvot.*"

Rae was undeterred by her family's unenthusiastic response. Through the years she has been a source of strength and willing helpmate to the Rabbi. Wherever they lived, their home was open to the congregation for official events connected with the synagogue or to join the Goodman family for Shabbat, holidays and normal socializing. In addition to her duties as "*rebbetzin*" and mother to three children born in Chicago, Rae earned a M.A. in Special Education and worked in that field.

From 1952-54 Rabbi Goodman served as the first Jewish chaplain at Ft. Sheridan, IL. While still in the chaplaincy, he taught in the Hebrew School at the north suburban Synagogue Beth El of Highland Park, Il.

Through contacts in Chicago Rabbi Goodman was offered his first pulpit with a two-year-old merged congregation, Rodfie Sholom-Or Chodosh, on Chicago's South Side. It was a challenge to become the first fulltime rabbi of a struggling synagogue.

During his 12-year tenure, the congregation grew from 250 families to 700, and was able to build a large facility on Euclid Avenue. It was a time for the young rabbi to hone his skills and

Certificate of membership in Israeli Bar Association. 1973

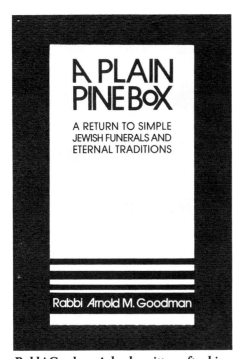

Rabbi Goodman's book written after his involvement with the organization of Adath Jeshurun's Chevra Kevod Hamet Society.

develop his personal leadership style.

It was also a time when he completed two post-graduate degrees; an M.A. in Educational Administration from the University of Chicago (1955) and a Law Degree from DePaul University (1962). He became a member of the Illinois Bar but, unfortunately, Louis Goodman did not live to see his son fulfill his wish.

After 12 very productive years in Chicago, Rabbi Goodman accepted the pulpit of Adath Jeshurun Congregation in Minneapolis, MN, in January, 1966. Then beginning its 83rd year, Adath Jeshurun is a large congregation which has a long history of leadership in the Midwest within the Conservative movement. Rabbi Goodman's presence there for the next 16 years greatly enhanced that reputation.

One of his outstanding innovative programs was the development of a Shabbat Morning Program for children between the ages of eight and 13, inte-grated into a series of *kallot* (retreats) for different age groups during the year. Not merely a Junior Congregation, the program also involves post Bar and Bat Mitzvah students as tutors. As a result of the *kallot* activity, the Congregation eventually built its own Retreat Center in a suburb of Minneapolis. The daily preschool, Gan Hayeled, was located there.

Another activity widely recognized was the organization of a Chevra Kevod Hamet (Society to Honor the Dead). In addition to the traditional Chevra Kadisha, which prepares a deceased for burial, the Society included *shomerim* to sit with the body until the funeral, people to ensure that there was a meal following the burial, and those who actually built the wooden caskets and sewed the white shrouds.

The Chevra was the subject of an ABC documentary titled "A *Plain Pine Box,*" which is also the title of a book written by Rabbi Goodman.

Both programs endeavored to create

146

Addressing USY Pilgrims after Shaharit service in Jerusalem's Conservative Synagogue.

Conservative Rabbinical Assembly To Install Rabbi Arnold Goodman

NEW YORK, N.Y. — 600 Conservative rabbis from all parts of the world will participate in a massive study program seeking answers to ultimate questions such as life and death, good and evil, the economy and nuclear arms at their 82nd Annual Convention, April 25 to 29, at the Concord Hotel, New York.

The Rabbinical Assembly represents 1,200 Conservative rabbis serving 1.5 million congregants in the United States, Canada, Israel, Europe, Latin America and Japan.

Rabbi William Frankel, Chicago, the convention's Program Chairman, announced that 20 study sessions will be held. The Convention will be keynoted on opening day, April 25, by a special prayer "A Declaration for Peace" coinciding with Israel's withdrawal from the Sinai and the return of this land to Egypt.

Special discussions will be held on the Middle East. Yehuda Blum, Israel's Ambassador to the United Nations, will address the meeting on Monday. An assessment of current concerns of the American Jewish community will be presented by the R.A.'s President, Rabbi Seymour Cohen of Chicago.

Several sessions will discuss how the economic crisis has curtailed Jewish social and educational programs in this country. On Monday evening, an analysis of the political right and left will be debated by Dr. Leonard Fein, editor of "Moment" magazine, and Dr. David Sidorsky, Columbia University.

RABBI ARNOLD GOODMAN

"Modern Man's Struggle with Prayer" will be presented by Paul Cowan, writer, and Rabbi Lawrence Hoffman, Hebrew Union College, New York. The Rabbinical Assembly recently published a new High Holiday Prayerbook, a new Haggadah, "The Feast of Freedom," which sold out the entire first edition of 20,000 copies, and plans this year a new Daily, Sabbath and Festival Prayerbook.

A report discussing the continued shortage of rabbis and future demographic projections for congregational life in the U.S. and Canada will be distributed at the Convention, compiled by Rabbi Gilbert Epstein, the R.A.'s Director of Community Services.

Senator Rudy Boschwitz of Minnesota will address the Convention Wednesday evening, Israel's Independence Day, and help install the R.A.'s incoming President, Rabbi Arnold M. Goodman of Minneapolis' Adath Jeshurun congregation.

A special tribute commemorating the 80th anniversary of Dr. Solomon Schechter's arrival in the United States, the founder of Conservative Judaism and its principal institutions, will be held on Tuesday. Leading the celebration will be Rabbi Gerson Cohen, Chancellor of Jewish Theological Seminary.

Election to presidency of Rabbinical Assembly. April, 1982

Traditional Burial Service Receives some Criticism

MINNEAPOLIS (AP) — Lifestyle has a way of influencing how a body is treated in death. An inexpensive, simple burial doesn't seem quite proper for a person of accomplishment and affluence.

But Al Sudit cherished traditions of his faith more than modern custom. When he died in 1977, at 75, he was given a simple burial by the Chevra Kevod Hamet (society to honor the dead) of Adath Jeshurun Congregation.

Not everyone understood. Some thought it barbaric that mourners shoveled dirt onto the cheap wooden coffin containing Sudit's body.

Last September, when the Chevra buried Morris Weiner, 81, relatives neither heard nor sensed criticism.

But has the controversial Chevra won acceptance?

Rabbi Arnold M. Goodman, Adath Jeshurun's spiritual leader, says Chevra volunteers handle nearly half the funerals of congregation members. The most in any year was 14.

Goodman believes his Conservative congregation of 1,150 families was a pioneer in setting up a total model for traditional, simplified funerals. He says congregations in Highland Park, Ill., Portland, Ore., and Washington, D.C., have adapted it.

Rabbi Max Shapiro of Temple Israel (Reform), is unimpressed. If the Chevra had merit, he reasons, it would have spread by now to other Twin Cities synagogues.

Shapiro feels most of the Minneapolis Jewish community sees "something ghoulish" in volunteers providing service normally done by "professionals conditioned to that activity."

His congregation, Shapiro adds, isn't interested in "going backward, to a time when there were no morticians."

"Nationally the movement has gone nowhere," adds Rabbi Bernard Raskas of Temple of Aaron (Conservative), St. Paul. Raskas says "amateurs" at Adath Jeshurun handle sensitive death matters that should be left to experts.

Another critic, Rabbi Marc Shhaber (Conservative), publisher of the weekly American Jewish World, says change from recent burial practice adds to a family's grief. The Chevra, he says, "returns to a

PART OF RITUAL — Rabbi Arnold M. Goodman, spiritual leader of Adath Jeshurun Congregation in Minneapolis, holds a seven-day mourning canel which is used in part of the simple burial service of the Chevra Kevod Hamet (Society to Honor the Dead). (AP Laserphoto)

Months of study convinced committee members that a simple wood coffin should be used, the body should be washed in a ritual process called tahara and, because dust is to return to dust as quickly as possible, there should be no formaldehyde in the veins, no nails in the coffin.

a shroud sewn by Chevra members, and placed in a wooden coffin.

—Shomrin (guards) watch over the body, in blocks of two hours, until burial. In silence, they study meditational literature and reflect on their own lives.

—The coffin with rope handles is light enough to be borne

Rabbi Arnold Goodman to Leave Adath Jeshurun

AMERICAN JEWISH WORLD — August 27, 1982

Rabbi Arnold M. Goodman, who has served as spiritual leader of Adath Jeshurun Congregation over sixteen years, will leave Minneapolis next month to assume the pulpit of Congregation Ahavat Achim in Atlanta, Georgia.

A farewell evening honoring Rabbi and Mrs. Rae Goodman is planned by the congregation 8 p.m. Thursday, September 2 at Adath Jeshurun.

During his tenure, Rabbi Goodman sparked many innovative programs, the most famous of which is the Congregation's Chevra Kevod Hamet (literally, Society to Honor the Dead). Its program of the Congregation providing a traditional funeral without charge has been widely reported and been the subject of articles and TV specials. The history of the Chevra was recorded by Rabbi Goodman in his book "A Plain Pine Box."

During his years at Adath Jeshurun, the Congregation committed itself to remain within the city limits of Minneapolis. Its newly-renovated facilities have enabled the Congregation to serve its membership in the site where it has been located since 1928.

Among Rabbi Goodman's achievements was the building of a Kallah Center in Minnetonka. It is a site for retreats as well as the place where Gan Shelanu, the Congregation's nursery school, meets.

At recent United Synagogue conventions the Congregation earned a national reputation by receiving Solomon Schechter awards for excellence for the Chevra Kevod Hamet, the Shabbat Morning Program, the TAMID cultural series, youth activities and Gan Shelanu.

In the community Rabbi Goodman served as statewide chairman of the twenty-fifth anniversary celebration of the State of Israel, and chairman of the Hillel Study

RAE and RABBI GOODMAN

Committee. He was a member of the Mt. Sinai Hospital medical ethics committee. Rabbi Goodman also was the first lecturer of Jewish Studies at the College of St.

(Continued on Page 10)

Rabbi Goodman
(Continued from Page 1)

Catherine, a position he has held for fifteen years.

Rabbi Goodman was elected this year to the presidency of the Rabbinical Assembly, the international body of Conservative Rabbis.

In a farewell message to his congregation, he wrote, "For Rae and me these were years of growth. Rae completed her graduate work at the "U" and developed her career in special education. This was in addition to her being a one-person welcoming committee to newcomers on Shabbat, the secretary of the study groups, and a positive presence at the Synagogue.

"As I reflect on my years here, I think of the many new and exciting programs that came into being. There was a positive symbiosis between Rabbi and Congregation which made possible the many innovations that are now part and parcel of our Synagogue. To the extent that I was involved in their creation and development, a part of me will always be here."

From Minneapolis to Atlanta

Ceremony Set May 22
The Neighbor May 13, 1983

Goodman New Rabbi At Ahavath Achim

RABBI GOODMAN
Ahavath Achim To Install

Rabbi Arnold Goodman will be officially installed as rabbi of the Ahavath Achim Synagogue in Sandy Springs during weekend ceremonies planned for May 20-22.

He replaced the Rabbi Harry H. Epstein, who served the congregation for 54 years, in September.

Goodman was ordained by The Jewish Theological Seminary in 1952. His career has included service as chaplain in the United States Army, as Spiritual Leader of Congregation Rodfei Sholom-Oir Chodesh in Chicago, and Adath Jeshurun in Minneapolis. He has been actively involved in civic and Jewish communities through numerous organizations; at present, Goodman is president of the Rabbinical Assembly, the international organization of Conservative Rabbis in the United States, Israel and throughout the world.

"Whatever I will accomplish, I will be building on existing structures," Rabbi Goodman commented about the future at Ahavath Achim. "I have come to a strong and active congregation."

Highlights of the weekend festivities include a Shabbat Service Friday, May 20, with Rabbi Stanley Schacter, vice-chancellor of the Jewish Theological Seminary of America, delivering the sermon. Following the services an Oneg Shabbat in honor of the Goodman family will be hosted by Ahavath Achim Sisterhood.

A gala evening is planned for Sunday, May 22, when the annual meeting, election of officers, installation ceremonies and dinner dance will be held. Presiding at the installation will be Rabbi Seymour Cohen, immediate past president of the Rabbinical Assembly and Spiritual Leader of the Anshe Emet Synagogue in Chicago.

For more information about weekend activities and reservations to the dinner dance, call Ahavath Achim at 355-5222.

The Congregation of
Ahavath Achim Synagogue
cordially invites you to attend a

Festive Week-End
featuring the installation of

Rabbi Arnold M. Goodman
as Rabbi of our congregation

Special Shabbat Service
Friday

Formal Installation
Sunday to be followed by a

Dinner Dance

The Election
and Installation
of Officers
To precede on Sunday evening
at 6:30 o'clock

Friday Evening, May 20, 1983 • Sivan 8, 5743
Sunday Evening, May 22, 1983 • Sivan 10, 5743
Sunday Evening, May 22, 1983 • Sivan 10, 5743

Installation festivities for Rabbi Goodman, May 20-22, 1983.

Cheryl Finkel (r) Headmaster of The Epstein School and Roz Cohen, assistant principal.

Jerre Friedman Askenazie recognized for 30 years of service to the Congregation. 1985

in a very tangible way a sense of community within the congregation. Both activities were recognized with Solomon Schechter Awards.

Despite a demanding congregational schedule, Rabbi Goodman involved himself in numerous community and organizational affairs.

He served twice as president of the Minnesota Rabbinical Association, and was statewide chairman of the 25th anniversary celebration of Israel's independence. Active in the affairs of the Rabbinical Assembly, the international organization of Conservative rabbis, he was a member of the Committee of Jewish Law and Standards as well as Resolution Chairman for the National Convention.

In April, 1982, Rabbi Goodman was elected president of the Rabbinical Assembly. The group represents 1,200 of the world's rabbis.

Immersed in numerous activities, Rabbi Goodman remained true to his title, teacher — the literal translation of "rabbi." For the regular worshippers on Shabbat morning he developed a "pulpit-pew" dialogue facilitated by a weekly Study Guide based on the *sidra*. Torah study became an exciting part of the weekly service.

He also led six monthly home study groups which averaged 20 to 30 persons in each group. For many years he was a

lecturer in Jewish Studies at the College of St. Catherine for Women in St. Paul, and was the featured speaker on a wide range of Jewish subjects in the Twin Cities area.

Rabbi Goodman is a man of great energy and drive. Beneath his warm smile and low-key demeanor there is a personality which is not afraid to tackle new challenges and chart unknown waters. Described by his former congregants as "dynamic...a strong personality...an idea-oriented person," Rabbi Goodman was a candidate worthy to fill the pulpit of Ahavath Achim as Rabbi Epstein's successor.

The first months in Atlanta were hectic and exciting for Rabbi Goodman and the Congregation. Slowly, notices of new programs appeared in the *Bulletin* and on committee agendas. Young couples were invited to his home to celebrate Sukkot, families were encouraged to attend Shabbat morning services by providing infant and child care, a 6th grade Kallah was discussed, and a College Student Homecoming Brunch instituted.

In addition to Rabbi Goodman, Jerre Friedman Ashkenazie was appointed Director of Administrative Services (February, 1982), and Brian Glusman became Youth Director. Cheryl Finkel became the headmaster of the Epstein School in the fall of 1983.

On Shabbat Chanukah, Dec. 11,

Sisterhood women and Rabbi Goodman join other members of Southern Branch at biennial convention of Women's League for Conservative Judaism. Concord Hotel, 1982

1982, the Congregation gathered once again to honor Rabbi Epstein and Reva. During the Shabbat service both lay and professional leadership participated. Rabbi Epstein was honored with the Maftir Aliyah and chanted the Haftorah. Joel Lobel, president of the Congregation, officially dedicated the Sanctuary in honor of the Epsteins. That evening a gala dinner was held and the title "Sh'litah"* (given to revered rabbis and teachers) was conferred on Rabbi Epstein.

It was almost impossible to imagine Rabbi Epstein not in complete command of Ahavath Achim. Approaching his 80th brithday and blessed with no diminution of his intellectual vigor or serious health problems, Rabbi Epstein was still **the** Rabbi for many congregants.

His impact on the Congregation as well as the Atlanta community had been enormous. He guided Ahavath Achim during times of economic disaster, World War, the destruction of one-third of world Jewry, social upheaval and the creation of Israel.

But he was more than a mere helmsman who keeps a vessel afloat.

Rabbi Epstein and Reva gave direction and established new channels for a whole community. Their lives were dedicated to the building of an institution and its members. Their influence will always be present.

After nine months of "active duty," Rabbi Arnold Goodman was installed officially in conjunction with the 96th Annual Meeting of Ahavath Achim, May 22, 1983. A festive reception and dinner followed the installation. After the formalities in the Epstein Sanctuary, there was music and cameraderie in Srochi Auditorium.

It was an historic night for the Congregation and the Jewish community. The leadership of one of the foremost religious institutions of the city had been placed in new hands. There was an atmosphere of excitement and energy among members as they anticipated the beginning of a new era in their long and distinguished history.

In his installation address Rabbi Goodman assured the members that he "would not advocate change out of pique or boredom or fear, but neither would he fear to advocate change." He also promised that the Ahavath Achim

*Hebrew acronym for "May he live a long life, amen."

Beverly and Sam Shonson with children and grandchildren. . .
three generations of members. 1982

Louis Smith and grandsons: Adam (l) and Ivan.

Brickman family (l to r): Teresa, Perry, Lori, Shirley, and Jeffery. 1982

Joseph Aronoff (left) celebrates the engagement of his
granddaughter Gloria Meltzer to Harold Minsk
with his family.

Bridal couple Marcy Goldstein and Eran Bellin in Srochi Auditorium.

Ordaining women enriches Jewish life, rabbi says

By Billie Cheney Speed
Religion Editor

The decision of the faculty of the Jewish Theological Seminary to open its ordination program to women is seen by Rabbi Arnold M. Goodman as "making available to our communities a large source of talent which will do much to strengthen and enrich Jewish life."

Goodman is president of the Rabbinical Assembly, made up of 1,200 Conservative rabbis who serve 1.5 million members. He said the step taken by the faculty of the seminary in New York City is consistent with the position of the vast majority of Rabbinical Assembly members, who are on record as favoring the ordination of women to the rabbinate.

"They regard this as the natural extension of egalitarianism, which is today reflected in virtually all of the American society," he said.

Goodman, who is also spiritual leader of Aha-

Presently, there are 175 women studying in the various programs at the Jewish Theological Seminary.

vath Achim Synagogue in Atlanta, said most of the Rabbinical Assembly members serve congregations where equality of sexes is an accepted reality.

"Whether it be the bat mitzvah of girls, or accepting women on the pulpit for a Torah honor, or including them in the minyan (quorum for prayer), the Rabbinical Assembly membership has provided opportunities for equal education and worship for men and women as consistent with the Traditional view of Jewish law," Goodman said.

There are three distinct groups within the Conservative movement: the Jewish Theological Seminary, which trains the rabbis and teachers; the Rabbinical Assembly, made up of rabbis, most of whom are graduated from the Jewish Theological Seminary; and the United Synagogue of America, which is made up of lay people.

The Rabbinical Assembly has gone on record in favor of ordination of women as rabbis, but until the seminary agreed to admit women as candidates for ordination to the rabbinate, this could not take place.

The historic decision to make the change came last Monday, when the faculty voted 34-8, with one abstention, to admit women to the ordination program effective September 1984.

Presently, there are 175 women studying in the various programs at the seminary.

Goodman said he has not talked with any woman in his congregation who has said she wanted to study for the rabbinate.

However, in his former congregation at the Adath Jeshurun Synagogue in Minneapolis, Minn., there were four women who expressed a strong desire to become rabbis.

"It was painful for them to realize that the option was not open to them in the Conservative movement," Goodman said. "One of them entered a Reform seminary, a second one chose to attend a Reconstructionist seminary, and two of them pursued other careers."

The Conservative Judaism movement is generally considered a middle course between the more liberal Reform Judaism movement and the various branches of Orthodox Judaism.

Reform Judaism and the smaller Reconstructionist movement have been ordaining women rabbis for a decade.

'NATURAL EXTENSION'
Rabbi Arnold Goodman

Rabbi Goodman speaks out in favor of the ordination of women.
1983

Phyllis Freedman, president, Women's Division, Council of Jewish Federations, greets Israeli Prime Minister Menachem Begin on his arrival in Los Angeles. 1982

Award from SE Region, United Synagogue for Excellence in Synagogue programming. 1984

pulpit "shall always stand for the values of Judaism."

As the editor of *The Southern Israelite* wrote in the issue of May 27, 1983, it was "A night to remember."

New programs were introduced during the year and there was an attempt to establish the "pulpit-pew" dialogue on Shabbat morning, but the most dramatic changes in the service were evident during Rabbi Goodman's second High Holiday season in Atlanta. Teenage Torah readers, a regular occurrence at festival services, participated for the first time on Rosh Hashanah and Yom Kippur. And now there were **female** readers.

The issue of egalitarianism within Ahavath Achim had smoldered among small pockets of women for some time. Many years before, Rabbi Epstein had counted women for a *minyan* and allowed them the honor of opening the Ark. Girls had participated in Bat Mitzvah since 1941 but the ceremony was held on

Friday night so the issue of being called to the Torah was avoided.

The steady growth of feminism in the general community certainly influenced Jewish women in all branches of Judaism to look critically at their own standing. Reform Judaism ordained its first female rabbi, Sally Preisand, in the early Seventies. Voices in the Conservative movement began to advocate the same change. The decision to admit women to the Rabbinical School of the Seminary was finally reached after years of discussion and controversy, in the fall of 1983.

For many years Rabbi Goodman had been a strong advocate of the full participation of women in the synagogue. He immediately began to schedule Bat Mitzvahs on Saturday morning, and granted *aliyot* to women in addition to including them in the *minyan*.

Other changes noticed during the High Holiday Season of 1983 were English readings led by congregants, the

Invitation to PEP havdallah service.

Rabbi Richardson in costume attending USY Purim Carnival.

PEP

YOU ARE INVITED
TO OUR

SECOND HAVDALLAH SERVICE

AT THE HOME OF ALAN AND TERRIE BRYAN
SATURDAY - DEC. 8, 1984
5:30 - 7:00 P.M.

BRING YOUR FAMILIES

REFRESHMENTS WILL BE SERVED!!!

R.S.V.P. BY DEC. 6, 1984
396-4344   MAP ATTACHED

Annual College Reunion Brunch held at the Goodman's home.

Hebrew School Graduation

Mothers and grandmothers prepare Minyonaire breakfast.

USY Reunion

153

Rabbi Goodman and Rae cuddle infants whose parents discussed Jewish customs relating to childbirth before their birth. This was their one year reunion.

Dr. Herbert Karp, Ahavath Achim's expert shofar blower.

Rabbi Marvin Richardson

question-and-answer period on Yom Kippur afternoon, and Havdalah chanted jointly by boys and girls scheduled to celebrate Bar and Bat Mitzvah in the coming year.

The process of reaching out to all segments of the Congregation continued. Single parents, expectant couples, engaged couples, newlyweds and singles were included in programming. Many of these groups met in Rabbi Goodman's home where they could develop rapport in an informal setting. Rae is the gracious hostess for these gatherings.

After serving in Detroit, Charlotte, Miami and Denver, Jerrold Leeson returned to Ahavath Achim as Educational Director in the fall of 1983. Since leaving Atlanta he had earned an M.A. in Education Curriculum and Guidance, and gained valuable experience in administration.

An interesting subject discussed by the Board concerned the type of music used at weddings in the Synagogue. It was generally felt that the use of the well known Wagner Wedding March had no place at a Jewish wedding, given the virulent anti-Semitism of the composer. A standing rule was approved which specified that "all music performed during a wedding ceremony in the Synagogue be of Jewish character. . .appropriate for a Jewish wedding."

In response to the increasing problem of the homeless and the hungry in growing Atlanta, the Congregation joined other civic and religious organizations working to alleviate the situation. In cooperation with Congregation Shearith Israel, which opened a Women's Shelter, Ahavath Achim members provide meals and staff for a month each year. A grant is also made to this project.

Twice each year, Sukkot and pre-Pesach, canned goods are solicited from the Congregation and donated to the Atlanta Food Bank. This important project is especially meaningful to the children, a tangible expression of *tzedekah*.

Rabbi Marvin Richardson came to the Congregation in the fall of 1984 as the Assistant Rabbi. A native of Charlotte, NC, Rabbi Richardson had been active in USY and was a frequent visitor to Ahavath Achim.

After graduating from Johns Hopkins University in 1974, he pursued a career in Jewish education and youth activities and served congregations in New York, St. Louis and Chicago. He entered Rabbinical School and was ordained in the spring of 1984. He was the recipient of awards in both Talmud and homiletics, and won a Graduate Service Award.

His first project was to plan and conduct an experimental parallel service for the High Holidays. Held in Ellman Chapel, the service was designed for teenagers and those who found that the vastness of the main sanctuary made personal involvement difficult.

Members were invited to participate by accepting *aliyot* and leading Hebrew or English prayers. Blessed with a rich, melodious singing voice and an engaging teaching style, Rabbi Richardson conducted a most meaningful service. The

David Stern presiding at International Convention, USY. 1985

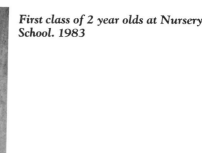

parallel service was well received and has continued.

Since Rabbi Goodman's arrival, the Congregation has participated with neighboring northside churches in a Thanksgiving Day Service held each year in a different instutition. Rabbi Goodman was invited to deliver the sermon at Northside Drive Baptist Church on Nov. 22, 1984.

Many Ahavath Achim teenagers have been active on a regional level in USY, serving as officers and committee chairmen. Beginning in 1983, Atlanta teens were active on a national level.

Jonathan Draluck was a committee chairman and vice president, and in December, 1984, David Stern became the first member of Ahavath Achim to be elected president of International USY. In congratulating David, Rabbi Goodman noted that "His election brings honor upon his family and upon Ahavath Achim."

Ahava, a monthly luncheon program and social gathering for retirees, was begun in February, 1985. Each meeting features a speaker on a subject of interest, entertainment or a holiday celebration. Dot Cohen has coordinated the project since its inception. Ahava is yet another program serving a significant segment of the community.

Dana Scott assumed the duties of Youth Director in the fall of 1985. A trained social worker with many years of experience in USY and camping activities, Dana came to Ahavath Achim from Congregation B'nai Amoona in St. Louis.

Ahava members (l to r) Tanya Goldstein, Betty Lerman and Dorothy Perrell with Epstein School students.

President of the Congregation Sidney Kaplan (left) and his wife Alice and Sisterhood President Gail Levitt (seated right) and her husband Maurice attend the Centennial Ball. May 17, 1987

As regular activities began in 1985, a committee was organized to begin the planning for the celebration of the Centennial, which was to begin on Rosh Hashana, 1986, and continue through May, 1987. Past Presidents Dave Alterman and Norman Diamond were appointed co-chairmen.

Among the events and activities planned were needlepointed Torah mantles, a cantorial concert, three Centennial exhibits, a Centennial Ball, a special concert and reception, a Centennial lecture series, a taped interview with Rabbi and Reva Epstein, and the Centennial Pictorial History Book - which you hold.

Torah Mantle Stitchers: (l to r) Sue Winner, Joyce Smilack (seated), Toby Rosing, Frances Saperstein, Leah Maizer (Chairman), Jan Fields, Vita Schulman, Pauline Cohen (seated), Bea Kessler, and Faye Cohen (Project Secretary). Missing from photo: Bunny Center, Peggy Ellman, Dee Kline, Elaine Siegel, and Diane Silverboard.

Centennial Co-Chairmen Dave Alterman (left) and Norman Diamond who coordinated the year's special events. Kol HaKavod to both of them for their efforts.

The Next Hundred Years

"Nothing is done; everything in the world remains to be done or done over."

Unknown

The Ahavath Achim Congregation of 1987 bears no resemblance to the Ahawas Achim of 1887.

The 4,762 men, women and children who are today's members are vastly different from the five young men who signed the original charter.

The ample homes and apartments in every part of the city cannot be compared to the rented rooms and behind-the-stores living spaces of long-ago Decatur Street.

The structure on Peachtree Battle Avenue which can seat 2,600 worshipers on any Shabbat morning bears no resemblance to the rented room on Gilmer St.

Nor is present-day Atlanta similar to the railroad town of a century ago. Instead of a single horse-drawn rail line there is modern rapid transit. In place of nondescript one-and-two-story buildings there are innovative structures of every size and description. The deep-throated chugging of railroad engines has been replaced by the roar of jets, and a population of less than 50,000 a century ago has now grown to more than 2 million in metro Atlanta.

The Jewish ambience has also changed. Atlanta is on the verge of becoming a major Jewish city instead of merely a modest outpost.

Among its 60,000 known Jews, there exists a range of belief from ultra-religious to secular. Fourteen synagogues and temples are scattered from Riverdale in Clayton County to Marietta in Cobb. There are four Jewish elementary schools and one high school in addition to the congregational schools.

A full range of social services under Jewish auspices exists and all major Jewish organizations are represented by

Atlanta's newest and tallest office building, the IBM Tower, rises 50 stories above the trees on the corner of W. Peachtree and 14th Sts. May, 1987

Officers of the Congregation: (l to r) Phillip Haber, Sidney Kaplan, Rae Alice Cohen, Carl Rosenthal, and Robert Gerber. Mrs. Cohen is the first woman elected to office in Ahavath Achim's history.

Sisterhood officers serving during the Centennial Year, 1986-87

substantial membership. Community leaders are invited to join national policy-making bodies and elected to office in these institutions and organizations. The community is self-confident, vibrant and ready to meet the challenges of the future.

Ahavath Achim has been a vital part of the development of the community throughout its history. In its early years, it augmented the size of the small Jewish population and established a center of traditional Judaism.

Early lay and rabbinic leadership were the spokesmen for Zionism in Atlanta at a time when the belief in a Jewish state was hardly the norm. They were influential in establishing important institutions such as the United Hebrew School and the Free Loan Society.

As they prospered, members assumed leadership roles in Jewish organizations such as B'nai B'rith, and in secular groups such as the Masonic Lodges. Small merchants whose hard work and business expertise enabled their ventures to succeed were generous in their support of the Synagogue and the community.

Rabbi Epstein and Reva's dedication to Ahavath Achim and the Jewish people has inspired an entire generation of men and women to step forward and accept the burden-and-joy-of leadership in Jewish life. Their presence in the community has truly been "for a blessing." There is no Jewish organization or cause which has not benefitted from the participation of the Epsteins and Ahavath Achim members.

Reaching its centennial is a historic moment for an institution, for within this milestone there is a synthesis of the past and the future. Each structure of the past is the springboard for the future. If an idea succeeds, it is continued; if it fails, a new idea takes its place. Each member of the past century is the prototype for the members who will shape the future; their example, good or bad, established a path to follow or avoid.

Jewish tradition teaches that humankind is in a constant state of becoming. Institutions, because they are a human product, are likewise in a constant state of being shaped and formed.

The Ahavath Achim of the next century will bear the stamp of the past but will be the work of future.

Let the work begin as we go **"From Generation to Generation."**

Ahavath Achim Synagogue

Synagogue Staff: (Seated l to r) Cantor Isaac Goodfriend, Rabbi Arnold Goodman, Rabbi Marvin Richardson. (Standing l to r): Jerry Ashkenazie, Jim Purcell, Dana Scott, Cheryl Finkel, and Jerrold Leeson.

Administrative Staff: (l to r) Edith Waronker, Bailey Olim, Bernice Mendel, Sylvia Friedberg, Marsha Elvidge, and Jerre Ashkenazie, Executive Director.

Six Hundred Peachtree Battle Avenue, Northwest/Atlanta, Georgia 30327/(404) 355-5222

Rabbi Epstein presents award to Nora and Charles Rinzler at Israel
Bond Dinner. Nov., 1986

Presiding clergymen at annual Thanksgiving Day ecumenical service
hosted in 1987 by Ahavath Achim.

AHAVATH
ACHIM
SISTERHOOD
GOLD
BOOK
1987

Sisterhood's special Centennial
Gold Book.

Rae and Rabbi Goodman host many
groups in their home.

Janie Gavron behind the counter of the
Sisterhood Gift Shop which she has
managed for many years.

Ahavath Achim. . .1986-1987

Epstein Sanctuary, Thanksgiving Day Service.

Cornerstones from the two previous synagogue buildings.

Magnificent stained glass window, Ellman Chapel.

Interior, Ellman Chapel.

Rabbis, Cantor and Congregational Officers before the chanting of Kol Nidre.

Side entrance with Centennial Sign in the garden

Sanctuary flooded with afternoon sunlight during the Torah Siyum. Dec., 1986

Bimah and cantor's pulpit, Ahavath Achim Synagogue.

Procession of the Torahs, copper sculpture by Perli Pelzig.

Wedding, Ellman Chapel.

Pre-school and Kindergarten

Religious School Activities

PEP. . .Parents and Children Learning Together

Glimpses of Hebrew School

The Rabbi Harry H. Epstein/ Solomon Schechter School of Atlanta

The Torah Mantles

In honor of the 100th Anniversary of Ahavath Achim an entire set of
Torah Mantles depicting the Sons of Jacob were designed and
exquisitely stitched in needlepoint. Asher is represented twice
as he is connected with fertility and abundance.
The mantles are arranged on these pages coinciding with the order
in which Jacob blessed his sons before his death. Genesis 49:3-27

Reuben
Stitched by Jan Fields
Donated by Jacqueline & Harvey Sacks
and Annette & Ted Marcus

Simeon
Stitched by Diane Silverboard
Donated by Eddie Silverboard, Children
& Grandchildren

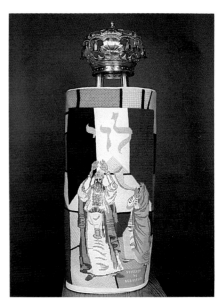

Levi
Stitched by Bea Kessler
Donated by Seymour Kessler

Judah
Stitched by Sue Winner
Donated by Jonathan & Sue Winner

Zebulun
Stitched by Pauline Cohen
Donated by Ruth & Morris Arnovitz

Issachar
Stitched by Vita Schulman
Donated by Vita & Dave Schulman

Dan
Stitched by Bunny Center
Donated by Bunny Center

Gad
Stitched by Toby Rosing
Donated by Leonard Meyer and Scott,
Roger, & Richard

Asher
Stitched by Peggy Ellman
Donated by Peggy & Harold Ellman

Asher
Stitched by Elaine Siegel
Donated by Louis Mazier, Children,
& Grandchildren

Naftali
Stitched by Frances Saperstein
Donated by Marion & Philip Perling

Joseph
Stitched by Dee Kline
Donated by Dee & Gerald Kline
and Kay & Richard Greenstein

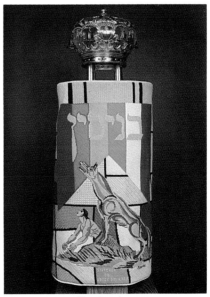

Benjamin
Stitched by Joyce Smilack
Donated by Zale Smilack

Siyum Hatorah. . .December 7, 1986

With ceremony and rejoicing, the Congregation completed the writing of a new Torah donated in honor of the Centennial by Marion and Philip Perling.

The procession forms on Peachtree Battle Avenue.

Covered by a Chuppa, the new scroll is escorted into the Synagogue.

Cantor Goodfriend carrying the scroll.

Marion and Phil Perling place the Torah in the Ark.

Past presidents Joel Lobel and Herb Karp complete letters.

Lois and David Kuniansky with Rachel and Michael participate in the Siyum.

Activities of the Centennial Year

Nobel Laureate Elie Wiesel inaugurates the Leo Eizenstat Memorial Lecture. Seated on the Bimah (l to r), Rabbi Epstein, Elie Wiesel, and Stuart Eizenstat.

Zoog (Young Couples) attends Chanukah Party at the Goodman's home.

Elie Wiesel addressing the audience which filled the Sanctuary. May 4, 1987

Youth Director, Dana Scott, leads USYers during convention.

Sunday morning Minyonaire Service conducted by teenagers.

Young and old participate in the first annual Fun Walk to raise funds for Youth activities scholarships.

Kadima president Cary Siegel introduces the chapter at a regional event.

Past president Joe Cuba with his daughter and granddaughter registers for the Fun Walk.

Finale of the Sisterhood's outstanding Donor Show, One Hundred Years Remembered written by Diane Clein. Feb. 10, 1987

Special Events of the Centennial

Doris Goldstein, Shirley Brickman, and Jane Leavey (l to r) ready the first of three Centennial Exhibits, Oct., 1986

Cantorial Concert soloists with chairmen.
March 10, 1987

Guest artist Robert Merrill and his wife (left) visit with Dave Alterman and Ann and Norman Diamond at the first major event of the Centennial. Oct. 29, 1986

Centennial Donors

(In addition to Centennial History and Torah Mantles)

Rabbi Epstein & Reva Tape
Sanford & Barbara Orkin

Sanctuary Ark Cover
Charles & Ida Borochoff

Chapel Ark Cover
Stanley & Marlene Rinzler
Robert & Renee Rinzler

Centennial Lecture Series
William & Barbara Schatten

Centennial Kiddush Cup
Richard & Susan Orenstein & Children

Torah Pointers
Saul & Geraldine Ashkenazie
Max & Helen Kuniansky
Harley & Lillian Ross & Family

Torah Stands
Children of Morris Arnovitz
Bernard & Rae Alice Cohen

Norman Diamond congratulates Sisterhood president Gail Levitt at the gala Centennial Ball. May 17, 1987

Leah Maizer and Fay Cohen receive Centennial awards at the 100th Congregational meeting for their work on the Torah mantle project. May 31, 1987

Reva and Rabbi Epstein greet Sisterhood past president Nessie Rich at the Centennial Ball.

From Generation to Generation

In time honored tradition, mothers and fathers lovingly hand down the treasures of Jewish living and learning to their children.

Congregation Ahavath Achim
Centennial Year Members

Abelman, Charles and Ethel
Abelson, Charnye
Abgott, Meyer and Jeanette
Abrams, Davis and Sandy
Abrams, Sam and Edith
Abramson, George and Esther
Adair, Abe and Frances
Adair, Harold and Sandra
Adair, Irving and Jayne
Adair, Jeffrey and Sheryl
Addlestone, Ruth
Adelman, David and Sheila
Adelman, Nelson and Donna
Adler, Saul and Rosalyn
Aftergut, Edith
Aftergut, Fred and Cookie
Albert, Anna
Alexander, Frank and Evelyn
Allen, Barry
Alon, Michael and Etti
Alperin, Carolyn
Alperin, Cheryl
Alperin, Herb and Ann
Alperin, Irving and Mimi
Alperin, Jeffrey
Alperin, Joseph and Helen
Alter, Elliott and Bernice
Alterman, A.A. and Elizabeth
Alterman, Daniel and Cathy
Alterman, Dave and Sara
Alterman, Esther
Alterman, Malcolm and Janice
Alterman, Max and Rosalyn
Alterman, Richard and Marty
Alterman, Sam and Chippie
Alterman, Stephen and Renee
Alterman, William and Florence
Altman, Michael and Nina
Andrews, Sam and Cheryl
Andrews, Simpson and Mae
Anker, Diane
Appel, Donald and Norma
Appelson, Irving and Blanche
Appleman, Elliott and Barbara
Aranson, Peter and Donna
Arlook, Martin and Elinor
Arnold, Deborah
Arnold, Hal and Dorita
Arnold, Joseph and Phyllis
Arnold, Sam
Arnovitz, David and Andria
Arnovitz, Eliot and Ellen
Arnovitz, Harold and Delores
Arnovitz, Morris and Ruth
Aronin, Howard
Aronin, Shirley
Aronoff, Joe
Aronoff, Louis
Aronovitz, Gerson and Avis
Aronovitz, Pamela
Aronson, Wayne and Joan
Aronstam, Annette

Ashendorf, Dorothy
Ashkenazie, Saul and Geraldine
Ashkinazy, Alan and Robyn
Auerbach, Jay and Martha
Austern, Lillian
Austern, Marvin
Axelrod, Harry and Dorothy
Ayal, Judy

Babbit, Joel and Barbara
Bach, Ben and Fannye
Bach, Milton and Bernice
Bachman, Gilbert and Lee
Backer, Marc and Susan
Baer, Edward and Ruth
Bagen, Leonard and Sara
Baird, Ronald and
    Barab, Benita
Balows, Albert and Patricia
Balser, Arnold and Claire
Balser, Jake
Balser, Lena
Balser, Meyer and Rosalyn
Banner, David
Baranovitz, Jack and Rosalind
Barashick, Harold and Margaret
Barenblit, Naomi
Barkan, Leonard and Mae
Barkin, Edna
Barnett, Leah
Baron, Harold and Claire
Baron, Hyman and Rosalind
Baron, Joseph and Roslyn
Baron, Murray and Eva
Bartell, Lena
Baum, Stuart and Iris
Bauman, Jack and Adeline
Bauman, Joel and Susan
Baumrind, Emil and Marcia
Baumrind, Seymour and Grace
Becker, Bruce and Cindy
Becker, Ralph
Becker, Saul and Sylvia
Beeber, David and Elaine
Beerman, Ida
Begner, Selwyn and Charlotte
Beinart, Neil and Rhonda
Belger, Morris and Miriam
Belvin, Rose
Benamy, Fredric and Gloria
Benamy, Lauren
Benamy, Maury
Benda, Gerald and Faith
Bender, Lena
Bennett, Sharon
Bennett, Stephen and Robin
Benveniste, Morris and Marilyn
Berch, Lois
Berchenko, Jack and Elizabeth
Berg, William and Carol
Berger, Eddie and Doris

Berger, Edwin and Dora
Berger, Esther
Berger, Joseph and Debra
Berger, Leon
Berger, Louis and Annette
Berger, Rose
Berger, Shirley
Berger, Sidney and Beverly
Bergman, Charles and Polly
Bergman, Mollie
Berk, Alan and Suzanne
Berke, Charles and Sheri
Berke, Herbert and Gloria
Berkman, David and Betty
Berkman, Steven
Berkowitz, Arthur and Rose
Berkowitz, Rose
Berkowitz, Sam and Sylvia
Berlin, David and Sarah
Berlin, Irving
Berlin, Jack and Dolores
Berlin, Martha
Berlye, Jay and Judy
Berman, Abe
Berman, Anne
Berman, Elliott and Rose
Berman, Ephie and Minnie
Berman, Fannie
Berman, Jerome and Betty
Berman, Leon and Polly
Berman, Merrill
Berman, Ralph
Berman, Robert and Sally
Berman, Stephen and Candy
Berman, Steven and Gita
Bernard, Perry and Jerry
Bernath, Albert and Sara
Bernath, Charles and Marilyn
Bernath, Ronnie and Penelope
Bernath, Stanley and Sybil
Bernath, Terry and Julia
Bernes, Gary and Debra
Bernknopf, David
Bernstein, Alfred and Patricia
Bernstein, David
Bernstein, Lillian
Bernstein, Marvin and Diane
Bernstein, Rick and Peggy
Blase, Jack
Blase, Sidney
Blass, Allen and Betty
Blass, Evelyn
Blass, Michael and Eleanor
Blass, Saul and Bea
Blau, Jennie
Blomberg, Sol and Goldie
Blonder, Gerald and Lois
Blonder, Pauline
Blondheim, Herbert and Martha
Bloom, Aaron and Wilma
Bloom, Bernice
Bloom, Bitsy

Bloom, David and Marian
Bloom, Leon and Dorothy
Bloom, Louis
Bloom, Marshall
Blumenfeld, Vicki
Blumenthal, Caroline
Blumenthal, David
Blumenthal, Jerome and Elaine
Blumenthal, Mark and Patricia
Blumenthal, Philip and Mona
Blumenthal, Sol
Blyden, Linda
Bock, David and Candy
Bock, Leonard and Barbara
Bock, Michael
Bock, Victor
Bodner, Arthur and Rita
Bogart, Anna
Bogart, Sherman and Harriett
Bonnardel, Deborah
Boorstin, Ronald
Borenstein, Aaron and Hedy
Borenstein, David and Julie
Borenstein, Herman and Shirley
Born, Richard and Sylvia
Borochoff, Charles and Ida
Borochoff, Lance and Sara
Borochoff, Pauline
Boros, Melvin and Phyllis
Borowitz, Rae
Borstein, Paul and Bessie
Boss, Elsie
Bove, Ruth
Brandi, Bruce and Rhonna
Brandt, Deobrah
Braun, Ernst and Margie
Braunstein, Ellen
Braunstein, Harry and Frieda
Braver, Helen
Bravman, Irving and Marilyn
Bredow, Bessie
Breen, E.O. and Bea
Breen, Lester and Betty
Bregman, Carolyn
Bregman, Keith and Jill
Bregman, Susan
Breiner, Joel and Margaret
Brenner, Leah
Bresler, Josh and Rosalyn
Bress, Dorothy
Bressler, Frances
Bressler, Hirsch and Sharon
Bressler, Richard and Linda
Brickman, Perry and Shirley
Brill, Walter and Gerrilyn
Briskin, Randy and Ceci
Brochstein, David and Barbara
Brodie, Laura Lee
Brody, Sam and Lee
Bromberg, Nathan and Bella
Bromberg, William and Miriam
Broudy, Michael and Elizabeth

Broudy, Nancy
Brouner, Barry and Leslie
Brown, Celia
Brown, Edith
Brown, Hannah
Brown, Joe and Edna
Brown, Larry and Arlene
Brown, Larry and Patty
Brown, Morris and Kathe
Brunner, Michael and Inez
Bryan, Alan and Terrie
Bryan, Bernard
Buchman, William and Joyce
Buchwald, Helaine
Buchwald, Ira and Laurie
Buford, Austin and Linda
Burnat, Lawrence and Rita
Burnham, Alan and Adele
Burnham, Gertrude
Bush, Phillip and Doris
Butler, Joel and Eleanor
Butler, Julia

Caller, Susan
Cammy, Debra
Canter, Edward and Lynn
Canter, Herman and Lucille
Canter, Jerry and Vicky
Canter, Linda
Canter, Louis and Ella
Canter, Sarah
Cantor, Betty
Capilouto, Eli and Barbara
Caplan, Beverly
Caplan, Mitchell and Cindy
Caplan, Myer and Evelyn
Caplan, Sylvia
Carasik, Vivian
Carl, Eugene and Fannie
Carl, Richard
Cavalier, Ben
Cavalier, Sidney and Helen
Center, Charles
Center, Dave and Bunny
Chazan, Marvin and Sally
Chinkes, Hy and Flora
Chisen, Sylvia
Chorches, Michael and Anne
Citron, Steven and Linda
Clark, David and Ruth
Clayman, Henry and Juliette
Clein, Harold
Clein, Harry and Esther
Clein, Irving
Clein, Jack and Annette
Clein, Robert and Dian
Clein, Sidney and Rose
Clein, Sol and Charlotte
Coan, Mark and Ruth
Codner, Saul
Coffsky, Brian and Terri
Coffsky, Jay and Sandy
Cohen, Adrienne
Cohen, Alan and Pamela

Cohen, Alan and Barbara
Cohen, Andy
Cohen, B.D. and Sara
Cohen, Barbara J.
Cohen, Bennie and Bertha
Cohen, Bernard and Rae Alice
Cohen, Brian and Lisa
Cohen, Bruce and Jeril
Cohen, Byron and Lou
Cohen, David and Lisa
Cohen, Don and Beth
Cohen, Edward and Elaine
Cohen, Etta
Cohen, Fannie
Cohen, Frieda
Cohen, Gerald and Helen
Cohen, Gilbert and Pauline
Cohen, Gilbert and Sarabel
Cohen, Harold and Diane
Cohen, Harvey and Debbie
Cohen, Helen
Cohen, Helene
Cohen, Ida
Cohen, Isadore
Cohen, Isidore and Fay
Cohen, Jack and Yvonne
Cohen, Jack and Sylvia
Cohen, Jan and Heidi
Cohen, Janice
Cohen, Joan
Cohen, Joe and Myrtice
Cohen, Leah,
Cohen, Leon
Cohen, Lester and Augusta
Cohen, Lillian
Cohen, Mark
Cohen, Mark and Tova
Cohen, Martin and Mildred
Cohen, Marvin and Sandra
Cohen, Murray and Roz
Cohen, Myrrium
Cohen, Nathan
Cohen, Patricia
Cohen, Pearl
Cohen, Philip
Cohen, Ralph and Benita
Cohen, Ruth
Cohen, Sam
Cohen, Samuel and Esther
Cohen, Sarah
Cohen, Seraphina
Cohen, Sheldon and Dorothy
Cohen, Sherman
Cohen, Stanley
Cohen, Steve
Cohen, Victor and Tillie
Cohen, Walter and Phyllis
Cohen, Walter and Melissa
Cohen, William
Cohn, Anne
Cohn, Ben
Cohn, Jerald and Carol
Cohn, Robert and Phyllis
Cohn, Sanford and
   Gershon, Ruth

Cohn, Trissy
Colby, Janette
Cole, Stephen and Judy
Coleman, Martin and Mary
Coolik, Adolphus and Eileen
Cooper, Jerry and Hannah
Cooper, Lawrence and Carol
Cooper, Lonnie
Cooper, Sylvia
Coplan, Charles and Dorothy
Corenblum, Michael and Debbie
Cowen, David and Betty
Cowen, Gary and Nina
Cowen, Rebecca
Crafton, Ernest and Mildred
Cristal, Mary
Cristol, Nathan and Shula
Cristol, Richard and Ronni
Cristol, Sidney and Jean
Cuba, Joseph
Cuba, Minnie
Cuba Philip
Cullen, Frances

Damon, Ben and Rita
Daniels, Irving and Harriett
Daniels, Morris and Rose
Daniels, Stanley and Brenda
Danneman, Anne
Danneman, Betty
Danneman, Dale
Danneman, Donald and Ida
Danneman, Edward and Rosamond
Danneman, Fred and Rosa Lee
Danneman, Jackie
Danneman, Julius and Sarah
Danneman, Marcus and Yetta
Danneman, Milton and Miriam
Danneman, Stephen
Davidoff, Alex
Davidow, Arthur and Harriet
Davidson, Bernard and Faye
Davis, Alfred
Davis, Andrew
Davis, Bruce and Sandi
Davis, Charles and Gloria
Davis, Edwin
Davis, Eva
Davis Stephen and Freda
Davis, Suzanne
Dayan, Edmond and Frenchy
Dayan, Joe and Florence
Deboisblanc, Debbie
Delman, Helen
Diamond, Alex and Gertrude
Diamond, Arthur and Shirley
Diamond, David
Diamond, Deborah
Diamond, Don and Margery
Diamond, Douglas
Diamond, Isadore and Lorraine
Diamond, Jeffrey and Felicity
Diamond, Jeffrey
Diamond, Leonard and Shirley

Diamond, Leslie
Diamond, Norman and Ann
Diamond, Richard
Diamond, Shea and Nettye
Diamond, Tessie
Diamond, Theresa
Dietz, Rose
Dillon, Ronald and Sondra
Dinerman, Samuel and Selma
Dinnerstein, Allan and Gail
Dolob, Abe and Martha
Dorfman, Randi
Draluck, Aaron and Bonnie
Draluck, Marvin and Barbara
Draluck, Merrill
Draluck, Sam and Harriet
Dunn, David and Joan
Dworetz, Edward and Miriam
Dwoskin, Harry
Dwoskin, Myron and Laura Lee
Dwoskin, Paul and Ileana
Dyckman, Edward and Lynne
Dziewinski, Herman and Maria

Eckstein, Sam
Edelstein, Bruce
Eden, Mark and Margie
Edlin, Andy and Karen
Edlin, Leonard and Rita
Edlin, Shiel and Margo
Ehrlich, Kurt
Eichel, Milton and Sara
Eisen, Gerald and Dottie
Eisenman, Ronald and Lauren
Eisenstein, Clara
Eizenstat, Berry and Bessie
Eizenstat, Stuart and Fran
Eizenstat, Sylvia
Elkan, Mary
Ellin, Martin and Aleta
Ellis, Seymour and Natalie
Ellman, Harold and Peggy
Elson, Eileen
Elson, Mae
Elson, Shia and Lynn
Ely, Bernard and Marian
Empel, Jay and Elise
Eplan, Elaine
Eplan, Elise
Eplan, Leon and Madalyne
Epstein, Burton and Sandra
Epstein, Daniel
Epstein, Harry and Reva
Epstein, Howard and Sondra
Epstein, Jacob and Marcia
Epstein, Leon and Carol
Epstein, Marvin
Epstein, Mildred
Epstein, Sam and Alice
Epstein, Sandy and
   Appley, Elizabeth
Epstein, Sunny
Epstein-Blankenship, Julie
Erbesfield, Carl and Terry

Erbesfield, Jerry
Erbesfield, Morris
Estroff, Abram and Linda
Ezor, Robert and Elisa

Fagelson, Mamie
Falck, Ruth
Falk, Charlotte
Feinberg, Helen
Feinberg, Marvin and Cynthia
Feingold, Louis and Susan
Feinstein, Robert and Lori
Feit, Albert
Feldman, Arnold and Natalie
Feldman, David and Diana
Feldman, M.A.
Feldman, Martin
Feldser, Robert and Goldie
Felton, Philip and Bessie
Fenton, Mark and Elaine
Feuer, Bruce and Maria
Fiedotin, Arnoldo and Rosa
Field, Ellen
Fields, Jerry and Janis
Fields, Ronnie
Fierman, Frances
Fierman, Robert and Lori
Fiksman, Alex and Diane
Filsoof, Fred and Mahnaz
Fine, Joe and Virginia
Fine, Pauline
Fine, Robert and Patricia
Fine, Stuart and Mary Jane
Fineman, Manuel and Myra
Fineroff, Isadore
Finkel, Edward and Cheryl
Finkel, Paul and Judith
Finkelstein, Alvin
Finkelstein, Bruce and Sally Jo
Finkelstein, Blume
Fischhof, Richard and Joan
Fishel, Julia
Fisher, Robert
Fisher, Scott and
   Bass, Marcy
Fishman, Herman and Nina
Fishman, Leonard and Rebeca
Fishman, Lillian
Fitterman, Abe and Jennie
Fix, Steven and Ellen
Fixelle, Alan and Marianne
Fleisher, Charlotte
Fleshner, Mae
Fleshner, Ruth
Flig, Steven and Candice
Floersheim, Richard and Elaine
Floersheim, Stanley and Rita
Fogel, Warren and Carol
Franco, Joseph and Rachel
Franco, Ramon and Jody
Franco, Richard and Phyllis
Franco, Robert and Sara
Frank, Harold and Doris
Frank, Larry and Lois

Frank, Maurice and Mickey
Frank, Rae
Frank, Sherry
Fred, Jack and Irene
Frederick, Fay
Freedman, Douglas and Genie
Freedman, Ely and Ramona
Freedman, Harriet
Freedman, Jack and Phyllis
Freedman, Kenneth and Robyn
Freedman, Milton and Irma
Freedman, Norman and Judith
Freedman, Sidney and Anita
Freedman, Steven and Susan
Freedman, Sylvia
Freedman, Sylvia
Freireich, Ronald and Bonnie
Friedberg, Leonard and Sylvia
Friedberg, Stephen and Nancy
Friedland, Jennye
Friedlander, Charlotte
Friedman, Bessie
Friedman, Elaine
Friedman, Esther
Friedman, Faye
Friedman, Gerald and Sandi
Friedman, Gus and Edie
Friedman, Harvey and Rhalda
Friedman, Murray and Lynn
Friedman, Sharon
Friedman, Stanley and Diane
Friedman, Stanley and Sylvia
Friedman, Stephen and Andrea
Friend, Stuart and Elayne
Frisch, Eli and Annette
Froug, Melvin and Sara
Fryer, Joel and Jane
Fryer, Keith and Marsha
Fryer, Matt and Linda
Fuller, David and Karyn

Gadlin, Bruce and Karen
Gaines, Peggy
Galanty, Ellen
Galanty, Fannye
Galishoff, Stuart and Frances
Gallant, Steven and Nancy
Gamsey, David and Carrie
Garber, Alfred and Geraldine
Garber, Dianne
Garber, Frank and Grace
Garber, Judith
Garber, Mildred
Garber, Stephen and Marianne
Garfinkle, Gail
Garten, Jay and Jody
Gartner, Larry and Carolyn
Gastwirth, Harold and Ann
Gavron, Janie
Gelb, Ronald and Faye
Geldbart, Jack and Barbara
Gelernter, Melvin and Marlene
Genser, Ronelle
Genz, Gina

Gepner, Ida
Gerber, Bernard and Toby
Gerber, Robert and Louise
Germain, Sophie
Gershon, Burton and Muriel
Gershon, Charles and Mollie
Gershon, Charles
Gershon, David and Irene
Gershon, Gina
Gershon, Herbert and Evelyn
Gershon, Nathan and Shifra
Sershon, Sylvan
Gerson, Joe and Evelyn
Gerson, Maury
Gerson, Ronald and Darriel
Gerstein, Joe and Doris
Gerstel, Marshall and Susan
Gettis, Melissa
Ghitis, Sara
Gilarsky, Bruce and Corinne
Gilbert, Gary and Karen
Gilbert Jerome and Henrietta
Gilbert, Joyce
Gill, Ed and Arlene
Gillman, Alan and Gerry
Gillman, Bernard and Florence
Gillman, Brad and Anne
Gillman, Rebecca
Gilman, Cary and Pamela
Gilner, Anne
Gilner, Donald and Celia
Gimbel, Kenneth and Madeleine
Gimpel, Amnon and Lynn
Gimpelson, Stephen and Riedy
Gingold, Alan
Ginsberg, Jean
Ginsberg, Max and Mary
Ginsberg, Robert and Thelma
Ginsburg, Samuel and Eva
Gladstone, Emanuel and Jackie
Glass, Ronald
Glass, Sam and Florence
Glassman, Harry and Anne
Glassman, Larry and Sandee
Glassman, Sidney and Myrna
Glatzer, Lawrence and Judy
Glazer, Barbara
Glazer, Jennie
Glazer, Jennifer
Glazer, Jerry
Glazer, Joseph and Rachel
Glazer, Michele
Glazer, Molly
Glazer, Scott
Glenn, Jimmy and Dale
Glickson, Miriam
Gluck, Emanuel and Rosalie
Gluck, Shirley
Glusman, Brian and Lisa
Gofman, Boris and Tamara
Gold, David and Ida
Gold, Lawrence and Natalie
Gold, Michael and Muriel
Gold, Perry and Carolyn
Goldberg, Elliott and Sarah

Goldberg, Emanuel and Sarah
Goldberg, Ervin and Esther
Goldberg, Eva
Goldberg, Gabriel and Mollie
Goldberg, Janette
Goldberg, Jay and Elsa
Goldberg, Robert and Sharon
Goldberg, Sidney and Sara Jo
Golden, Ben and Ruth
Goldenberg, Mark
Goldfine, Eric and Jody
Goldhammer, Ginger
Goldin, Paul and Linda
Goldin, Paul and Estelle
Goldman, Bluma
Goldman, Ethel
Goldman, Richard and Susan
Goldman, Robert and Toby
Goldsmith, Robert and Carolyn
Goldstein, Anne
Goldstein, Barbara
Goldstein, Eddie and Naomi
Goldstein, Ellyn
Goldstein, Fannie
Goldstein, Frances
Goldstein, George and Bernice
Goldstein, Helen
Goldstein, Herbert and Mary
Goldstein, Jennie
Goldstein, Joel and Eve
Goldstein, Joseph
Goldstein, Leon and Betty
Goldstein, Martin and Doris
Goldstein, Marvin and Rita
Goldstein, Morris
Goldstein, Philip
Goldstein, Philip and Roz
Goldstein, Robert and Liz
Goldstein, Ronald and Judy
Goldstein, Rubye
Goldstein, Stanley and Rita
Goldstein, Stanley and Carolyn
Goldstein, Steven and Karen
Goldstein, Tanya
Gole, Robert and Stacy
Goldwasser, Murray and Mollie
Goldwasser, Robert and Shirley
Golsen, Carey
Golsen, Charles and Barbara
Golsen, Richard and Julie
Goodfriend, Isaac and Betty
Goodhart, Glenn and Donna
Goodman, Arnold and Rae
Goodman, Margery
Goodman, Oscar
Goodman, Rose
Goodman, Terri
Gordon, Charles and Edith
Gordon, Harry and Charlotte
Gordon, Judith
Gordon, Larry and Janis
Gordon, Meyer
Gordon, Neil and Susan
Gordon, Richard and Bonnee
Gordon, Sam and Rae

Gould, Myles and Lynn
Gould, Stephen and Paula
Grablowsky, Oscar and Maxine
Graetz, Pearl
Graiser, Mitchell and Dorothy
Graiser, Sheldon and Estelle
Green, Lewis and Jackie
Green, Lois
Green, Max and Mary
Green, Ralph and Lillian
Green, William and Emily
Greenbaum, Irwin and Shirley
Greenbaum, Leonard
Greenbaum, Naomi
Greenberg, Alvin and Margie
Greenberg, Earle and Ruth
Greenberg, Fannie
Greenberg, Harry
Greenberg, Ira and Gail
Greenberg, Larry and Reva
Greenberg, Martin
Greenblatt, Don and Barbara
Greenblatt, Jeff and Sharon
Greene, Gary and Sally
Greenfield, Mary
Greenfield, Thomas and Lynne
Greenhill, Joel and Janet
Greenstein, Marla
Greenstein, Richard and Kay
Greenwald, Julius and Theodora
Greenwald, Robert
Greenwood, Martin and Audren
Griffith, Vivian
Groont, Edward and Frances
Gross, Arnold and Josephine
Gross, Israel and Ruth
Gross, Leon and Susan
Gross-Edelstein, Etta
Grossman, Adele
Grossman, Sidney and Sylvia
Gruber, Burton and Dandra
Gruber, Michael and Lillian
Gruber, Morton and Ellen
Grusin, Alyson
Gruskin, Sanford and Sue
Gruss, Beatrice
Guggenheim, Stephen
Gunter, Brian and Nancy
Gurin, Gerry and Arlynne
Gurin, Julius and Fannie
Gurwitch, Bert and Mary Jane
Gurwitch, Rebecca
Guttenplan, Mitchell and Linda

Haber, Ira and Wendy
Haber, Phillip and Rosalind
Haberman, Julius and Barbara
Habif, Michael and Gail
Habif, Morris and Susie
Hager, Sandra
Hahn, Frank and Helen
Hahn, Irving and Mildred
Hahn, Julian and Marion
Halberg, Harry and Patricia

Halbreich, Ivan and Martha
Halperin, Eva
Halperin, Frederick and Renie
Halpern, Aaron and Mary
Halpern, Alvin and Sherry
Halpern, Jack and Lynne
Halpern, Jay and Barbara
Halpern, Larry and Lisa
Halpern, Martin and Lisa
Halpern, Murray and Natalie
Halpern, Richard
Halpern, Shirley
Hamburger, Steven and Sharon
Hammer, Claire
Hammer, Elliot and Sandra
Hammer, Jay and Meryl
Hammerman, Martin and Gail
Handler, William and Karen
Harber, Philip and Delcy
Harber, Ruth
Harris, Bess
Harris, Helen
Harris, Joyce
Harris, Lee and Susan
Harris, Marvin and Natalie
Harrison, George and Linda
Harrison, Jean
Hartman, Ethel
Hartman, Freda
Hartman, Irving and Beatrice
Hartman, Morris
Haskins, Sidney and Dot
Haver, Bernard
Hayet, Philip and Eileen
Hazan, Joe and Irma
Hecht, Howard and Gloria
Hecht, James and Ilissa
Hefter, Ira and Barbara
Heiman, Bertha
Heiman, Leonard and Gloria
Heiman, Richard
Helbraun, Abraham and Ruth
Hendelberg, David and Linda
Herman, Freda
Herman, Madelyn
Hersch, Harold and Helen
Hersch, Rochelle
Hersh, Theodore and Rebecca
Hershberg, A.L. and Mildred
Hershberg, Harold and Roslyn
Hershberg, Martin and Shirley
Hess, Jack and Anita
Heyman Jr., Lyons and Gail
Hildebrand, Janet
Hillman, Arthur and Bibi
Hillman, Harvey
Hillman, Jack and Michal
Hillman, Ralph and Sara
Hiltzik, Laurence and Amy
Hirsch, Fred and Sylvia
Hirsch, Henry and Etta Rae
Hirsch, Marshall
Hirsch, Murray and Hannah
Hirschberg, Mark
Hirschberg, Walter and Rosalie

Hirsh, Bertha
Hirsh, Jack and Esta Jean
Hirsh, Josephine
Hirsh, Lawrence
Hirsh, Lee and Laurie
Hirsh, Marvin
Hirsh, Sadye
Hirshberg, Aline
Hochberg, William
Hoelting, Maurice and Renee
Hoffman, Anne
Hoffman, Celia
Hoffman, Joe and Sissy
Homburger, Kurt and Harriette
Horowitz, Frederick and Marjorie
Horowitz, Gerald and Pearlann
Horowitz, Maurice and Ida
Horowitz, Robert
Horowitz, Tanya
Horwitz, Dave
Horwitz, Lillian
Horwitz, William and Frances
Hurtig, Judy
Hurtig, Karen
Hurwitz, Marilyn
Hurwitz, Herschell
Hyman, Ben and Evelyn

Iny, Khalil and Adrianne
Isaacs, Phil and Cheryl
Isaacson, Edith
Isaacson, Herschel and Beth
Isaacson, Lewis and Nancy
Isenberg, Esther
Isenberg, Joel and Nancy
Isenberg, Martin and Harriet
Isenberg, Marvin and Barbara
Isenberg, Sam and Agnes
Isenberg, Sam and Regina
Ish, Elmir and Lena
Isikoff, Otis and Sylvia
Iteld, Guta
Iteld, Sholem and Eva
Itzkowitz, Martin and Michael

Jackson, Ann
Jackson, Gary and Kathi
Jackson, Kenneth and Lenore
Jacobi, Edward and Sharlene
Jacobs, David
Jacobs, Gary and Sandra
Jacobs, Harris and Kitty
Jacobs, Joe and Joann
Jacobs, Leroy and Hannah
Jacobs, Raymond
Jacobson, Bessie
Jacobson, Burton and Loretta
Jacobson, Erwin and B.J.
Jacobson, Milton and Arlene
Jacobson, Richard and Marcia
Jaffe, Dennis and Marcia
Jaffe, Robert and Bette
Jaffe, Sherry

Janis, Gertrude
Janko, Adele
Janko, Isaac and Lillian
Janus, Leah
Jay, Ferman and Esther
Jay, William
Jennings, Barbara
Jeroslow, Robert and Sondra
Joel, Robert and Rita
Joffe, Stanley and Avril
Joffre, Jane
Joffre, Lyonel and Phyllis
Joffre, Robyn
Joffre, Steven
Johnson, Diane
Johnson-Whatley, Jeanne
Jones, Allen and Edith
Joondeph, Rose
Joseph, Larry and Eileen
Jurofsky, Allen and Sylvia

Kagan, Jeffrey and Deborah
Kahanow, Jerome and Clara
Kahn, Bernard and Joan
Kahn, David and Ruby
Kahn, Joel and Mindy
Kahn, Ralph and Rhalda
Kalan, Eleanor
Kalin, David
Kaliser, Mike and Minnie
Kalish, Joseph and Irene
Kalish, Murray and Joan
Kaminsky, Allen and Charlotte
Kaminsky, Lawrence and Harriet
Kaminsky, R.M. and Shirlee
Kamor, Abe and A. Vincent
Kamor, Manuele and Regina
Kamor, Stanley and Pamela
Kanfer, Arthur and Jackie
Kaplan, Alan and Barbara
Kaplan, Arthur and Frances
Kaplan, Ben
Kaplan, Bernard
Kaplan, Beth
Kaplan, Eugene and Linda
Kaplan, Henry and Adele
Kaplan, Isadore
Kaplan, Jay and Susan
Kaplan, Kusiel and Paula
Kaplan, Lawrence and Leah
Kaplan, Lillian
Kaplan, Mark
Kaplan, Marvin and Polly
Kaplan, Philip and Sally
Kaplan, Ronald and Angela
Kaplan, Scott and Shelley
Kaplan, Shirlee
Kaplan, Sidney and Alice
Kaplan, Theodore and Anne
Karlan, Morton and Marilyn
Karp, Barbara
Karp, Harold and Sylvia
Karp, Herbert and Hazel
Karp, Herbert and Estelle

Karp, Sam and Freda
Kasriel, Robert and Ernestine
Kasriel, Sarita
Katt, David and Ida
Katz, Bradley and Bernice
Katz, Daniel and Ellen
Katz, Ira and
    Wertheimer, Mindy
Katz, Israel and Annette
Katz, Jay and Hazel
Katz, Marian
Katz, Michael and Patricia
Katz, Susan
Kaufman, Bruce and Jenny
Kaufman, Howard and Susan
Kaufman, Jeffrey and Alison
Kaufman, Kenneth and Sandra
Kaufman, Marilyn
Kaufman, Saul and Bess
Kaufman, Sidney and Carolyn
Kauffman, David and Jody
Kay, Michael and Ann
Kaye, Dora
Kaye, Norman and Annie Ruth
Kelly, Terry and Brenda
Kelman, Leslie and Marilyn
Kern, Fred
Kern, Lee and Jessica
Kersh, Gloria
Kersh, Harriet
Kessler, Ethel
Kessler, Jerry
Kessler, Seymour and Bea
Kessler, Walt
Ketzky, Lillian
King, Ella
King, Kevin and Claire
Kingloff, Daniel and Barbara
Kinsler, Mollie
Kinstein, Fannie
Kleber, Garvin and Barbara
Kleber, Steven
Klee, Ronald and Rita
Klein, Frances
Klein, Herman and Rose
Klein, Howard and Marilyn
Klein, Paul and India
Klenberg, Max and Nancy
Kline, Gerald and Dee
Klingler, Debra
Klotz, Minnie
Klotz, Sol and Rose
Knopf, Jay and Roberta
Knopf, William and Randy
Kogon, Larry and Lisa
Kogon, Martin and Judy
Kolesky, Marlene
Kolesky, Sylvia
Kolkin, Aaron and Lee
Kolodkin, Alan and Elaine
Kolodkin, Minnie
Konsker, Abraham and Rifki
Kopelman, Kenneth and Arlene
Kopelman, Mitchell
Koplin, Beryl and Doris

Koplin, Kal and Charlene
Koplin, Simon and Gertrude
Kornman, Jacob
Kornman, Joan
Kornmehl, Bernard and Jill
Krafchick, Harold and Beverly
Krafchick, Michael and Laura
Kraft, Irving and Esther
Kraft, Jerry and Phyllis
Kraft, Raye
Kramarow, Nathan and Ruth
Kramer, Milton and Beryl
Kramer, Russell and Cheryl
Krasnoff, Cindy
Krasnoff, Robert and Barbara
Krasnoff, Steve
Kraut, Joseph and Bonnie
Krebs, Richard and Lana
Kreisberg, Michael and Jana
Krinsky, Joseph and Ethel
Krinsky, Lee and Lori
Kroll, Bernard
Kroll, Lorraine
Kruger, Sarah
Krugman, Lovie
Krugman, Seymour and Marjorie
Kuniansky, David and Lois
Kuniansky, Douglas and Andrea
Kuniansky, Max and Helen
Kupshik, Hilton and Janet
Kurtz, Arthur and Irene
Kushner Jr., Robert and Brenda
Kutner, Stephen and Jean
Kwatinetz, Neil
Kwatinetz, Martin and Mildred

Labovitz, Albert and Debra
Lafkowitz, Larry and Elissa
Lahman, Rose
Landau, Sol and Dorothy
Lande, Arnold and Starr
Lander, Anna
Landis, Alan
Landis, Evan
Landis, Kerry and Linda
Landis, Paul and Rhona
Landy, Michael and Audrey
Lansky, Murray and Lucy
Lansky, Rubin and Lola
Lasky, Andy and Helaine
Lavietes, Paul and Marilyn
Lavine, Dorothy
Lavine, Steven and Lauri
Lawson, Brian and Jean
Leademan, Adam and Shirley
Leaf, Bruce and Michelle
Leavey, Robert and Jane
Lebovitz, Robert and Edith
Lederman, Hyman and Esther
Leeson, Jerrold and Joyce
Leeson, Sophie
Leff, Henry and Ida
Leff, Isadore and Dorothy
Leff, Moses

Leff, Peter and Sandra
Lefkoff, Anne
Lefkoff, Harold and Evelyn
Lefkoff, Louis and Hessie
Lefkoff, Marvin and Frances
Leighton, Leslie and Deborah
Lessner, Jerry and Teddy
Lev, Julius and Esther
Levenson, Alan and Renay
Leventhal, Ronald and Dorothy
Levetan, Phillip and Liane
Levi, Robert and Sharon
Levin, Amy
Levin, Doris
Levin, Ed and Brenda
Levin, Eleanor
Levin, Harold and Elaine
Levin, Jonathan
Levin, Kenneth and Beverly
Levin, Leonard and Margie
Levin, Marc
Levin, Michael and Ann
Levin, Mary Lee
Levin, Rose
Levin, Rose
Levin, Sol and Sally
Levin, William and Valerie
Levine, Barbara
Levine, Leon and Irene
Levine, Manuel and Rita
Levine, Marshall and Nancy
Le Vine, Michael and Rita
Levine, Michael and Esther
Levine, Morton and Phyllis
Levine, Nathan and Balfoura
Levine, Steven
Levinson, Abe and Iris
Levinson, Robert and Wilhelmina
Levitas, Elliott and Barbara
Levitas, Ida
Levitas, Theodore and Miriam
Levitt, Jacob and Betty
Levitt, Julius and Toby
Levitt, Maurice and Gail
Levow, Alan and Renee
Levy, Annie
Levy, Charles and Nancy
Levy, Dorothy
Levy, Ethel
Levy, Hannah
Levy, Kenneth and Sherry
Levy, Meyer and Elsie
Levy, Neilan and Anita
Levy, Selig and Bertha
Levy, Sidney and Randi
Levy, Ted and Meredith
Lewis, Bernie
Lewis, Frank and Mimi
Lewis, Seymour and Harriet
Lewit, Lena
Lichtenstein, Aaron and Anne
Lichtenstein, Jack and Elsie
Lichtenstein, Mark and Brenda
Lieberman, Jack and Marilyn
Lieberman, Robert and Anita

Liebman, Paul and Naomi
Light, Steven and Wendy
Lincoln, Jack and Zelda
Lincoln, Linda
Lincoln, Sam
Linver, Sandra
Lipman, Marlene
Lippitt, Alan and Linda
Lippman, Marie
Lipsius, Joseph and Anne
Lipson, Nathan and Joan
Lipton, Nathan and Bernice
Lischkoff, Herman
Lisker, Arthur and Barbara
Liss, Robert and Annette
Lobel, David and Beverly
Lobel, Joel and Barbara
Lobel, Paul
Loff, Abbey and Sylvia
London, Bob and Sandy
London, Max and Mary
Lorowitz, Harry and Tracy
Lovell, Ralph and Carla
Lovinger, Nathan and Audrey
Lowenstein, Richard and Harriette
Lowy, Stephen and Benita
Lubel, Alan
Lubel, David and Suzanne
Lubin, Samuel and Frances

Madison, Rose
Makavitt, Thelma
Makover, Bernard and Anne
Makover, Stanford and Maxine
Makover, Sylvan and Frances
Malkin, Abraham
Manchel, Howard and Janet
Mandel, Benjamin
Mandel, Frank and Harlean
Mandel, Jerome and Rosalyn
Mandel, Mark and Michelle
Manes, Dave
Manes, Irving
Manning, Pauline
Maran, Scott and Vicki
Marbach, Lloyd and Peggy
Marcus, Joseph and Charlotte
Marcus, Ted and Annette
Margol, Howard and Esther
Margoles, Elias and Delia
Margolis, Michael and Sheila
Margolis, Stephen and Rhoda
Marks, Charles and Sylvia
Marks, Jack and Mozelle
Marks, Louise
Marks, Neal and Phyllis
Marks, Robert and Sue
Marmer, Robert and Natalie
Marsh, Gary and Sherry
Martin, Eva
Martino, Erna
Masor, Jonathan and Helen
May, Frederic
Mayson, Bill and Sara

Mayson, Thelma
Maziar, Harry and Sherry
Maziar, Howard and Patty
Maziar, Louis and Leah
Maziar, Neal
Maziar, Sunny
Maziar, Todd
McDaid, Marcia
Medintz, Coleman and Myra
Mell, Labe and Lorraine
Meller, Steven and Jody
Melnick, Daniel and Ellen
Meltz, Hyman and Irene
Meltz, Viola
Meltzer, Abe and Minnie
Meltzer, Harold and Sylvia
Mendel, Barbara
Mendel, Bette
Mendel, Donald and Pat
Mendel, Hal and Marcy
Mendel, Jerome and Joanne
Mendel, Laurie
Mendel, Paul and Leslie
Mendel, Richard and Bernice
Mendel, Sidney and Lee
Mendel, Simon and Dorothy
Mendelson, Morris and Mary
Merkel, Amanda
Merlin, Leon and Dottie
Metzman, Michael and Judy
Meyer, Leonard and Janet
Meyer, Ray
Meyers, June
Mezritch, Bernard and Marcia
Michelson, Robin
Miles, Robert
Millender, Ivan and Shirley
Millender, Sam
Miller, Ada
Miller, Alvin and Harriet
Miller, Eleanor
Miller, Ida
Miller, Jack and Rose
Miller, Jody
Miller, Jon and Ilene
Miller, Ronald and Cathy
Miller, Wayne and Lori
Millner, Bess
Mills, Monty and Harriet
Mills, Sally
Minin, Larry
Minkin, David and Glenda
Minsk, Alvin and Shirley
Minsk, Eric
Minsk, Harold and Gloria
Minsk, Jonathan
Mislow, Annie
Mislow, Sam and Sandra
Mitchell, Richard and
   Kupferberg, Susan
Mizell, Albert and Flora
Mizell, Harold
Mizell, Rachel
Moattar, Edward and Marcialyn
Moldow, Sidney and Barbara

Molkner, Betty
Moog, Charles and Zelda
Moog, Sam and Dora
Moore, Dan and Ina
Moret, Daniel and Gail
Moret, Ethel
Moret, Macy and Jennie
Moret, Muriel
Moret, Robert and Eula
Morgan, Richard
Morgan, Sol and Sadye
Morris, Adell
Morris, Lewis and Lynn
Morris, Perry and Anita
Morris, Ralph and Rae
Morris, Rose
Morris, Steven and Vicki
Morse, Muriel
Morton, Andrew and Jill
Moscow, Joel and Lynne
Moscow, Robert and Estelle
Moscow, Sarah
Moss, Fred
Moss, Joel and Karen
Moss, Robert
Moss, Ruben Richard
Moss-Englett, Mary
Muchnick, Dorothy
Mushnick, Herman and Evelyn

Nach, Rose
Nadel, Herbert and Janet
Nadel, Lyn
Nassau, Saul and Tootsie
Nathan, Martin and Patty
Neiman, Howard and Phyllis
Nelson, Earle
Nerenbaum, Daniel and Marilyn
Nerenbaum, Marshall and Ona
Nerenbaum, Sophie
Neuhaus, Sylvia
Neumark, Gerald and June
Neuwirth, Herbert and Barbara
Neuwirth, Wayne
Newman, Philip and Donna
Ney, Robert and Hilda
Ney, Stanley and Dubby
Nochumson, Frank
Nochumson, Howard and Janice
Nodvin, Marvin and Sandra
Nord, Dina
Novak, Jack
Novak, Jonas and Frances
Novak, Leon and Brenda
Nye, Madolin

Okun, Lois
Okun, Phillip and Margie
Olim, Bailey
Olim, Max and Ann
Ollins, Robert and Ruth
Oppenheimer, Stephen and Carolyn
Orenstein, Irving and Doris

Orenstein, Linda
Orenstein, Marvin and Elise
Orenstein, Max and Bernice
Orenstein, Richard and Susan
Orenstein, Temme
Orenstein, Walter and Diane
Orkin, Kenny
Orkin, Sanford and Barbara
Orlin, Scott
Oroshnik, Amy
Oser, Nettye
Oxman, Bennett and Hank
Oxman, Jerome and Sonia
Oxman, Richard and Sharon

Pachter, Lillian
Pack, Frances
Pack, Louis and Linda
Padawer, Randy and Heddy
Palefsky, Charles and Sherry
Paller, Gerald and Gerry
Paller, Jack and Gail
Paller, Lottie
Paller, Robert and Caryl
Paradies, Dan and Billie
Paradies, James and Judy
Parker, Alex and Pauline
Parks, Bertha
Parks, Harry and Sylvia
Parks, Steve and Peggy
Parks, Sidney and Eleanor
Parnes, Irwin and Linda
Patinkin, Mark and Shannon
Patt, Ira and Charlotte
Paul, Alan and Judy
Pazol, Elissa
Pazol, Richard and Sherry
Pazol, Sidney and Jackie
Pearlstein, Allen and Pearline
Peck, Howard and Harriet
Perkel, Michael and Helen
Perling, David and Peggy
Perling, Michael and Dori
Perling, Philip and Marian
Perling, Sam
Perlman, Robert and Freda
Perlmutter, Frank and Mary
Perrell, Isadore and Dorothy
Peskin, Mary
Peskin, Phillip and Betty
Pett, Harry and Sylvia
Pfeffer, Albert
Philipson, Hal and Lisa
Piassick, Joel and Karen
Pichulik, Charlie and Lena
Pichulik, Louis and Jo
Pichulik, Rubin and Sarah
Picker, Karol
Piel, Erwin and Frances
Piem, Albert
Piem, Sarah
Pilzer, Alan and Edith
Pine, Jonathan and Marci
Pinsker, Alan and Sally

Pinsky, Alice
Pitt, Louis and Lillian
Planer, Richard and Barbara
Plasker, Michael and Susan
Pliner, Stuart and Barbara
Podber, Morris and Ann
Podhouser, David and Fannie
Podhouser, Morris and Cindy
Pollock, Bernard and Elaine
Polstein, Leon and Sharon
Pomerance, Lorraine
Popky, Patsy
Port, Helen
Posner, Rubye
Powell, Gussie
Prusin, Barry and Lynn
Ptaschnik, Richard and Jill
Purser, Faye

Rachelson, Ira and Ducie
Rainbow, Glenn and Lynn
Rand, Michael
Rauzin, Milton and Ruth
Regitsky, Jonathan and Stacy
Reinhardt, Burton and Diana
Reisman, Bruce and Vickie
Reisman, Donald and Shirley
Reisman, Howard and Linda
Reisman, Nathan and Margaret
Reisner, Andrew
Renas, Susan
Resin, Alexander and Iva
Resman, Gary
Rice, Ben and Bess
Rich, Arnold and Shirley
Rich, Maurice and Shirley
Rich, Nessie
Rich, Stephen and Sandra
Rich, Sydney
Richardson, Marvin and Maureen
Richman, Harry and Lillian
Richman, Jack and Zira
Rickles, Harvey and Jennifer
Rifkin, Henry and Sherrie
Rifkin, Sidney and Helen
Rinzler, Charles and Nora
Rinzler, Florence
Rinzler, Lisa
Rinzler, Robert and Renee
Rinzler, Stanley and Marlene
Ritchkin, Frances
Rittenbaum, Jerry
Rittenbaum, Louis
Rittenbaum, Max and Miriam
Rittenbaum, Scot and Karen
Robbins, Ian
Robbins, Morris and Sylvia
Roberts, Gary and Julie
Robinson, Gus and Sylvia
Robkin, Max and Ozna
Rodbell, Leonard and Thelma
Rogers, Peter and Alice
Rogin, Norman and Mollie
Romano, Sarah

Ronick, Robert and Tina
Ronin, Frances
Rose, Doran and Carolyn
Rose, Sidney and Gertrude
Rosenbaum, Jack and Mildred
Rosenbaum, Melvin and Shirley
Rosenbaum, Sarah
Rosenberg, Allan and Marcia
Rosenberg, Ben
Rosenberg, Charles and Bunny
Rosenberg, Chester and Jill
Rosenberg, Dave and Libby
Rosenberg, Donald and Sally
Rosenberg, Fredric and Robin
Rosenberg, Gershon and Mimi
Rosenberg, Helen
Rosenberg, Phil and Blume
Rosenberg, Sam and Sara
Rosenberg, Stephen
Rosenblum, Dorothy
Rosenfeld, David
Rosenfeld, Tillye
Rosenthal, Carl and Rosalie
Rosenthal, David and Anne
Rosenthal, Herman and Selma
Rosenthal, Morris and Joanne
Rosh, Adel
Rosh, Doris
Rosh, Karl and Linda
Rosing, Faye
Rosing, Michael
Rosing, Tom and Toby
Ross, Alma
Ross, Harley and Lillian
Ross, Michael
Rossner, Stephen and Joan
Rothberg, Lil
Rothfarb, Dave and Ruth
Rothman, Lee and Ray
Rothman, Mitzi
Rottersman, William and Lena
Rouben, David and Maxine
Rubel, Herbert and Ruth
Rubel, Julia
Rubenstein, Lynda
Rubin, Abraham and Muriel
Rubin, Bertha
Rubin, Bonnie
Rubin, Cary
Rubin, Jerry and Donna
Rubin, Meyer and Lillie
Rubin, Perry and Evelyn
Rubin, William and Sariece
Ruden, Isadore
Ruskin, Louis and Shirley

Sachs, Howard and Kathy
Sackett, Herbert and Elaine
Sacks, Harvey and Jacqueline
Sacks, Ralph and Sadie
Sadow, Steven and Susan
Safra, Mark and Clara
Saginar, Edwin
Saks, Kate

Salby, Harry and Esta
Saltzman, Alan and Sandy
Salzman, Martin and Beth
Sanders, Abe and Betty
Sanders, Alice
Sanders, Arthur and Herta
Sandler, Jack and Sylvia
Sandler, Steven and Marcia
Sandfelder, Martin and Paula
Saparow, Annette
Saparow, Herschel and Susan
Saperstein, Max and Frances
Sasine, Jeffrey and Janice
Sasine, Stanley and Irene
Sauers, Nancy
Saul, Bertha
Saul, Edmund and Norma
Saul, Irving and Celia
Saul, Michael and Karen
Saul, Milton and Virginia
Saul, Ruth
Schaffer, Carolyn
Schaffer, Jeff
Schaffer, Joel and Lynda
Schaffer, Sam and Betty
Schaffer, Tom and Sallie
Schatten, Kenneth and Amy
Schatten, Samuel and Janet
Schatten, William and Barbara
Schear, Abe and Linda
Schechter, Leonard
Scheer, Rita
Scheinbaum, C.N. and Helen
Scheinfeld, Harry and Jane
Scherr, John and Ruth
Scheuer, Marie
Scheuer, Sigmund and Charlene
Schiff, Arthur and Patricia
Schiff, Irving and Norma
Schlansky, Stuart and Susan
Schlosser, Jay and Jill
Schlossman, Frances
Schmerler, Alan and Robin
Schmidt, David and Nancy
Schneider, Les and Deborah
Schoenbaum, Raymond and Susan
Schoenberg, Arthur and Sara
Schreiber, Judy
Schube, Keith and Maxine
Schube, Stanley and Brenda
Schulman, Alan and Judy
Schulman, David and Vita
Schulman, Howard Lee
Schultz, Arthur and Ruth
Schultz, Myron and Selma
Schussel, Robert and Gladys
Schwartz, Alfred and Eleanor
Schwartz, Daniel and Barbara
Schwartz, Fred and Marilyn
Schwartz, Herbert and Kathy
Schwartz, Irene
Schwartz, Jeff
Schwartz, Lauren
Schwartz, Meyer
Schwartz, Meyer and Gayle

Schwartz, Raleigh
Schwartz, Robert
Schwartz, Robin
Schwartz, Steven and Cathy
Schwartz, William and Anne
Schwartz, William and Marlene
Schwartzberg, Ben and Sara
Schwartzberg, Hilda
Schwarz, Erwin and Susi
Schwarzman, David
Scott, Dana
Segal, Dorothy
Segal, Joan
Segal, Joe and Jill
Segal, Mendel and Mynette
Segall, Nathan and Susanne
Seitz, Harry and Mary
Seitz, Inez
Seitz, Kenneth and Betty
Seldes, Morene
Selfridge, Bette
Seligman, Fred and Sylvia
Seligman, Leonard and Irene
Seligman, Preston and Maxine
Selmonosky, Carlos and Sonia
Senoff, Judy
Sens, Alan and Lynda
Shafer, Barry and Sharon
Shaffer, Joe
Shaffer, Marie
Shaffer, Morty
Shaffer, Murray
Shaffer, Sarah
Shafferman, Jeanette
Shafton, Minnie
Shainker, Charles
Shalloway, Inda
Shapiro, Bernard and Selma
Shapiro, Jay and Andrea
Shapiro, Jeffrey and Sharon
Shapiro, Jonathan and Cathy
Shapiro, Joseph and Cookie
Shapiro, Mark and Jean
Shapiro, Martin and Donna
Shapiro, Ronald
Shapiro, Samuel and Gina
Shavin, Norman and Phyllis
Shavin, Samuel and Ruth
Shaw, David and Sherry
Shell, Dorothy
Shenk, Linda
Sheron, Alec and Marion
Sherwinter, Julius and Carol
Shimm, Jonathan and Judith
Shmerling, Gary and Shelley
Shmerling, Sanford and Beverly
Shonkoff, David and Julie
Shonson, Brian and Karen
Shonson, Sam and Beverly
Shoob, Marvin and Janice
Shovers, Andrew and Carole
Shulman, Gertie
Shulman, Harry
Shulman, Irving and Irma
Shuman, Joseph and Rose

Shusterman, Leon and Betty Ann
Siegel, Abe and Tillie
Siegel, Alvin and Mimi
Siegel, Alvin and Dorene
Siegel, Arthur and Arlene
Siegel, Bea
Siegel, Calvin
Siegel, Harry Lane and Elsie
Siegel, Harvey and Vicki
Siegel, Isadore and Eva
Siegel, Louis and Lorraine
Siegel, Paul and Elaine
Siegel, Richard
Siegel, Rose
Siegel, Sophie
Siegel, Stanley and Ruth
Sifen, Paul and Sonia
Silberstein, Kenneth and Felice
Silberstein, Milton and Eileen
Silberstein, Paul and Rita
Silver, Arthur and Carla
Silver, Barry
Silver, Esther
Silver, Irving and Ronnie
Silver, Louis and Margie
Silver, Nancy
Silver, William and Susan
Silverboard, Edward and Diane
Silverboard, Lewis and Evelyn
Silverboard, Stanley and Helaine
Silverman, Alan and Bonnie
Silverman, Ida
Silverman, Julius and Edie
Silverman, Marvin
Silverman, Marvin and Nan
Silverman, Lisa
Silverman, Robert and Eileen
Silverman, Rose
Silverman, Sidney and Lee
Silverman, Stephen
Silverman, Victor and Saba
Silverstein, Hyman and Gussie
Silverstein, Ida
Simmons, Ella
Simmons, Howard
Simon, David and Barbara
Simon, Sam and Faye
Sims, Dave
Singer, Eric and Carla
Singer, George and Selma
Singer, Gordon
Singer, Herbert and Joanne
Singer, Richard and Sandra
Singer, Sol and Ruth
Sisselman, Sidney and Lena
Skoke, David and Sandra
Skorecki, Adam and Jodie
Sloan, Louis
Sloman, Bernard and Rella
Slosman, Rene
Slutzky, Joe and Betty
Slutsky, Morton and Ina
Smilack, Zale and Joyce
Smiley, David and Gloria
Smith, Al and Elinor

Smith, Anne
Smith, Bernard and Edith
Smith, Dora
Smith, Earl and Shirley
Smith, Harris
Smith, Isadore and Hilda
Smith, Jacob and Judy
Smith, Joel and Donna
Smith, Martin and Judy
Smith, Mollie
Smith, Myron and Merle
Smith, Nathan and Edith
Smolen, Lee and Janice
Smolen, Perry and Claire
Snyder, Gary and Gale
Snyder, Sol and Rose
Socoloff, Esther
Socoloff, Morris and Susan
Soden, Allen and Judy
Solin, Maurice and Babe
Solloway, Lewis
Solloway, Raye
Solnik, Pinkus and Bella
Solodar, Seymour and Helena
Solomon, Archie and Kaethe
Solomon, Jerome and Rebecca
Solomon, Marshall and Gail
Solomon, Richard and Susan
Solomon, Samuel and Frances
Spanier, Jacob and Harriet
Spector, Bernard
Spector, Bobby and Rosalind
Spector, Maurice and Fritzi
Spector, Ruth
Spector, Scott
Speert, Jay
Spiegelman, Betty
Spielberg, Jack and Sarah
Spielberg, Sol and Gisela
Spielberger, D.L. and Jessie
Spielberger, Larry
Spielberger, Selma
Spikler, Elihu and Pamela
Spilky, Goldye
Spindel, Edna
Spizman, Willy and Robyn
Srochi, Alan and Rebecca
Srochi, Annette
Srochi, Lane
Srochi, Samuel
Srochi, Stanley and Joan
Stahl, Robert and Claire
Stark, Stanley and Margie
Stein, Allen and Merna
Stein, Benjamin and Iris
Stein, Bert
Stein, Bessie
Stein, Howard and Irene
Stein, Ken and Ellen
Stein, Max and Mathilda
Stein, Melissa
Stein, Milton and Ragolda
Stein, Saul and Bea
Stein, Sol and Bess
Stein, Stanley and Judy

Steinberg, Carole
Steinberg, Harvey and Donna
Steinberg, Nancy
Steinberg, Toby and Ileen
Steinbook, Jeff and Sandra
Steinmark, Stuart and Phyllis
Stepakoff, Joel and Elaine
Stern, Martin and Sunny
Stine, Herbert and Joyce
Stollerman, Burt and Pearl
Stone, Irving and Shirley
Stone, Jules and Harriett
Storch, Jack and Janine
Storch, Marty and Dorothy
Strauss, Walter and Estelle
Streve, Pauline
Streve, Renie
Strickman, Andrew
Strongwater, Jay and Elizabeth
Struletz, Annette
Struletz, Cheryl
Sturm, Hiram and Ruth
Sturman, Milton
Sturman, Sidney
Sucan, Stanley and Joan
Sugarman, Harry and Margaret
Sugarman, Ida
Sugarman, Marvin and Rose
Sunshine, Alan and Betty
Sunshine, Kalman and Dora
Sunshine, Philip and Janet
Suzman, Cedric and Wendy
Swerdlin, Richard and Cathy
Szporin, Munio and Edzia

Tamli, Meir and Ann
Tantillo, Eileen
Taratoot, Abe and Bea
Taratoot, Dorothy
Taratoot, Isadore and Evelyn
Taratoot, Joseph and Beatrice
Taratoot, Kim and Janet
Taratoot, Louis and Amy
Taylor, Herbert and Esther
Taylor, Rose
Tedoff, Ira and Carol
Tenenbaum, Abe and Alice
Tenenbaum, Stanley and Shirley
Teplis, Nathan and Monica
Teplis, Paul and Betsy
Tepper, Robert and Jeannie
Tepper, Rubin and Selma
Tesler, Sidney and Ruth
Tetenbaum, Ronald
Theise, Lee
Tillem, Bella
Tillem, Jerry and Yvonne
Tillem, Melvin and Franceen
Tobin, Steven and Abbe
Topper, Ron and Eileen
Torch, Evan and Robin
Tracy, Patrick and Cindy
Traub, Rick and Goldie
Trauner, Robert and Bobbi

Travis, Elsa
Tuchman, Fred and Rose

Ulman, Bernard
Ulman, Boris and Tonia
Ulman, Stanley and Margie
Ullman, Sarah
Unell, Gary and Renee
Unell, Harry and Ruth

Vantosh, Jeff and Jill
Velkoff, Abraham and Evelyn
Vener, Arthur and Ronnie
Visner, Sidney and Marjorie
Vitner, Charlotte
Vitner, Fannie
Vitner, Saul and Joan
Vizzini, Thomas and Lynne
Voll, Eva
Vrono, Charles and Marsha
Vrono, Harold and Eleanor
Vrono, Louis and Jennie

Wachtel, Celia
Walcoff, Sara
Wald, Gertrude
Wallen, David
Wapnick, Janice
Waronker, Edith
Waronker, Steven and Mitzi
Waronker, William and Cecelia
Warshauer, Michael and Caryn
Warshaw, Morris and Harriette
Wassman, Suzan
Weinberg, Celia
Weinberg, Eva
Weinberg, James and Sandy
Weinberg, Sam
Weinberg, Sara
Weiner, Barry and Linda
Weiner, Charles and Laurel
Weiner, Daniel and Sheila
Weiner, Irwin and Lynne
Weinman, Joe and Evelyne
Weinman, Milton and Patsy
Weinroth, George
Weinstein, Alan and Renee
Weinstein, Mark and Barbara
Weinstein, Milton and Vi
Weinstein, Morris and Sadye
Weinstein, Robert and Marjorie
Weintraub, Ronald and Leslie
Weintraub, William and Veronica
Weiss, Barbara
Weisser, Harry and Anita
Weissman, Samuel and Sylvia
Weissmann, Ben and Hilda
Weissmann, David
Weitz, Greg and Aletta
Weitz, Izzy and Shirley
Weitz, Norman and Mitzi
Wender, Marvin and Diane

Wender, Robert and Lorraine
Wendkos, Philip and Carol
Wenger, Julius and Nanette
Werbin, Samuel and Renne
Wetstone, Jordan and Sherrie
Wexler, Alan and Barbara
Wexler, Norma
Whitlock, Morris and Deanne
Whiteman, Arnold
Whiteman, Frank and Eva
Whiteman, Sarah
Wildstein, Gilbert
Wildstein, Walter and Arlene
Wile, Debra
Wilensky, Edwin and Rhoda
Wilensky, Julius and Ida
Wilensky, Larry and Sheila
Wilensky, Robert and Ava
Wiley, Joan
Willen, Harold and Beakie
Willen, Frances
Wind, Joseph and Bronia
Wineburgh, Michael and Adele
Winner, Jonathan and Sue
Winston, Ronald and Marilyn
Winter, Irwin and Ruth
Winter, Lewis
Winter, Mark and Brenda
Wise, Eli and Karen
Wise, Isaac and Rachel
Wise, Sam and Ida
Wisebram, Diane
Wisebram, Henry and Jeanne
Wisebram, Herschel and Ruth
Wisebram, Steve
Wolbe, Bea
Wolbe, Daniel and Judy
Wolbe, Sara
Wolensky, Michael and Sandra
Wolf, Irving
Wolf, Marty and Bonnie
Wolf, Sidney and Ida
Wolfe, Adele
Wolfe, Bernard and Linda
Wolfe, Larry and Lynda
Wolff, Sam and Sandra
Wolff, Susan
Wolkin, Alan and Pepi
Wolkin, Larry and Susan
Wollner, D.L. and Catherine
Wolson, Bertha
Wooten, Diane
Wright, Michael and Nancy

Yarfitz, Raymond and Marcia
Yerlow, Charles and Irma
Yerlow, Mildred
Yerlow, Minna
Yerlow, Richard and Eileen
Young, Barry and Debra
Young, Jerome and Miriam
Yudelson, Anne
Yudelson, Harold and Jane

Zaban, Erwin and Judy
Zadoff, Andrew
Zaglin, Joe and Margo
Zaglin, Lawrence
Zbar, Jack and Leda

Zebrack, Arthur and Rachel
Zeitlin, Allan and Barbara
Zier, Steven and Ilene
Zimmer, Morris
Zimmerman, Esther

Zimmerman, Lawrence
Zimmerman, Rosalie
Zion, Sam and Annette
Zivitz, Donald and Leona
Zuckerman, Max and Shirley

Zukor, Michael and Jeannette
Zwecker, Jack and Sophie
Zweig, Arnold and Carolyn
Zwerner, Herbert and Grace
Zyman, Sergio and Rebecca

Membership. . . .1900

The following handwritten list was deposited in the cornerstone of the Gilmer St. shul on Oct. 4, 1900. Due to age, some of the names are not completely legible. In cases where the proper spelling is known, the name has been listed correctly.

Officers
J. Dorfan, Pres.
H. Mendel, Vice Pres.
F. Weinberg, Treas.
M. Ney, Fin. Sec.
? Lichtenstein, Rec. Sec.

Trustees
M. Clein
J. Golden
D. Saul
I. Wein. . . . .
N.A. . . . .

Building Committee
L. Fresh, Chairman
M.M. Cohen
M. Lichtenstein
Sam Rosendorf
A. Rosenblum
J. Shein
P. Elson
J. Levin

N. Abelson
J. Balser
J. Bersnstein
W. Cohen
P. Cohen
M. Ellman
Z. Frong
M. Goldberg
L. Goldstein
J. Gottlieb
G. Blatt
J. Hirschovitz
L. Hirschovitz
A. Jaffe
S. Klein
S. Kabatsky
A. Landsberger
H. Lichtenstein
I. Meyer
M. Nissenbaum
I. Strom. . . .
A. Springer
J. Simonoff
J. Saul

H. Yalovitz
L.G. A. . . .
M. Blumberg
J. Bok..tzky
I. Cohen
G. Constangy
S. Feldman
? Felix
J. Goldberg
Chas. Goldstein
? Goldwater
S. Ginsberg
A.B. Hat. . . .
M. Hirschovitz
A. Jacobs
L. Katzoff
Louis Klein
Joe Locoff(?)
B. Levy
P. Mendel
H. Roughlin
M. Savolovitz
S. Stein
S. S. . . . lyan

A. Solansky
D. Burges
H. Bressler
Issac Caplan
Wolfe Cohen
Sam Cline
S. Feen
L. Friedman
A.J. Grudinsky
A. Ginsburg
Joe Goldberg
I. Grudberg
H. Heiman
J.N. Hirsch
M. Kaplan
N. Keilson
Chas. Levcoff
M. Morris
S. Marks
L. Rosenthal
J. Schechter
I. Schiff
S. Susamn (?)
I. Simocovitz.

M. Bercovitz
. . . . . . .uchmann
J. . . . .onsky
D. Czaban (?)
L. Eplan
M. Frankel
? Grudsinsky
P. Glass
M. Goldfarb
S. Goldstein
J. Hirschberg
H.L. Harris
H. Klein
S. Kisch
I. Kalish
A.J. Lehrman
Joe Lichtenstein
A. Moscovitz
A. Rabinovitz
M. Srochi
M. Shirman
Mike Schurman
W. Tutac (?)

RELIGIOUS LEADERS

RABBIS

1886—1902	*No ordained Rabbi; services led by lay readers and Rev. Abraham Jaffe and Rev. Jacob Simonoff*
1901—1907	*Rabbi Berachya Meyerowitz*
1907—1915	*Rabbi Joseph M. Levine*
1915—1919	*Rabbi Hyman Yood*
1919—1928	*Rabbi Abraham Hirmes*
1928—1982	*Rabbi Harry H. Epstein*
1982	*Rabbi Arnold Goodman*

CANTORS

Abraham Jaffe	*Aaron Lipitz*
I.M. Lubel	*Max Landman*
N. Abelson	*A. Paskin*
M. Rabinowitz	*Joseph Schwartzman*
Solomon Goldstone	*Isaac Goodfriend*
Abraham Selsky	

ASSISTANT RABBIS & EDUCATIONAL DIRECTORS

Rabbi Ralph DeKoven	*S. Hirsch Jacobson*
Alex Kaminetsky	*Yair Frankel*
Rabbi Samuel Langer	*Dr. Philip Wendkos*
Rabbi Raphael Gold	*Rabbi Leonard Lifshen*
Rabbi Alexander Graubart	*Rabbi Marvin Richardson*
Rabbi David Auerbach	*Jerrold Lesson*

CONGREGATION PRESIDENTS

1887-1888	I. Balagur	1946-1947	Charles Bergman
1888-1889	Leopold Fresh	1948	Simon Bressler
1889-1890	F. Rabinovitz	1949-1950	Max Cuba
1890-1891	A. Posner	1951-1952	Dr. Nathan Blass
1892-1893	N.A. Kaplan	1953-1954	Joseph Zaglin
1893-1894	Philip Elson	1955-1957	Joseph Cuba
1894-1895	J. Goldin	1958-1959	Abe Goldstein
Date Uncertain	S. Boorstein	1959-1961	Hyman Meltz
Date Uncertain	Leon Eplan	1961-1963	Dr. Irving Goldstein
Date Uncertain	D. Zaban	1963-1965	Max Rittenbaum
Date Uncertain	Morris Lichtenstein	1965	Michael Kraft
1900-1928	Joel Dorfan	1965-1968	Harry Lane Siegel
1928-1929	Joseph Goldberg	1968-1970	Sylvan Makover
1929-1930	Hyman Jacobs	1970-1972	David Alterman
1931-1932	Joel Dorfan	1972-1974	Dr. Marvin Goldstein
1933-1934	Hyman Mendel	1974-1976	Gerald Cohen
1935-1937	Oscar Gershon	1976-1978	Dr. William Schatten
1937-1939	I.J. Paradies	1978-1980	Norman Diamond
1940-1941	Meyer Rich	1980-1982	Dr. Herbert Karp
1942-1943	Abe Goldstein	1982-1984	Joel Lobel
1944-1945	Thomas Makover	1984-1986	Marshall Solomon

1986   Sidney Kaplan

SISTERHOOD PRESIDENTS

1920-1924	*Lizzie Jacobs Scheinbaum*	1957-1958	*Lois Makover*
1924-1927	*Lillie Faeman*	1958-1960	*Janet Meyer*
1927-1930	*Nessie Rich*	1960-1962	*Betty Levitt*
1930-1933	*Ray Meyer*	1962-1963	*Betty Ann Shusterman*
1933-1935	*Rose Klotz*	1963-1965	*Doris Koplin*
1935-1937	*Zelda Berman*	1965-1967	*Sherry Halpern*
1937-1939	*Annabelle Samet*	1967-1969	*Phyllis Cohen*
1939-1941	*Rubye Goldstein*	1969-1971	*Phyllis Levine*
1941-1943	*Gertie Bressler*	1971-1973	*Helene Cohen*
1943-1946	*Esther Friedman*	1973-1975	*Diane Bernstein*
1946-1947	*Frances Bressler*	1975-1977	*Doris Goldstein*
1947-1949	*Doris Levin*	1977-1979	*Miriam Levitas*
1949-1951	*Sylvia Parks*	1979-1981	*Shirley Minsk*
1951-1953	*Elizabeth Berchenko*	1981-1983	*Franceen Tillem*
1953-1955	*Rose Morris*	1983-1986	*Donna Smith*
1955-1957	*Dorothy Rosenblum*	1986	*Gail Levitt*

Honorary President: Mary Dwoskin

MR. & MRS. CLUB PRESIDENTS

Sheila & Aaron Cohen	*Marilyn & Morton Karlan*
Leita & Mickey Cole	*Doris & Beryl Koplin*
Harriet & Arthur Davidow	*Sadie & Ralph Sacks*
Ann & Norman Diamond	*Phyllis & Ralph Saul*
Jane & Joel Fryer	*Sonia & Paul Sifen*
Pauline & Herschel Isaacson	

BROTHERHOOD PRESIDENTS

Simon Mendel   Jack Isenberg

Sam H. Hirsh   Louie Rittenbaum

Joseph M. Brown   Monte Rosing

Dr. Irving Goldstein   Sidney Herzenberg

Joseph L. Goldberg   Abe Lewis

Abe Goldstein   Ephraim Berman

Sol Morgan   Dr. David Kahn

Sol Klotz   Sidney Goldberg

Sam Eplan   Dave Alterman

MEN'S CLUB PRESIDENTS

Steven Zier

Donald Field

Edwin Saginar

Abram Estroff

Melvin Tillem

STATISTICAL DATA — 1986

TOTAL MEMBERSHIP

Family Units	2,053
Individuals (including children)	4,762

AGE DISTRIBUTION

Under 18 yrs.	904	19%
College Age (18-22)	238	5%
Young Adults (22-34)	856	18%
Couples (35-65)	1807	38%
Over 65	952	20%
*Single Households (All Ages)	665	32%

*This statistic is separate from the above listing.

LOCATION IN METRO ATLANTA

Northwest (Zip codes 30305, 09, 27, & 42)	33%
Northeast (Zip codes 30306, 19, 24, & 29)	28%
Sandy Springs and Dunwoody (Zip codes 30328 & 38)	15.75%
Cobb County (Zip codes 30060 & 80)	6.66%
Doraville and Chamblee (Zip codes 30340, 41, & 45)	3%
Decatur and Stone Mountain (Zip codes 30330, 35, & 43)	2%
Roswell (Zip codes 30075 & 76)	1%
Out of Metro area	4%
Other	6.6%

Last panel from the 2nd Centennial Exhibit.